HIERONYMUS BOSCH

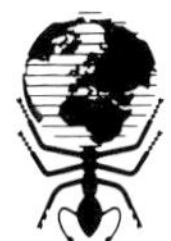

Books in the RENAISSANCE LIVES series explore and illustrate the life histories and achievements of significant artists, rulers, intellectuals and scientists in the early modern world. They delve into literature, philosophy, the history of art, science and natural history and cover narratives of exploration, statecraft and technology.

Series Editor: François Quiviger

Already published

Albrecht Dürer: Art and Autobiography *David Ekserdjian*
Aldus Manutius: The Invention of the Publisher *Oren Margolis*
Artemisia Gentileschi and Feminism in Early Modern Europe *Mary D. Garrard*
Blaise Pascal: Miracles and Reason *Mary Ann Caws*
Botticelli: Artist and Designer *Ana Debenedetti*
Caravaggio and the Creation of Modernity *Troy Thomas*
Descartes: The Renewal of Philosophy *Steven Nadler*
Donatello and the Dawn of Renaissance Art *A. Victor Coonin*
Erasmus of Rotterdam: The Spirit of a Scholar *William Barker*
Filippino Lippi: An Abundance of Invention *Jonathan K. Nelson*
Giorgione's Ambiguity *Tom Nichols*
Hans Holbein: The Artist in a Changing World *Jeanne Nuechterlein*
Hieronymus Bosch: Visions and Nightmares *Nils Büttner*
Isaac Newton and Natural Philosophy *Niccolò Guicciardini*
Jan van Eyck within His Art *Alfred Acres*
John Donne: In the Shadow of Religion *Andrew Hadfield*
John Evelyn: A Life of Domesticity *John Dixon Hunt*
Leonardo da Vinci: Self, Art and Nature *François Quiviger*
Leon Battista Alberti: The Chameleon's Eye *Caspar Pearson*
Machiavelli: From Radical to Reactionary *Robert Black*
Michelangelo and the Viewer in His Time *Bernadine Barnes*
Paracelsus: An Alchemical Life *Bruce T. Moran*
Petrarch: Everywhere a Wanderer *Christopher S. Celenza*
Piero della Francesca and the Invention of the Artist *Machtelt Brüggen Israëls*
Pieter Bruegel and the Idea of Human Nature *Elizabeth Alice Honig*
Raphael and the Antique *Claudia La Malfa*
Rembrandt's Holland *Larry Silver*
Rubens's Spirit: From Ingenuity to Genius *Alexander Marr*
Salvator Rosa: Paint and Performance *Helen Langdon*
Thomas Nashe and Late Elizabethan Writing *Andrew Hadfield*
Titian's Touch: Art, Magic and Philosophy *Maria H. Loh*
Tycho Brahe and the Measure of the Heavens *John Robert Christianson*
Ulisse Aldrovandi: Naturalist and Collector *Peter Mason*

HIERONYMUS BOSCH

Visions and Nightmares

NILS BÜTTNER

REAKTION BOOKS

Published by Reaktion Books Ltd
Unit 32, Waterside
44–48 Wharf Rd
London N1 7UX, UK
www.reaktionbooks.co.uk

First published in English 2016, reprinted 2017
Paperback edition first published 2023

Translated by Anthony Mathews

Printed and bound in India by Replika Press Pvt. Ltd

A catalogue record for this book is available from the British Library

ISBN 978 1 78914 792 6

CONTENTS

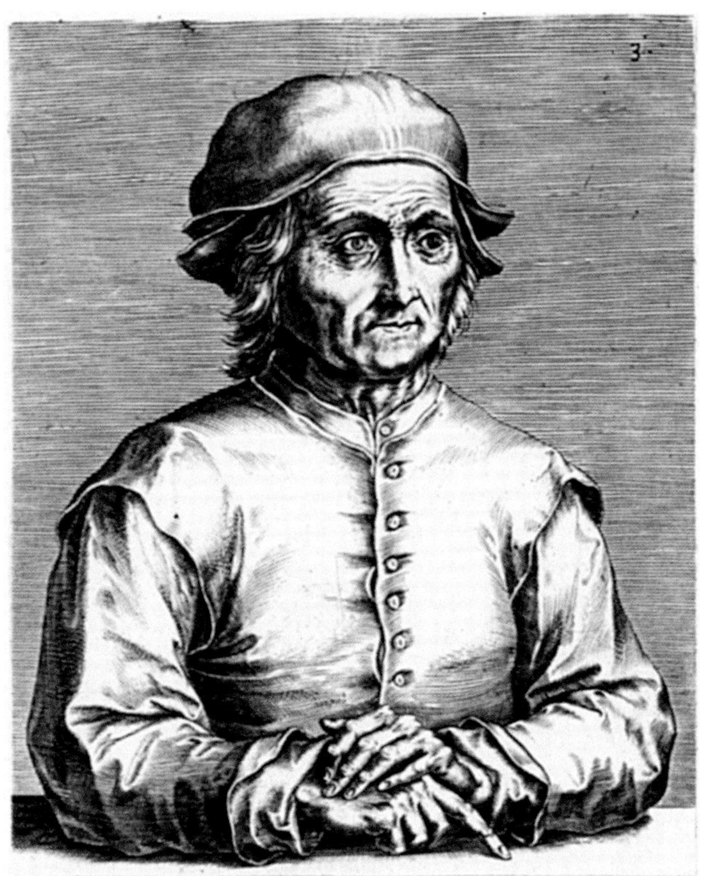

HIERONYMO BOSCHIO PICTORI.

Quid sibi vult, Hieronyme Boschi,   Aspiceres? Tibi Ditis auari
Ille oculus tuus attonitus? quid   Crediderim patuisse recessus
Pallor in ore? velut lemures si   Tartareasque domos· tua quando
Spectra Erebi volitantia coràm   Quicquid habet sinus imus Auerni
Tam potuit bene pingere dextra.

ONE

Visions and Nightmares

IERONYMUS BOSCH was famous throughout the world even in his own lifetime, and his works remained sought-after collectors' items long after his death. His pictures were appreciated not just in the Netherlands and Spain but also beyond the Alps, in Italy. He was one of the few northern European painters whom Giorgio Vasari thought worthy of mention in his widely read collection of artists' biographies. Vasari praised the originality of the painter from 's-Hertogenbosch, citing some of the works known to him from engravings, 'and so many other fantastic and wanton inventions that it would be tiresome to recount them all'.[1] The Ghent historian Marcus van Vaernewijck had already referred to Bosch, in a similar vein, as the 'devil maker'.[2] Ludovico Guicciardini, a representative of humanism in Italy who published a detailed description of the Netherlands in 1567, called Hieronymus Bosch 'a noble inventor and famous for his fantastic and bizarre things'.[3] Even before the end of the century the images considered typical of Bosch's work were interpreted as indicative of his psyche.[4] An early example of this can be seen in a poem by the painter and writer Dominicus Lampsonius, which gained wide circulation:

1 Johannes Wierix (?), *Hieronymus Bosch*, 1572, engraving.

Jeroon Bos, what means your frightened face
And pale appearance? It seems as though you just
Saw all infernal spectres fly close around your ears.
I think that all the deepest rings of miserly Pluto
Were revealed, and the wide habitations of Hell
Opened to you – because you are so art-full
In painting with your right hand depictions
Of all that the deepest bowels of Hell contain.[5]

These lines were used as the caption to an image first published in 1572 in a series of engravings edited by Hieronymus
Cock, which were frequently reprinted elsewhere (illus. 1).[6]
The posthumous portrait engraving was based on an original
that is now lost and corresponds to a drawing in what is
referred to as the *Recueil d'Arras*, a collection of portrait drawings put together by Jacques Le Boucq in 1560.[7] The same
face appears in a tiny painting in the Mead Art Museum in
Amherst, Massachusetts, which was presumably not done
until after the Arras drawing and the engraving, though in
a similar format.[8] The image of a painter possessed by
nightmare visions, familiar in writings on art, turned Bosch's
name into a synonym for all manner of devilish images and
depictions of Hell that came to be imitated far and wide.[9] A
good number of the works by his imitators and admirers
were inscribed with his name, which became synonymous
with the depiction of visual nightmares.

In the literary sphere, this is seen above all in the writing
of Francisco Gómez de Quevedo y Villegas, in whose *Sueños
y discursos* Bosch was closely identified with visions and nightmares.[10] Unlike many other authors, Quevedo may actually

2 Detail from right panel of 'Hell', Hieronymus Bosch, *The Garden of Earthly
Delights*, *c.* 1505, oil on panel (see illus. 4).

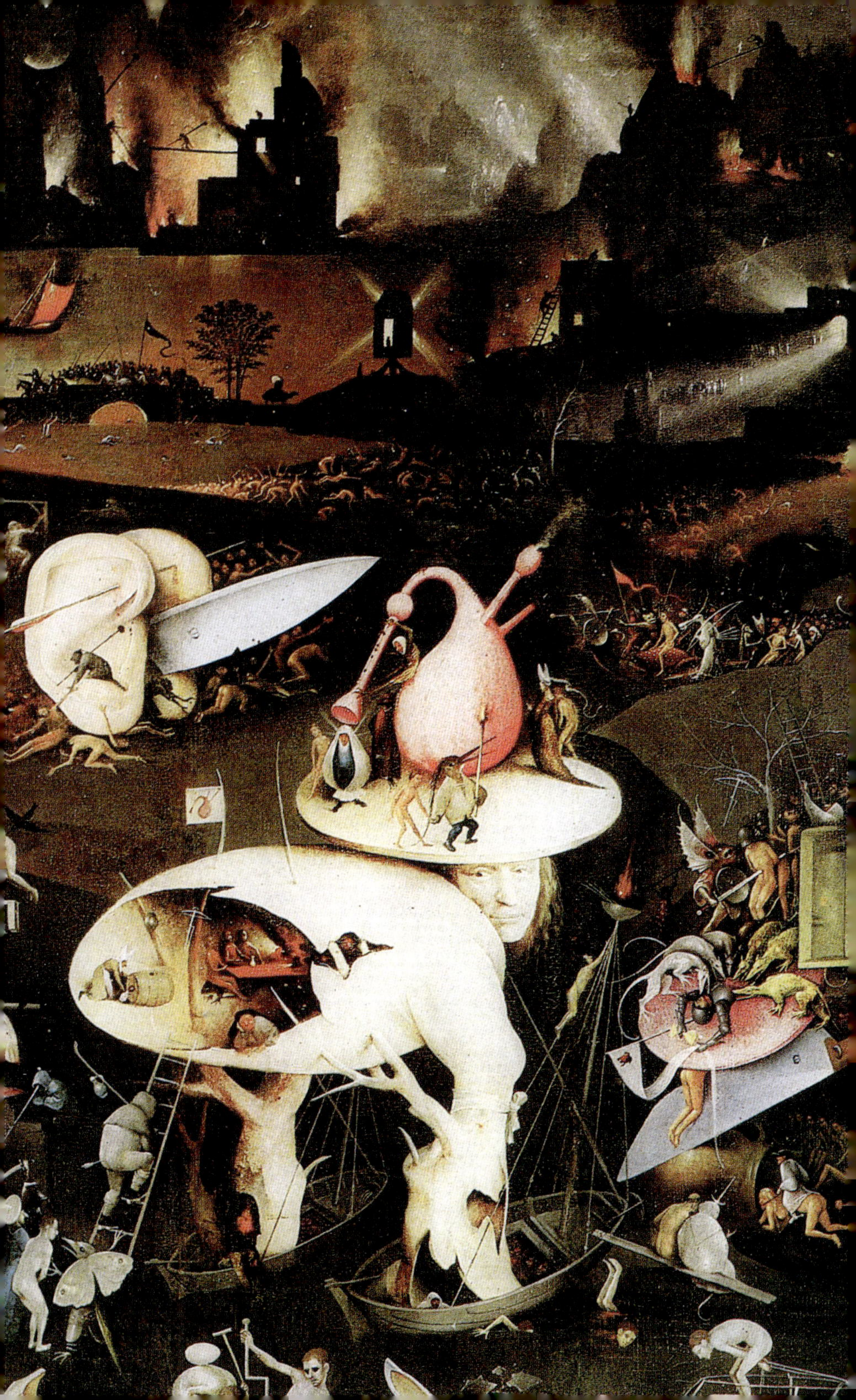

have been familiar with the original representations of Hell by Bosch, such as the wing depicting this subject in the so-called *The Garden of Earthly Delights* (illus. 2), at that time owned by the king of Spain. It was only some years previously that one of the most complete surviving sources of evidence about Bosch was published. It appears in the *Historia de la orden de S. Geronimo*, written in 1605, which is also a detailed chronicle of the monastery of El Escorial founded by Philip II of Spain. Four decades after the Council of Trent, which had explicitly condemned the pictures from the time of Bosch criticized by the Reformation, Fray José de Siguença attempted to account for the fact that this most Catholic of kings had a liking for these works. For Siguença, the king's authority was proof that Bosch's pictures were beyond all suspicion of heresy. 'The difference that, to my mind, exists between the pictures of this man and those of all others', Siguença writes, 'is that the others try to paint man as he appears on the outside, while he alone had the audacity to paint him as he is on the inside.'[11] Thus right from the start the pictures came to sum up the inner life of a painter, a life about which Siguença was as ignorant as his contemporary Karel van Mander. In his collection of biographical descriptions of the most celebrated Dutch painters, van Mander frankly declares, 'I have not been able to discover at which time he lived or died – only that it was very early on.'[12] We know considerably more about Bosch now. Today, his biography is better documented than most Dutch painters of the period, allowing us to gain an extremely detailed picture of his life.

At the end of the nineteenth century, art historians started to take an interest in Bosch's life and work. It is surely no coincidence that interest in Bosch increased considerably during the decades that also saw the discovery of the inner life of human beings and the growth of psychoanalysis.[13] The first monograph in book form in which Maurice Gossart catered for the growing interest in the 'faizeur de Dyables' appeared in 1907.[14] Since then well over a thousand publications on Hieronymus Bosch have appeared. They mainly attempt to account for his seemingly mysterious world of imagery and only rarely focus on his style; it is very rare indeed to find both things being taken into account.

The painter's home town, 's-Hertogenbosch, from which he took his name and which is mostly referred to by its inhabitants as Den Bosch, is situated in the Netherlands. It is as remote from Haarlem in Holland proper as it is from Antwerp in what is now Belgium. This fact is significant for the interpretation of Bosch's work; his alleged distinctiveness in the field of what is often called the art of the Early Netherlandish masters has been interpreted as a first indication of a specific northern Dutch characteristic by an art-historical approach based on national schools. It is the northern Netherlands that is also usually identified with the paintings of the so-called Dutch Golden Age. But Belgium did not yet exist in Bosch's day and the Netherlands was not to become a unified cultural area for some time. Bosch was strongly influenced by painters from the southern Netherlands, and he had a considerable following there; the exceptionally large number of copies and imitations that were produced in his lifetime are clear proof of this.

Apart from his pictures, Bosch did not leave anything of great interest to future interpreters. There are no diaries, letters or personal statements about himself or his art; he would be an ideal test case of claims about the 'death of the author'. However, instead of seeing his works in the context of the art and culture of the time, people have drawn conclusions about the person who created them. Clear distinctions have not always been made between paintings that are verifiably Bosch's own work and those created by imitators. Biographies of the artist in the style of the nineteenth-century cult of the genius have portrayed Bosch as both a groundbreaking precursor of Surrealism and a painter of heresy closely associated with secret sects. He has been identified with the heretical 'Brotherhood of the Free Spirit', whose mystical teachings provided him with motifs for his pictures.[15] He has been seen as an Adamite, a Cathar, an astrologer, an alchemist or a psychopath and was said to have used 'magic potions' or psychedelic drugs. People have also looked for explanations behind his paintings based on the interpretation of dreams, psychoanalysis and the collective unconscious.

Detailed art-historical analysis of Bosch's style has resulted in a considerable reduction in the number of his works that can be authenticated. In 1937, Charles de Tolnay could put a figure of 41 on the number of pictures by Bosch's own hand, but by 1965 he had dropped the number to 36.[16] Gerd Unverfehrt accepted a figure of 25 in 1980, and Stefan Fischer only twenty in 2013.[17] Scientific analysis and dating of the relevant painted panels by dendrochronology have been used to establish the limit.[18] Research has in the meantime identified no more than two dozen works by Bosch's own hand. Some of these are fragments of larger works that once went together and are now found in different museums.

The frequent reduction of the size of the oeuvre has had the effect of shifting the focus when it comes to subject-matter. In place of the darkly fantastical scenes of Hell populated by odd hybrid creatures, we now find an emphasis on the more traditional motifs of Christian iconography. A lot of works that were once seen as crucial are now attributed to imitators or admirers. As a result, the many interpretations based on the artist's biography and psychopathology have become increasingly suspect; they run counter to the wealth of documentary evidence providing clues to the everyday life of the painter. This book is based on these sources and on the paintings that have been established as the work of Bosch's own hand.

The following history is rooted in the practice of historical writing and is based first and foremost on extant material sources. This practice guarantees what the historian Reinhart Koselleck calls the 'right of veto on the part of the sources'.[19] Although the large body of surviving material evidence, the pictures, records and documents, do not determine what can or should be said about the historical context, they do determine what cannot be said. What follows can be said.

TWO

A Painter in Den Bosch

T WAS NOT THE FIRST TIME the painter Anthonius van Aken had gone to the town hall of Den Bosch ('s-Hertogenbosch) when, on 5 April 1474, he accompanied his daughter Katharina, at that time still a minor, to arrange the payment of a lease.[1] In addition to her father Anthonius, her brothers Goessen, Jheronimus and Johannes all gave their approval for the transaction. This seemingly insignificant legal document is the earliest record we have of the life of the painter who was later to be known all over the world by the name of the place where he painted his most famous pictures. Since the document mentions his name, Bosch must have been of age at the time; the legal age of majority was not fixed at 24 until the sixteenth century.[2] Bosch must therefore have been born between 1450 and 1455, though in his day people were probably considered to be of age earlier on. In addition, this document reveals for the first time how he wrote his first name. In 1604 van Mander, his first biographer, used the Dutch form of the name 'Ieronimus'; in the same period the Spanish Siguença gave the name as 'Geronimo'. Even if no individual signature has survived, we find the signature Jheronimus Bosch on a number of paintings. It soon became an internationally

recognized brand, even if not all the paintings bearing this name are now thought to have been painted by Bosch's hand. How Bosch himself wrote his name is not only shown by the remarkably uniform signatures on the pictures, but by a note in the records of the Brotherhood of Our Lady. The writer noted on 10 March 1510 that they had been guests at the house of Brother Hieronymus van Aken, the painter 'who himself writes his name as Jheronimus Bosch'.[3] The members of his family and his fellow citizens called him Joen, a form of the name attested in a number of documents, such as a financial contract made out on 26 July 1474.[4] Today the Latinized form of the name – Hieronymus Bosch – has become standard, and that is what will be used here.

Altogether, more than fifty official records providing information about Bosch's life have survived from a period of 42 years. There is no evidence relating to his education but he must have attended the (Latin) grammar school. This is not only reflected in his subsequent career, but can be assumed from his background. According to the town chronicle written by Albertus Cuperinus around the middle of the sixteenth century, it was customary in 's-Hertogenbosch for children either to be sent to school from an early age or taught a trade.[5] In Bosch's case both are true. He started his career as a painter working alongside others in his father's workshop; Anthonius van Aken was the second generation to run one of the most respected painting workshops in the town. His father, Jan van Aken, Hieronymus's grandfather, who was originally from Nijmegen, had established himself as a painter in the town in 1427, and here four of his five sons were also to become painters.[6] Jan was continuing a tradition started by

Bosch's great-grandfather, who had also been a painter. He had moved to the Netherlands from Aachen in Germany, hence the surname van Aken, settling in Nijmegen in 1404. It was not unusual for a number of the men in a family to follow the same occupation. Nevertheless there are no other examples of such a consistently fixed tradition in the Netherlands at that time.[7]

The house in which Bosch spent much of his childhood and youth was situated on the marketplace. In 1462, Bosch's father had acquired the property called Sint Thoenis (St Antonius), now with the address 29 Market Place. After the death of Anthonius van Aken in 1478, it became the property of Bosch's elder brother Goessen 'the painter', who in 1498 left it to his son Jan, who was working as a woodcarver.[8] Jan 'the painter', the brother of Goessen and Hieronymus, also lived and worked in this house until his death in 1499, as did Goessen's son, Anthonius 'the painter', who died in 1516.[9] Bosch's mother, Aleyt, and Goessen's wife, Katlijn, also lived there, no doubt along with servants and employees of the workshop.[10]

Evidence of the van Aken family of painters can be found in the records of the noble Brotherhood of Our Lady, who planned to commission an altarpiece from the Utrecht wood-carver Adriaen van Wesel in 1475–6. Anthonius van Aken 'and his sons' were also invited to the meeting held in a wine tavern in which the commission was to be discussed.[11] Five years later we also find the addition of 'the painter' in the records against Bosch's name for the first time. This was when for a small sum he acquired from the Brotherhood of Our Lady the wings of the old altarpiece that were now surplus to requirements.[12]

The legal documents that have survived refer mainly to property and financial matters, for example the sale of his share of the family house to his brother Goessen, recorded on 3 January 1481.[13] No records or documents survive from the period 1474–81 to provide evidence of Bosch's presence in his home town.[14] Whether he was travelling during those years or whether, as just an employee in his father's workshop, he had no legal status, is an open question.[15] Having sold his share of the family inheritance in this period, he must presumably already have been living with his wife. Given the situation with regards to accommodation in his parents' house, this would seem a sensible decision. It was presumably at the end of 1480 that Bosch, who was around thirty at the time, married Aleyt Goijaert van den Meervenne, who was a few years older than him.[16] She came from a well-off merchant family and brought with her money, property and a complex network of relations. Her father had died when she was only eleven years old, and her mother, with whom she had occupied a house on the Schilderstraat, died around 1474. In addition, she inherited from a number of sources a series of properties in the vicinity of 's-Hertogenbosch and a house on the marketplace that she rented out from 1477 for six years.[17]

From 1481 onwards the name of Bosch occurs only in legal documents in relation to the management of his wife's financial affairs. On 15 June 1481, for example, he sold Aleyt's inherited share in a country estate to his brother-in-law Godefridus, leading to an agreement three weeks later on 3 July, which resolved a dispute that had arisen in the interim.[18] Over the next few years the young couple sold a number of properties that Aleyt had inherited. The sales were recorded on 11 April 1482 and 21 March 1483, in both cases about a week before the start of the new year, which at that time finished after Easter.[19] On the money made from these sales one could live and run a household with a considerable degree of independence. In addition, it probably helped the couple set up an independent workshop. By 1483 Bosch and his wife had moved into the house on the marketplace that had been rented out earlier, situated only a stone's throw from Bosch's family home. The house, called In den Salvatoer (At the Sign of Our Saviour), had a frontage 19 ft wide – almost 5.5 m – with a stepped gable.[20] Its four storeys had a total surface area of 465 sq m. An additional rear building also provided living and working areas, giving the family 650 sq m of space in total.[21] A view of the Lakenmarkt (Cloth Market) of 's-Hertogenbosch dating from around 1530 (illus. 3) shows Bosch's impressive property (the seventh house from the right).[22] In 1553, by which time it had been occupied by other people for a good while, it had five fireplaces, a baking oven, a brewery and even a bath that could be heated.[23] Although these conveniences might have been installed at a later date, the house nevertheless provided enough room for a workshop and a household befitting their social standing. They would also have had a number of staff, such as the employees in Bosch's workshop – his *knechten* (assistants) – who according to a document from 1503–4 received six stuivers for producing three small coats of arms.[24] Five stuivers was a quarter of a guilder and was about the daily rate for a master craftsman. The family's domestic work would also have been assisted; the records speak of the 'servants in the kitchen' and the 'maids' who were paid extra for festive banquets.[25]

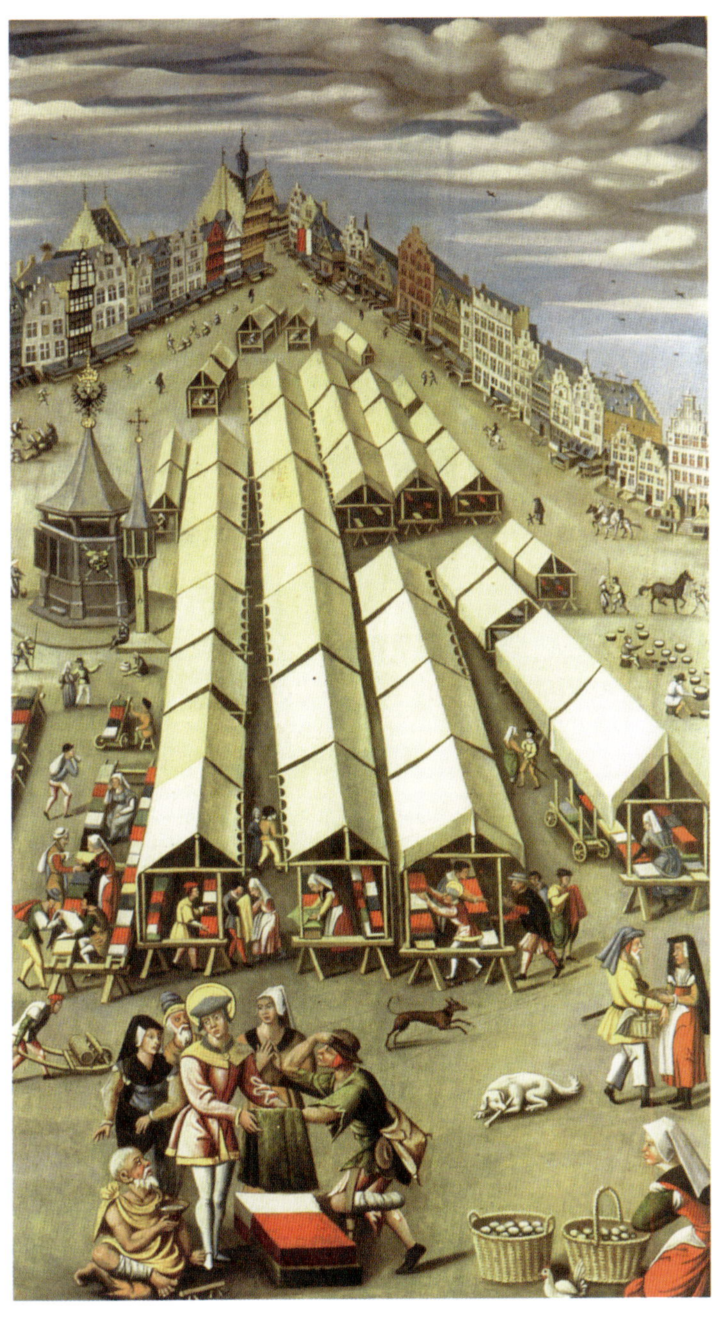

3 Anon., *The Drapers' Market in 's-Hertogenbosch with the Houses of Hieronymus Bosch and his Family on the Right Side*, c. 1530, oil on panel.

Municipal records bear witness to the prosperity Bosch and his wife enjoyed. In 1484 she had also inherited the country estate Ten Roedeken, at Oirschot near Eindhoven, which provided a considerable income from the sale of wood obtained from the forests belonging to it.[26] By this time Bosch was no longer obliged to work for a livelihood, and in 1487 was even in a position to lend money. In 1498 the painter and his wife were among the 2,000 most prosperous of the 20,000 citizens of 's-Hertogenbosch.[27] In the year 1502–3 Bosch was charged nearly five guilders in tax, nine times what most other people paid. From this point on, Bosch belonged to the small elite that provided more than half of the tax revenue and held almost all the property in Den Bosch.[28] In the case of both the *Ruytergelt* (cavalry money) – a tax levied in 1505–6 for the war against the duke of Gelderland – and the contributions levied annually, Bosch was always one of the highest taxpayers.[29]

Increasingly, Bosch's art may also have brought in a tidy sum. In September 1504, for example, he received a payment of 36 guilders for a triptych of the Last Judgment, commissioned by Philip the Handsome. The estimate for the completed work was 360 guilders, a considerable sum given that the annual income of a master stonemason in that period, paid at a daily rate, was around 55 guilders.[30] As the cost of living was high, this amounted to the annual needs of a well-off household in the town.[31] You could buy a trading ship for that price; a cog, the most common sea-going vessel at this time, cost between 30 and 150 guilders in Antwerp.[32] The fame enjoyed by the painter from Den Bosch is exemplified not only by the sale price appropriate for the social position of the buyer, but also by the fact that the Habsburg ruler, residing mainly in Brussels, commissioned him to paint such a significant piece of work.[33] Everything points to the fact that Bosch came to the notice of court patrons early on. For example, Margaret of Austria, the governor of the Netherlands, owned a *Temptation of St Anthony* during the painter's lifetime. Even Queen Isabella of Spain, who died in 1504, owned paintings by him, as did the Venetian cardinal Domenico Grimani, who died in 1523.[34]

As regards Bosch's position within the community in the town, it is highly significant that in the fiscal year 1486–7 he became a member of the Brotherhood of Our Lady, which is still in existence today.[35] This religious brotherhood, founded in 1318, had increased so much in popularity by the end of the century that there had to be a division made between the several thousand 'outer members' and the inner circle of 'sworn members'.[36] The sworn members, between fifty and sixty in number, were required, to avoid paying a fine, to take part in the Sunday services and the Tuesday and Wednesday Vespers, and to take part in Vespers and Mass on the nearly twenty religious feast days, as well as in the three annually staged processions.[37] Every six to eight weeks there were communal meals, which they were also required to attend, along with participation in the Passion plays that were organized at irregular intervals during the late fifteenth century.[38] The Brotherhood of Our Lady was closely linked to the other religious institutions of the town whose representatives met regularly for common meals. Contacts were kept up with the friars, who were recognized as brothers having a common way of life, with the Dominicans, who followed a strict order, and with the guilds in the town, such as the chamber of rhetoric, De Passiebloem, which also put on religious plays. Bosch may personally have known a good number of the 1,100 religious people living there.[39]

As a result of the close contact between the Brotherhood of Our Lady and the friars, Bosch probably came to know about the *Devotio moderna*, the religious reform movement that was modelled on the piety of the Desert Fathers and propagated a mystical and personal *imitatio Christi*. Bosch may therefore have known Thomas à Kempis's *The Imitation of Christ*, the book that exemplified this movement. One can at least say that there would have been talk in the circles in which Bosch moved about the books by Dionysius van Rijkel (Denis the Carthusian) written on the subject of 'Vices and Virtues', with titles such as *On Contemplation* or *On Contempt for the World*. Even if you had not read all the 187 books published by the founder of the Carthusian monastery of 's-Hertogenbosch, who died in 1471, you might still know about his religious beliefs. Bosch may even have met Erasmus of Rotterdam, who was interested in art and artists, and who studied in 's-Hertogenbosch between 1484 and 1487. Erasmus was later excused from Vespers at the Augustinian monastery of Steyn so he could paint between studying and praying.[40] Unfortunately nothing has survived of Erasmus's artistic efforts. Likewise, no evidence of Bosch's theological training has survived. But study of theology going beyond that which one got from attending the grammar school might explain not just the considerable gaps in Bosch's biography as an artist but the fact that he was promoted so quickly, joining the elite circle of the sworn brethren in the Brotherhood of Our Lady.

At the start of 1488 Bosch shared the costs for a formal meal with six other members of the Brotherhood to celebrate his having achieved an elevated social position.[41] According to the records of the Brotherhood, even the secretary to the future Emperor Maximilian I was invited.[42] It is presumed that Bosch had by then been accorded the status of a master painter, but there was no painters' guild in Den Bosch at this time.[43] In addition, unlike his grandfather Bosch is never referred to in documents as a 'master' but only as a 'painter'.[44] It was probably at this time that he became one of the sworn members of the Brotherhood, as he is mentioned as such on several occasions after this point.[45] Recognition of his status as a master of his craft was from then on no longer required since, as a brother who had taken the oath, he was relieved of all obligations to a guild.[46] Several other formal meals are documented in the records of the Brotherhood, including a banquet at some point in 1498–9 that Bosch helped pay for, at which two roasted swans were served.[47]

There is no reliable documentary evidence of what Bosch looked like and the surviving alleged portraits reveal more about Bosch's later fame than his appearance. Even if we do not know what he looked like (though many people have claimed to see him in the figures in his pictures), we can at least describe how he would have been dressed at certain times.[48] As a member of the Brotherhood of Our Lady, for ceremonial occasions he would have worn a cope, the colour and cut of which changed every year on 24 June, the feast of St John the Baptist. This red, violet, white, blue or green cope had a silver badge attached to it bearing a saying from the Song of Solomon, *Sicut lilium inter spinas* – 'As the lily among thorns'.[49] In addition to this, we can identify another detail of his appearance; as a sworn member of the Brotherhood, Bosch was a cleric. He was married, and unlike a priest or deacon was not required to be celibate. Nevertheless, having been received into one of the four lower orders of the *clericus*, it was ordained by the statutes of the Brotherhood that he should be given a *kruinschering* – a tonsure – at least at certain times, showing him to be a man of God.[50]

Presumably, like the majority of the sworn members, Bosch held a religious office. He might have acted as an ostiarius, keeping order in the church, or as a lector, reading from the Bible during divine service; or he might have been an exorcist or acolyte, serving generally at the altar.[51] In any case we can assume that he would have had a sound basic knowledge of theology. His works show evidence of a detailed knowledge of religious literature and a familiarity with both the lives of the saints and exegetical and mystical writings.[52] Among the thousands of members of the Brotherhood there were hundreds of priests, people from the lower nobility and the patrician class, merchants, apothecaries, doctors, craftsmen and representatives of the administration of the town. Only the poor were barred from membership of the Brotherhood as they were not even able to pay the modest admission fee of seven stuivers.[53] The members of the Brotherhood belonged almost exclusively to the upper classes. Bosch was the only painter among the sworn members, over half of whom were priests or *magistri*, theologians, physicians or lawyers who had gone through a period of study. For that reason Bosch's membership of the inner circle of the Brotherhood of Our Lady is evidence of both his education and his elevated social position. The Brotherhood provided Bosch not only with the commission to decorate Sint-Jan, St John's Cathedral in Den Bosch, but also, above all, with access to numerous potential patrons. The Brotherhood, which saw considerable expansion just before 1500, was a network linking the religious and secular elite, extending far into German territory. It counted the patrician class of the town among its members, along with high-ranking representatives of the nobility. During the years that Bosch was a member, between 1488 and 1516, they included two consecrated bishops of Liège along with six senior brethren from other dioceses.[54] Various holders of high office and rank were represented, even members of the Habsburg and Burgundian court.[55] The Palatine Count Robert of Bavaria and the Margrave Friedrich of Baden counted among the members, along with Diego de Guevara, the steward of Philip the Handsome and Hendrick III of Nassau, who may have commissioned *The Garden of Earthly Delights* (illus. 4).[56]

The surviving records give an insight into the everyday life and feasts of the Brotherhood. On 10 March 1510, for example, the funeral was held of the knight Jan Backx, whose coat of arms had been painted on a shield by Bosch's 'assistants' in 1503–4. After the solemn Mass the sworn members proceeded 'in pairs from the church to the house of our fellow brother Hieronymus van Aken who signs his name as Jheronimus Bosch'.[57] The copious supply of drinks is recorded and the food is described in such detail that a study on *Eating and Drinking at the House of Jheronimus Bosch* (2003) was able to provide recipes for the dishes presented.[58] The life of the members of the Brotherhood was shaped by a host of shared

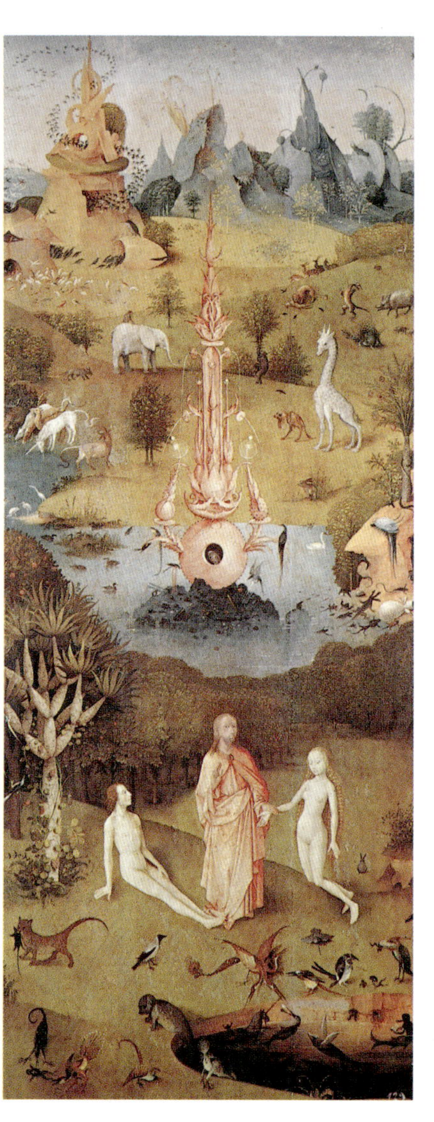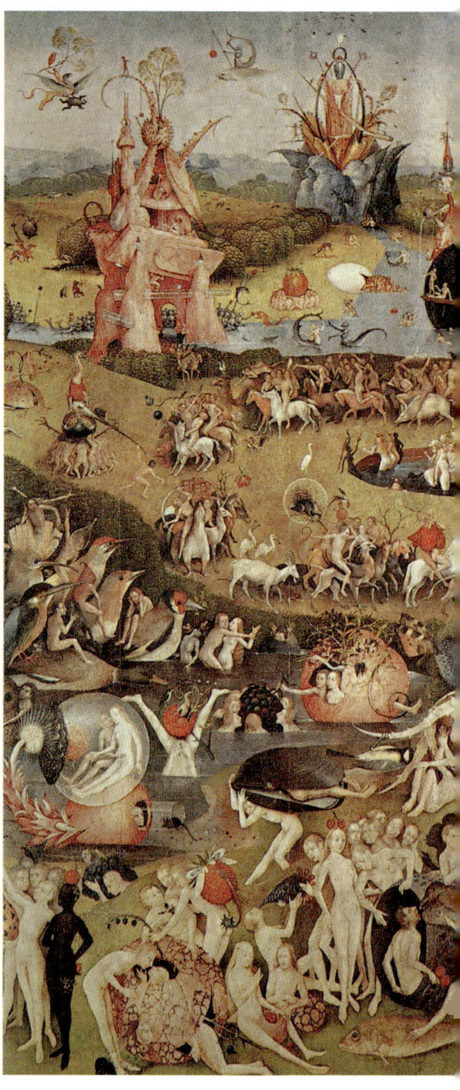

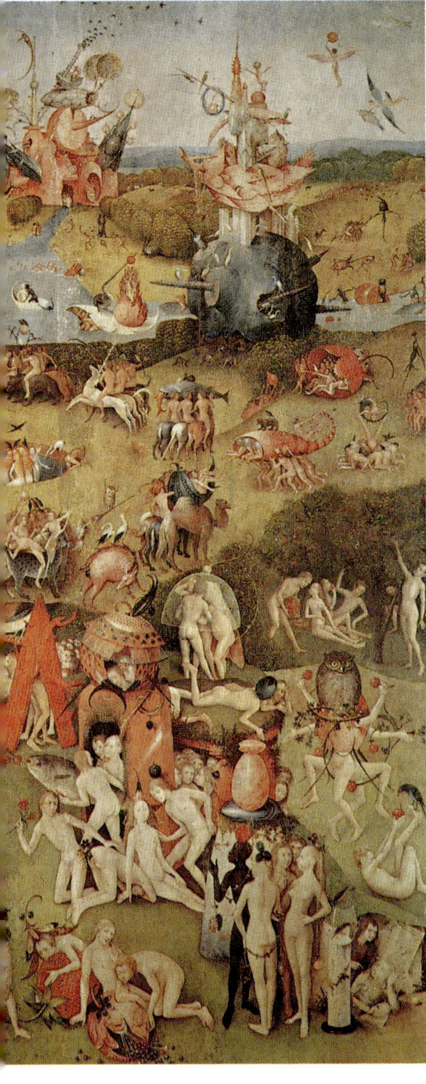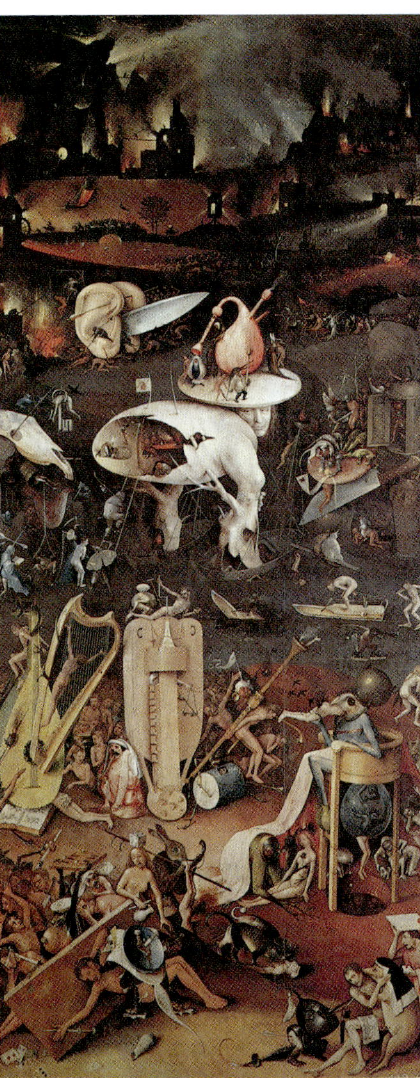

4 Hieronymus Bosch, *The Garden of Earthly Delights*, c. 1503, oil on panel.

activities that dominated the calendar and their daily round. Evading the duties to which all members of the Brotherhood were bound by oath was severely sanctioned.[59] There is no record of whether or not Bosch ever neglected to carry out any of his self-imposed duties. All signs point to his total integration into the religious life of the town, which permeated all aspects of life.[60]

There is no record of the day of Bosch's death, nor the cause. He may have died of an infection of pleurisy, then at its height in Den Bosch; according to the town chronicle, it carried off a great number of people 'like the raging of the plague'.[61] On 9 August 1516 he was given a Christian burial; the account book of the Brotherhood of Our Lady notes the cost of the funeral Mass: 'To Wilhelm Hameker, officiating, 1½ stuivers for singing of the Mass and ½ stuiver for his presence. For the Deacon and Sub-deacon 1 stuiver each. All the others, priests, singers, verger, church officers, grave diggers, bell ringers, organist, ½ stuiver each.'[62] Each member of the choir was given an obol coin and there was even a small gift of money for every pauper present. As their contribution, the Brotherhood provided Bosch's widow with the black material that covered the altar. In addition they supplied a suitable memorial in honour of the deceased. In a book produced towards the end of the sixteenth century bearing the names and coats of arms of all the sworn members, Bosch's name appears underneath an empty heraldic shield with the inscription *seer vermaerd Schilder* — 'celebrated painter' (illus. 5).[63]

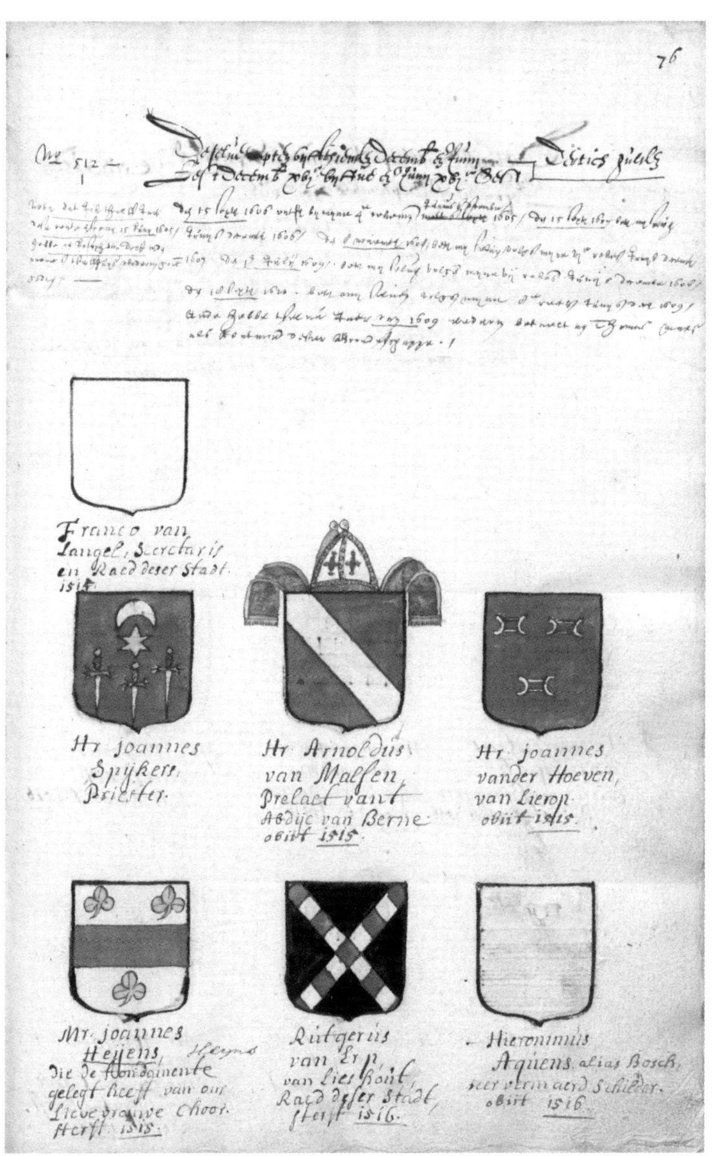

5 *Register van namen en wapens van de Lieve Vrouwebroederschap* (Register of names and coats of arms of the Brotherhood of Our Lady), *c.* 1742, 's-Hertogensbosch, fol. 76 recto. Bosch's shield is at the lower right corner.

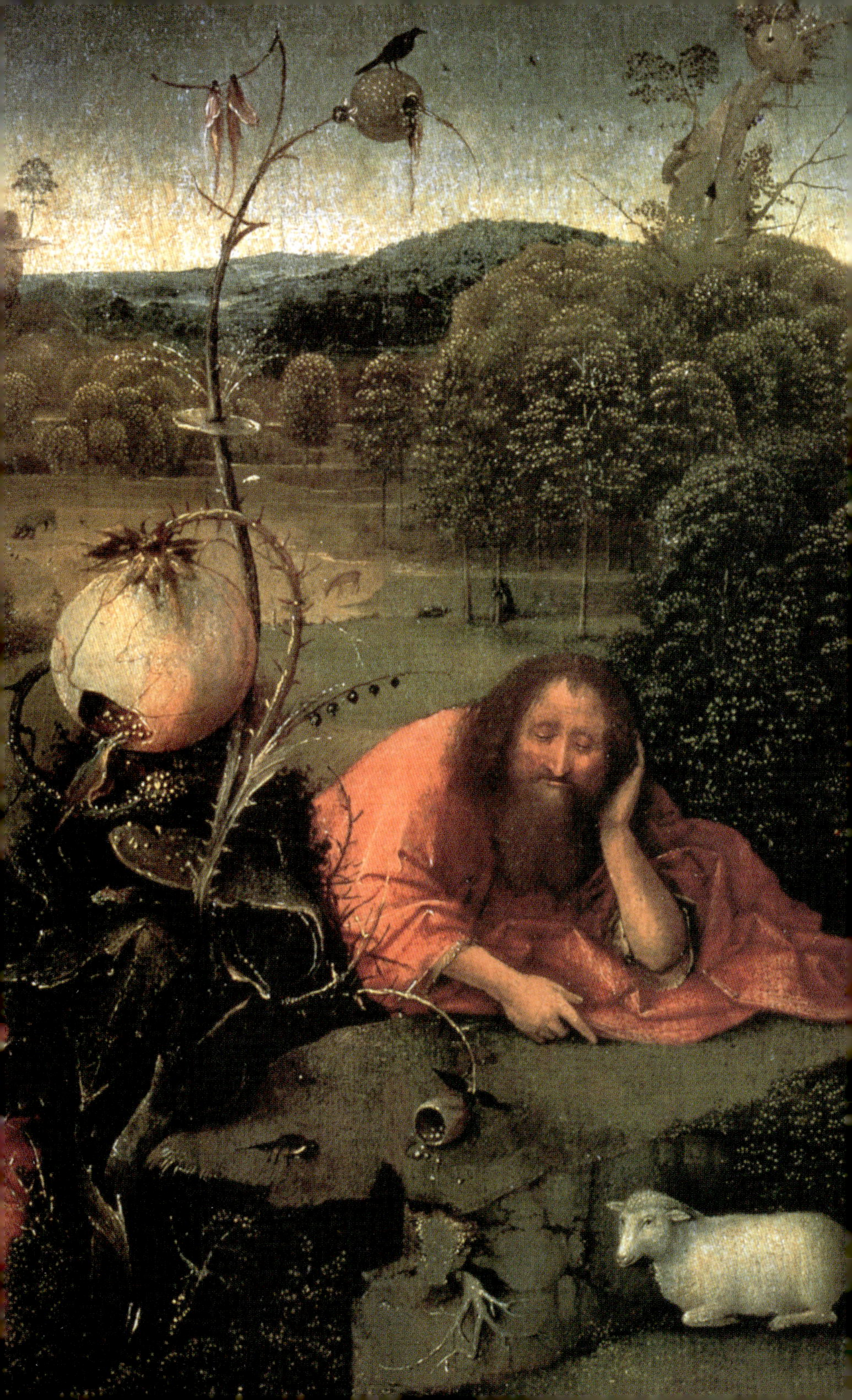

THREE

Pious Donations

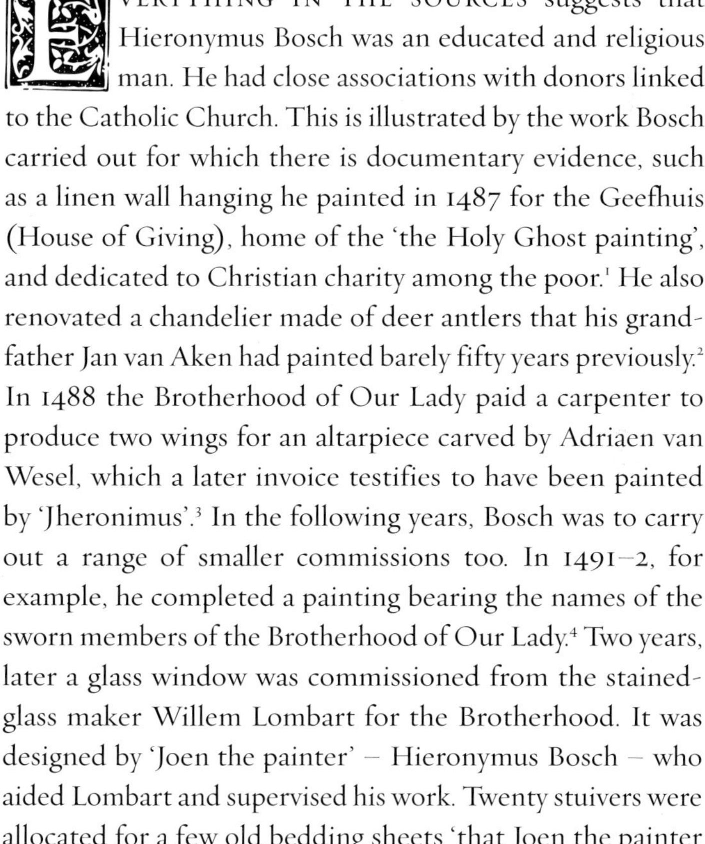

EVERYTHING IN THE SOURCES suggests that Hieronymus Bosch was an educated and religious man. He had close associations with donors linked to the Catholic Church. This is illustrated by the work Bosch carried out for which there is documentary evidence, such as a linen wall hanging he painted in 1487 for the Geefhuis (House of Giving), home of the 'the Holy Ghost painting', and dedicated to Christian charity among the poor.[1] He also renovated a chandelier made of deer antlers that his grandfather Jan van Aken had painted barely fifty years previously.[2] In 1488 the Brotherhood of Our Lady paid a carpenter to produce two wings for an altarpiece carved by Adriaen van Wesel, which a later invoice testifies to have been painted by 'Jheronimus'.[3] In the following years, Bosch was to carry out a range of smaller commissions too. In 1491–2, for example, he completed a painting bearing the names of the sworn members of the Brotherhood of Our Lady.[4] Two years, later a glass window was commissioned from the stained-glass maker Willem Lombart for the Brotherhood. It was designed by 'Joen the painter' – Hieronymus Bosch – who aided Lombart and supervised his work. Twenty stuivers were allocated for a few old bedding sheets 'that Joen the painter

6 Hieronymus Bosch, *St John the Baptist in the Wilderness*, c. 1505, oil on panel.

was to use for the design'.[5] Mention has already been made of the payment in 1503–4 to Bosch's workshop for painting a metal shield for the knight Jan Backx and two other members of the guild, as well as of the triptych of the Last Judgment commissioned in 1504 by Philip the Handsome. In 1508–9 the Brotherhood of Our Lady sought advice from 'Jheronimus' and the master builder Jan Heyns about the gilding and painting of an altarpiece that had not yet been carried out.[6] Presumably this was once again the Altar to Our Lady by Adriaen van Wesel. Clearly, however, the extremely costly enterprise was abandoned. Instead, two other smaller commissions are recorded over the next few years. In 1511–12 Bosch was remunerated for making a design 'of the Cross' – 'vanden cruce'.[7] Unfortunately there is no record giving any details about what this was. Perhaps it was, as many experts presume, an embroidery design for a cope. Apart from the note in the files, there is no mention of the design of 'vanden cruce', any more than of the brass chandelier for the design of which they were willing to pay Bosch 'as much as he should desire' in 1512–13.[8]

A large number of pictures by Bosch were still on display in Den Bosch long after his death, including in the chapel of the Brotherhood of Our Lady and on a number of the altars at St John's Cathedral. According to a description published by Jean-Baptiste Gramaye in 1610, this church was adorned with fifty altars,

> which lose nothing in comparison with the sculptures of Praxiteles and the pictures of Apelles. The most valuable one is that of the Upper Choir, the

Sacramental Altar, which is dedicated to the Holy Virgin, to St Catherine and St Barbara. Those panels in the altar of the Upper Choir and the larger altar of Our Lady [in the chapel of the Brotherhood of Our Lady] that were painted by Bosch with unique skill are still extant. They show the creation of the world in six days, likewise the legend of Abigail, humbly presenting gifts and goods, seeking pardon from David for the humiliation inflicted upon him, and Solomon being honoured by his mother Bathsheba. On the small altar the same artist has portrayed the presentation of the gifts by the Three Kings. The altar of the Archangel Michael shows the siege of Bethulia, the killing of Holofernes, the flight and destruction of the Assyrian army, the victory achieved by Judith, also the triumph of Mordechai and Esther, along with the triumph of the freed Jewish people.[9]

Only a few years later, in December 1615 a number of these pictures came in for some criticism on the occasion of an official visit. The naked figures in the picture of the creation of the world were found particularly displeasing.[10] In the municipal financial records there is a payment listed on 4 January 1671 to the verger of St John's church, who was given 75 guilders for the wings of the high altar.[11] There is no trace of these afterwards. The purchase by the town council may at least be taken as an indication that Bosch's works, having survived the sixteenth-century outbreak of iconoclasm unscathed, were seen to have artistic merit irrespective of their religious function. The high altar of the Dominican friary in Brussels was still adorned with an altarpiece by Bosch in the seventeenth century, and once a year a Mass was held there for the soul of the painter. This work too has vanished without trace, but there is a record of the Dominican Michael Ophovius endeavouring in vain to purchase it for 100 guilders after he was appointed the first bishop of Den Bosch on 22 June 1626.[12] The work was lost only a few years later.

It is now thought, at least, that what Gramaye calls the 'panels displaying the extraordinary art of Hieronymus Bosch' from the altar of Our Lady belonging to the Brotherhood of Our Lady have survived.[13] One of these shows John the Baptist in the desert, depicted alone in a wood (illus. 6); the other shows John the Evangelist, who in Bosch's day was thought to have written the Book of Revelation (illus. 7). It is logical to suppose that this panel was once the wing of an altarpiece, as it is also painted on the reverse (illus. 8).[14] Presumably this representation, consisting entirely of grey and blue shades and usually described as painted in grisaille, was once the everyday or outer side of the altar wing, enclosing a carved shrine. There is a pelican at the centre of the picture, surrounded by a circular pictorial shape suggesting an open but misty landscape in which a series of scenes from the Passion of Christ are arranged. Christ's suffering for mankind was widely symbolized in the medieval period by a pelican. The *Physiologus*, an early Christian compendium of animal symbolism, had misunderstood the behaviour of the pelican and interpreted it in terms of the Christian message.[15] This bird was thought to kill its offspring in anger; after three days it tore its own breast open with its beak out of remorse, so as to revive its progeny by sacrificing its own blood, just as Christ gave mankind eternal life through His sacrifice. The roundel showing the scenes from the Passion and the pelican stand out against a dark background that close inspection reveals to come alive with dark monstrous shapes. The inside of the wing shows St John, banished to the island of Patmos, where Bosch shows the saint writing down the apocalyptic visions that occurred there (Revelation 1:9). One of these 'revelations' was 'a woman clothed with the sun, and the moon under her feet, and upon her head a crown of twelve stars' (Revelation 12:2). In accordance with the accepted theological interpretations of this vision current in his day, Bosch shows an apparition of Our Lady as a halo of light in the sky. An ethereal-looking angel indicates this to John, who interrupts his writing. With his gaze directed upwards he does not notice the scene taking place at his feet. The eagle on the left-hand side of the picture, the animal symbolizing John the Evangelist, has its eyes fixed on a demon-like hybrid creature illustrated opposite it on the right. It has raised its stump-like hands, letting go of the meat hook, which it was perhaps going to use to steal the Evangelist's writing tools lying on the ground. A number of Dutch pictures of the Evangelist show demonic beings caught in this shameful act.[16]

The theologically based narrative of Bosch's painting has a good number of parallels in paintings and illustrations of the period. It has rightly been pointed out that the image of the Evangelist writing is paralleled in an engraving by Martin Schongauer from around 1480.[17] The relatively conventional iconography should not, however, detract from the originality

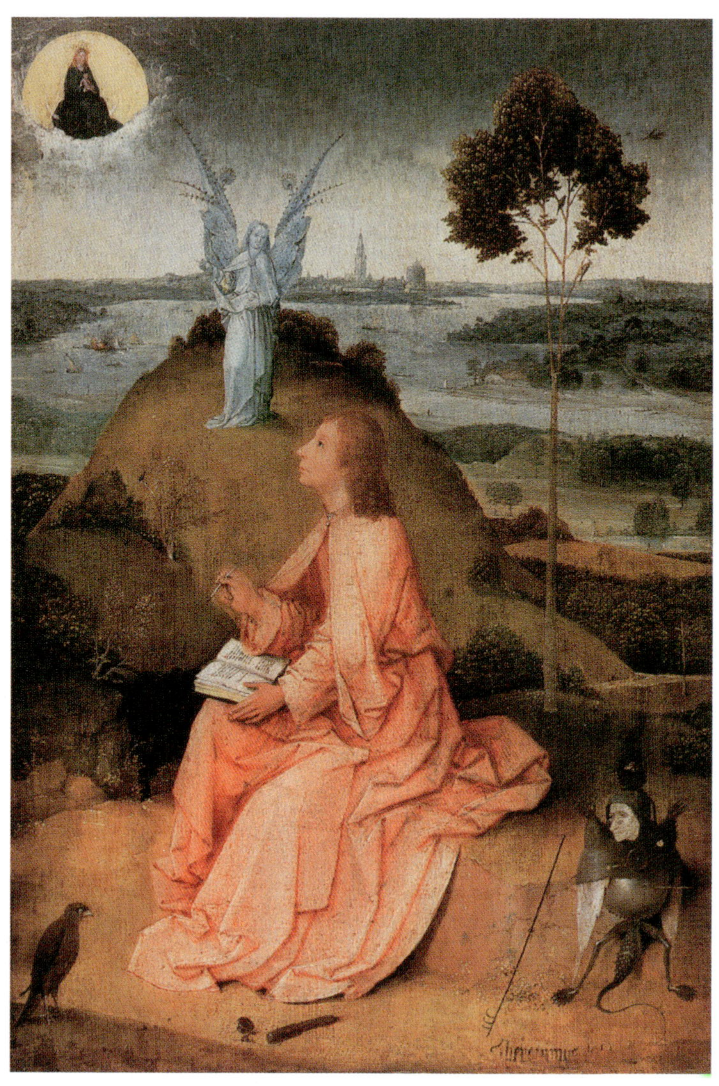

7 Hieronymus Bosch, *St John on Patmos*, c. 1505, oil on panel.

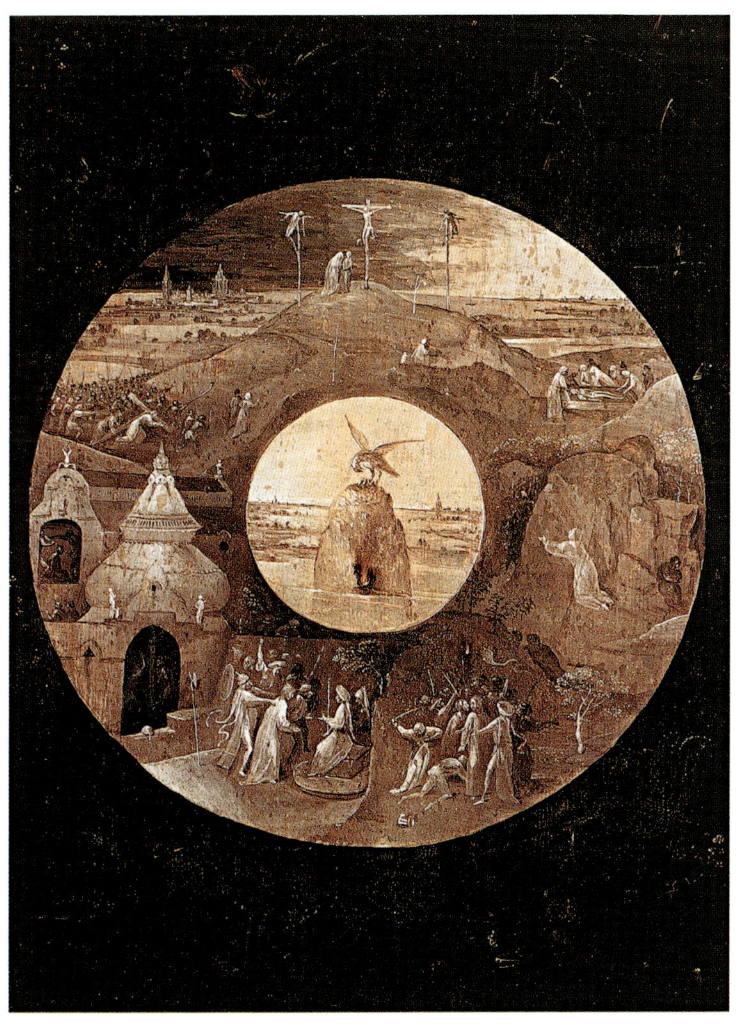

8 Hieronymus Bosch, *Scenes from the Passion of Christ*, c. 1500, reverse side of *St John on Patmos*.

of the representation; you do not need to look at the signature clearly added at bottom right to know that this painting is by Bosch. Just take a look at the little demon. Bosch presents us with a beetle-like hybrid creature identifiable as a messenger and official representative of Hell by a small badge on his clothing.[18] The spectacles on his nose remind one of a scribe, and would have been easily recognizable to contemporaries as an intellectual firebrand on account of the dimly smouldering object on his head. Unlike the little demon, who is highly individualized, the figure of the saint conforms to a stereotype. His facial features are pictured without any modelling of the muscles. His pointed nose turns the gaunt figure of the saint into one of those Bosch figures with mouse-like features, such as Christ in the Frankfurt *Ecce Homo* (illus. 9) or the naked figures in *The Garden of Earthly Delights* (illus. 10). The saint's robe, thanks to the strong exaggeration of the whiteness, gives the impression that it is made of pink metal sheeting. Unlike most other Dutch Old Masters, Bosch does not use the robe as an opportunity to show the qualities of the material and surface structure naturalistically, or to paint artistically ornamented folds; instead, clothing becomes a two-dimensional emblem of the state of being clothed, in which Bosch represents all that is necessary using outlines of pleasing decoration.

For Bosch, the pictorial space is not an observed slice of reality but a symbolically charged scene of action. His distant landscapes are unique for their time: Bosch avoids the representation of detailed landscape typical of other painters of the period, preferring to create in his own particular style. This can be seen particularly in the background landscape, which because of the raised horizon appears to

9 Hieronymus Bosch, *Ecce Homo*, c. 1495, oil on panel.

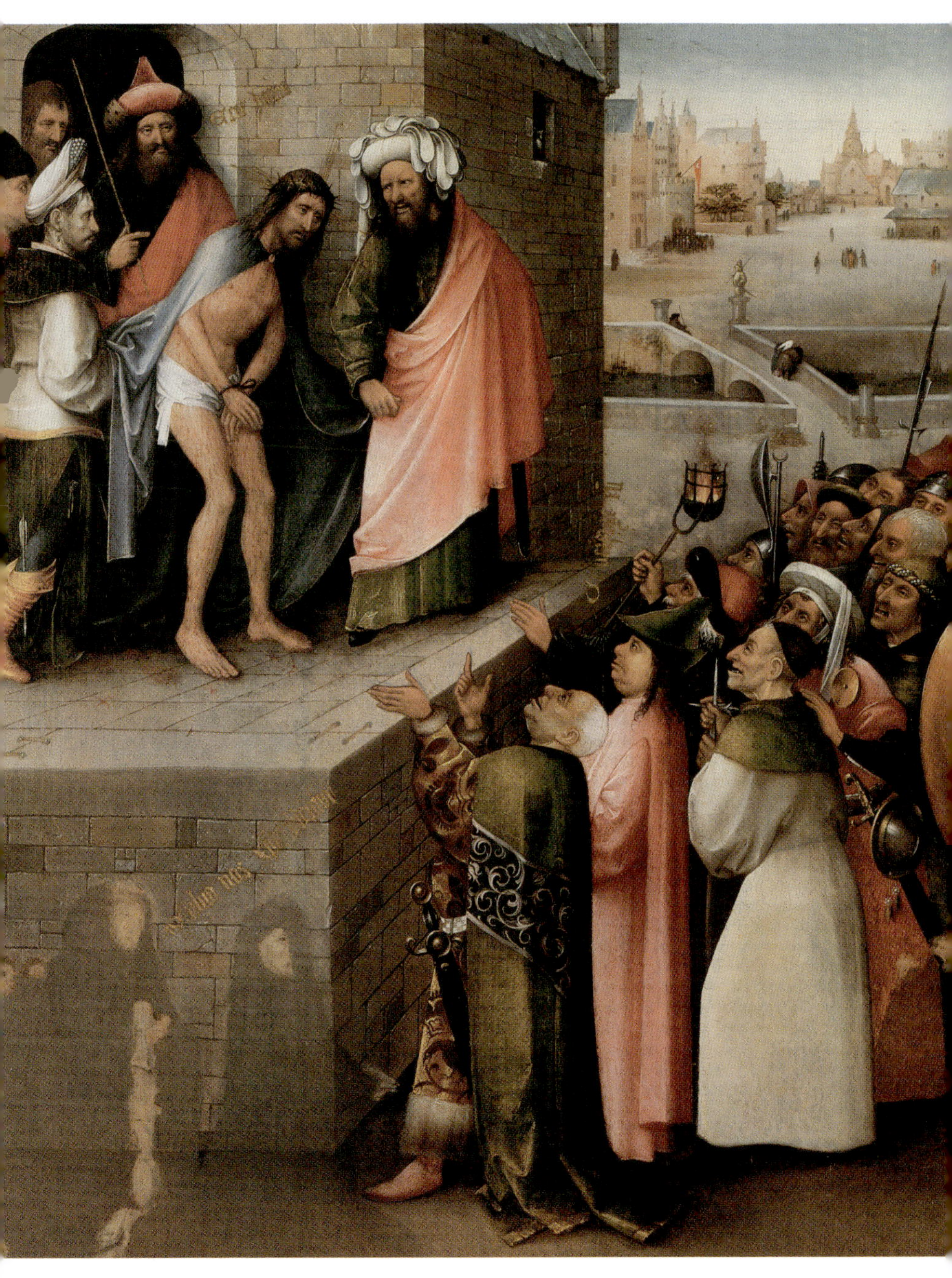

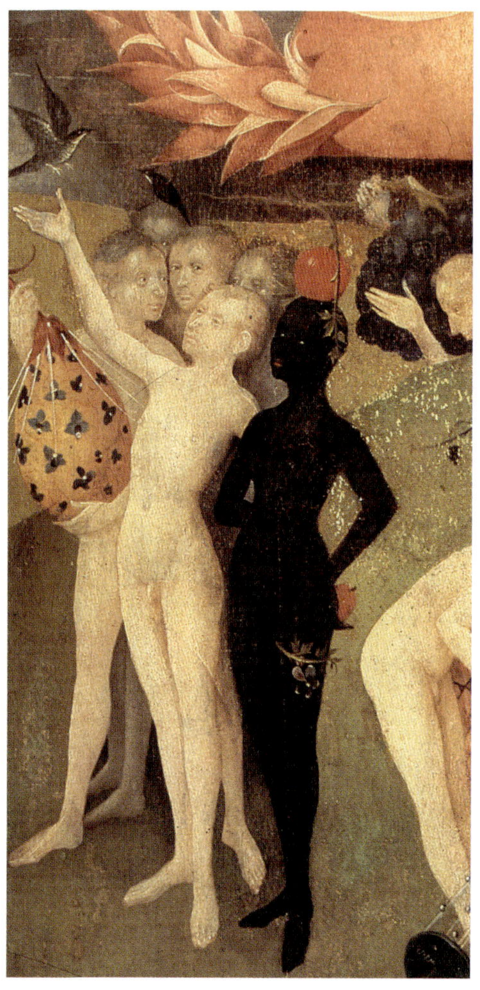

be viewed from a high tower. By the use of a restrained but acute painterly hand, the barren plain becomes furnished with plants, trees, houses and other clues as to the presence of human civilization. With the paint thickly applied, the dense foliage of the vegetation is suggested in

10 Detail from Hieronymus Bosch, *The Garden of Earthly Delights* (see illus. 4).

a non-naturalistic pointillist manner, the closely related shades of colour blending into one another in a fascinating way. Unlike Rogier van der Weyden or Jan van Eyck, who built their paintings up using a series of layered painting surfaces, Bosch worked with the paint while still wet. His pictures are in large part created all in one go.

This can also be seen in the Madrid *St John the Baptist in the Wilderness* (see illus. 6), in which the saint is depicted by Bosch as a thoughtful hermit in the wilderness. By means of a skilful gradation of areas of paint, an impression is given of an aerial view. The individual sections of the picture are unified, presenting a convincing depth of space animated by a host of animals and plants. The cliffs in the background of the Madrid picture and the monstrous vegetation emerging out of the wood on the right are typical of Bosch's landscapes. These fantastical elements – the hybrid species of vegetation, scornful of nature, and the geological forms blending animal, vegetable and mineral – expressed the conviction of the people of the time that the world around them was full of demonic trickery. These landscape details owe more to late-Gothic ornamentation than to precise observation of nature. Nevertheless, Bosch's pictures give a remarkable impression of spatial depth thanks to the skilful effects of their colouring. Particularly remarkable is the vegetation shown in the foreground with its alien-seeming shapes reappearing in the background. Recent technical analysis has shown that this place was originally occupied by the figure of a donor, only to be painted over a little later.[19] This overpainting was presumably carried out in Bosch's workshop, where one of his assistants chose a motif appropriate to the theological subject of the painting and so obliterated the figure of the donor, which was thought to be out of place.

In the medieval world of representation there was a profound belief that life meant temptation and earthly existence produced nothing but thorns and thistles. In keeping with this, the plants, to which the meditative saint pays little attention, could be a symbol for the world and its temptations. John stands out against them, deep in thought and clearly indicating the lamb symbolizing the innocence of God. Whether the painting, almost identical in form with the representation of John the Baptist, the back of which bears no trace of painting, once formed the other wing of the same altarpiece can be questioned on the basis of analysis by dendrochronology.[20] The dates of felling of the trees from which the panels were made are in fact some years apart. In addition, dendrochronology carried out on the panel showing St John on Patmos has shown that it must date from some time after 1495, as the tree from which this board was made can only have been felled in 1487 at the earliest. As unseasoned wood was not suitable for painting, it is difficult to square this result with the wings commissioned in 1488 by Adriaen von Wesel for the altarpiece of Our Lady. Even if it is somewhat unlikely, then, that the painting showing John the Baptist once adorned the altarpiece of the Brotherhood of Our Lady, there is no doubt that it was intended for a religious foundation to preserve the memory of a devout donor and bear testimony on behalf of his soul. The painted figures of donors suggest a practical function and purpose for the pictures and this has a bearing on any answer to the question of the original significance of these works.

One has to keep in mind here that for a devout Christian, death was not the absolute end. For Christians in the Middle Ages right through to the early modern period the doctrine of salvation contained in the Bible was a living presence, amounting to what you could rightly call certain faith. Paradise lost, Heaven for the blessed and Hell for the damned, were not, it is true, within everyone's reach but they were no less real for all that, and were part of the very air that they breathed. The final end of the world as it is, limited in time, was just as certain as the ensuing establishment of God's eternal order as foretold in the Bible. Whoever died continued to exist in life beyond the grave where, just as in this life, they awaited the Day of Judgment and Resurrection. Anyone searching for a coherent concept of what the beyond was like was faced with the question of where the dead who had died before the sounding of the Last Judgment had actually gone. An answer to this was provided by the doctrine of Purgatory, already developing in the twelfth century, making it possible to gain access to Heaven after a limited period. Those sinners who were truly evil went straight to eternal damnation, while in Purgatory all the rest could expiate their guilt resulting from Original Sin in its purifying fires and thus count on being quickly accepted into Heaven. In any case, you had a hope of salvation by the time of the Last Judgment.[21] To help bring this about, it was thought useful for prayers to be said for the soul of the deceased after his death in order to mitigate the suffering of the fires of Purgatory inevitably imposed by Original Sin. Recollection of the name of the deceased in the celebration of Mass aided in the process of purifying the soul in the beyond. The doctrine of Purgatory was central to medieval religious devotion. The institution of Masses for the souls of the deceased, such as those celebrated by the Brussels Dominicans for Hieronymus Bosch, made for a communion, renewed at every divine service, between the living and the dead. Remembering the dead informed social customs and everyday life, in a culture where memory played such a key role and which was focused on the life beyond.[22] This kind of culture based on memory extended well beyond the religious and liturgical sphere since acts concerning life in the hereafter affected the public realm. They served to enhance the standing of the donors and the legitimation of their social ambitions and social position. As visual manifestations of cultural memory, pictures were able not just to keep memory alive, but to legitimate claims to power and overlordship in the present.

Numerous pictures by Bosch have their origin in late medieval religious practices and in this culture of keeping alive the memory of the deceased, including a small picture of *Christ on the Cross with Donors and Saints* (illus. 11).[23] The Crucifixion group conforms to the common depiction of Crucifixion with donor, as established by Rogier van der Weyden, in which the figures, as so often in van der Weyden's case, only act on the narrow pictorial stage in the foreground.[24] Below the Cross, on which hangs the slight figure of the suffering Christ, stand Mary and the apostle John. It presents an appeal for sympathy in equal measure for both the crucified Lord and the donor, kneeling to the right dressed in fashionable clothing. Admittedly there is no coat of arms by which to identify the donor, but his sword shows him to be a noble. Peter, the saint after whom he is

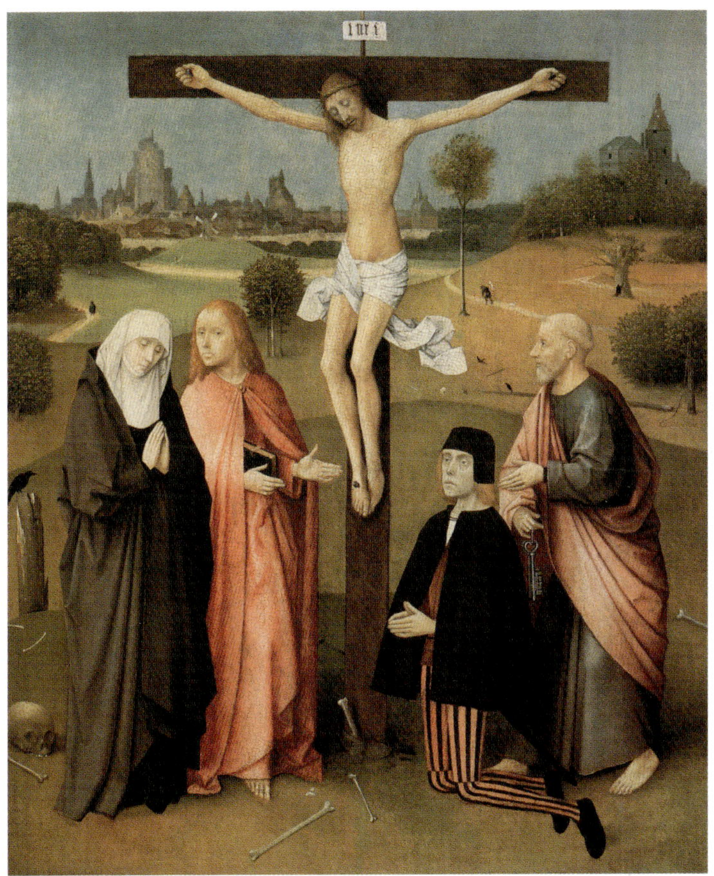

named and who is in possession of two keys, makes supplications in his favour (Matthew 16:19). Scattered bones reveal
the location of the scene to be the place mentioned in the
Bible as 'a place called the place of the skull, which is called
in the Hebrew Golgotha' (John 19:17). The proud outline of
Jerusalem stands out in the background, transformed into the
reality of Bosch's time and place.

11 Hieronymus Bosch, *Christ on the Cross with Donors and Saints*, c. 1490, oil on
panel.

The community of righteous believers, affirmed over and over again in imagery and in sermons, was taken in Bosch's day to be an affiliation modelled on the heavenly city of Jerusalem, home of the blessed. The eternal was located in the here and now, partly because the concept of faith associated the surviving holy relics with the actual presence of the individual saints. Christ himself was physically present within the celebration of the Mass by the transubstantiation of the bread and wine into His Body and Blood. Thereby the saint was assigned a fixed place in this world and this world a place in the salvific history that was not considered a thing of the past. God's plan of creation determined the present. The painted parts of the visible world in which the holy figures were shown thus depicted the unquestionable salvific significance for the present. Bosch's painting easily falls within this religious and pictorial tradition, though this should not detract from the fact that this is also a typical painting by Bosch. This can be seen in the painting technique and the use of colour, as well as the way in which the narrow trees are stippled and the blank faces are executed: 'We know these pointed, sickly heads', wrote Max J. Friedländer in 1927.[25]

Although there has never been any doubt that Bosch painted this work, it has attracted very little attention compared to his other works. This picture, which from the iconographic point of view is fairly modest, can at the same time be used to illustrate the characteristics of Bosch's painting. It has been pointed out that the attitude of Christ's head and the emotional restraint of the figures presented are paralleled by a mural in St John's Cathedral from around 1455 that has been convincingly attributed to Bosch's grandfather

Jan van Aken.[26] However, even though the overall composition and the details of the motifs are taken from other earlier examples of art, there is nothing comparable with Bosch's amazing use of his painting materials, nor his characteristic use of colour. The representation of the Crucifixion is linked to a painting dating from between 1490 and 1495, now in Frankfurt.[27] In terms of composition it harks back to an earlier work of art, a woodcut from about 1450.[28] The subject is 'Ecce Homo', the presentation of Christ before the people, described in detail in the Bible (John 19:4−6). After Christ's arrest and trial when He is scourged and reviled, He is brought before the Roman governor Pontius Pilate. Bosch shows Christ bound and wearing a crown of thorns, standing between two tormentors and a learned scribe who are pulling his clothing apart to reveal His naked, tortured body down to His loincloth, leaving spots of blood on the floor. Behind him, Pilate stands bearing a staff as evidence of his status as a judge, and his dialogue with the crowd is indicated by captions. The words 'Ecce homo' − 'Behold the man' − are coming out of his mouth. There is almost no need for the caption above the angry crowd: 'Crucife eum', they shout − 'Crucify him'. The red flag with the Turkish crescent fluttering in the background, the curious-seeming figure on the bridge, the architecture of towers looming up in an alien fashion, the toad on the shield belonging to the man on the right-hand side of the picture, along with the grotesque faces of the crowd, are symbols of evil. Bosch makes use of the pseudo-oriental motifs and the reference to the Turks − who in this period had brought practically all the holy sites of Christendom under their control − presenting to his contemporaries a comprehensive image of the enemies of Christ. Bosch's portrayal of the hideously distorted faces of the angry mob refers to the traditional gallery of grotesque faces of evil, straight out of a late medieval pattern book. They were not just intended to be a contrast to the figure of Christ, the embodiment of good. Their cruel reaction also provided a contrast to the figures of the donors, who were at one time clearly shown in full size in the foreground. They were removed and painted over, presumably in the sixteenth century. In the copies of Bosch's picture produced in this period they are no longer shown devoutly praying, as they are now revealed to have been in the original composition of only a few years earlier.

Careful restoration now allows one at least to get an idea of the original composition. On the left, below the dais where Christ is displayed, is where the paterfamilias was kneeling, painted particularly large in keeping with his importance. Opposite him, though one can hardly make it out any more, was where the women of the family were kneeling, right in front of the angry mob and in a sharp contrast to them. Behind the paterfamilias, and also larger than the five sons shown in the background, is another male figure. His tonsure shows him to be a man of religion. The dress of his order, perhaps a Dominican habit, can still be made out. He mouths the Latin prayer of the donors, which is inserted in gold letters in the picture: 'Salva nos Christe redemptor' – 'Christ, Redeemer, save us'. The figures of the donors represented, for the religious viewer of the picture, a direct counterweight to the negative example embodied in the baying mob. In the actual enactment of this prayer in front of the picture, which

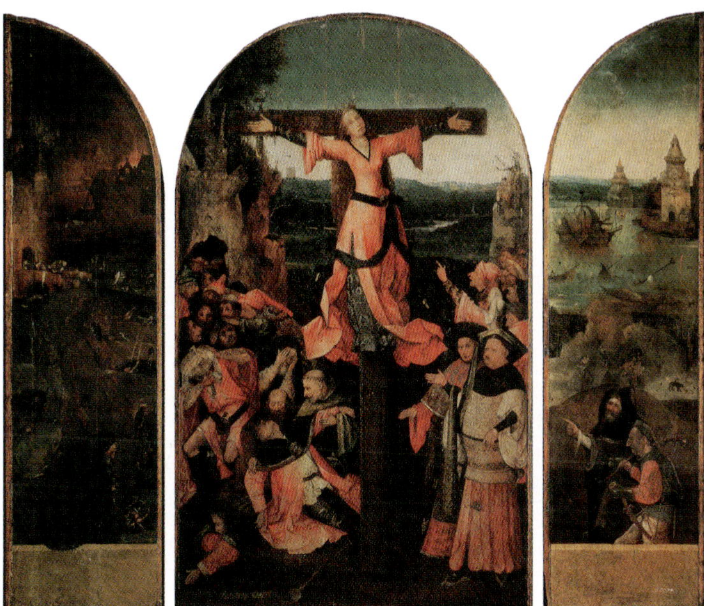

was presumably donated by way of an epitaph, the communion of the living and the dead became reality in the context of its original purpose. The removal of the figures of the donors is evidence of a changing role, and illustrates an aesthetic appreciation of Bosch, as do the copies of the Frankfurt picture surviving from this time. It was presumably owing to this new appreciation of his pictures as works of art, starting around 1500, that the figures of the donors on the triptych of *St Uncumber* (illus. 12) were painted over.[29]

12 Hieronymus Bosch, triptych of *St Uncumber*, c. 1505–15, oil on panel.

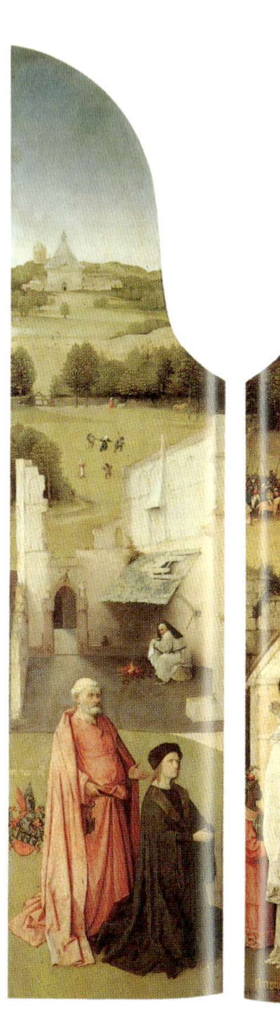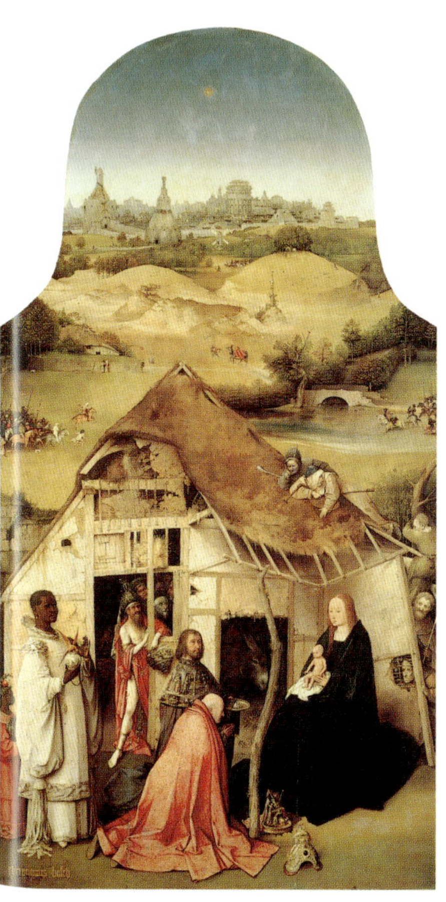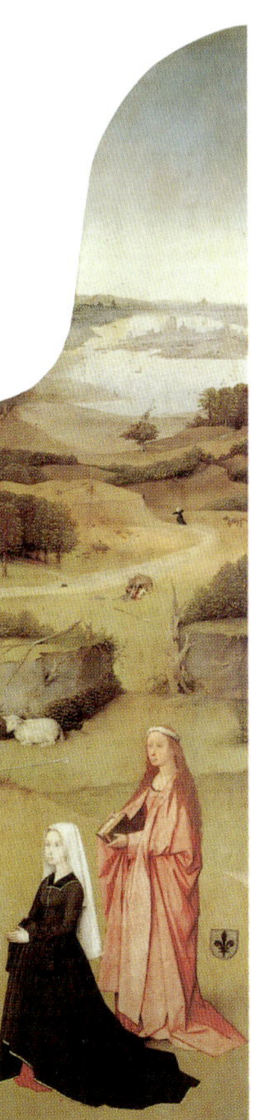

FOUR

From Christmas to Easter

I N ABOUT 1507 Hieronymus Bosch's younger contemporary Albrecht Dürer decided to write a manual of painting. In the introduction to this text, which never made it to print, he outlined what he considered to be the most noble function of painting. The art of painting, he writes, 'is used in the service of the Church, and through it the Passion of Christ is displayed, it also keeps the shape of men after their death'.[1] A similar view had already been put forward by the Italian Leon Battista Alberti, as well as by other painters, theologians and theorists of art. It was a widely held opinion that the noblest task of painting in the service of the Church was to illustrate the sufferings of Christ, an ideal with which Bosch would surely have concurred. A large number of his works bear testimony to this, since their main purpose was to contribute to the salvation of the souls of their wealthy donors. The events related in the biblical account of Christ's birth, suffering and death occupy a central role in Bosch's oeuvre, and his work is therefore a reflection of the religious devotion of the period.

One of the particularly impressive examples of this is an altarpiece showing the Adoration of the Magi (illus. 13).[2] The top of the central panel of this triptych, which was no doubt

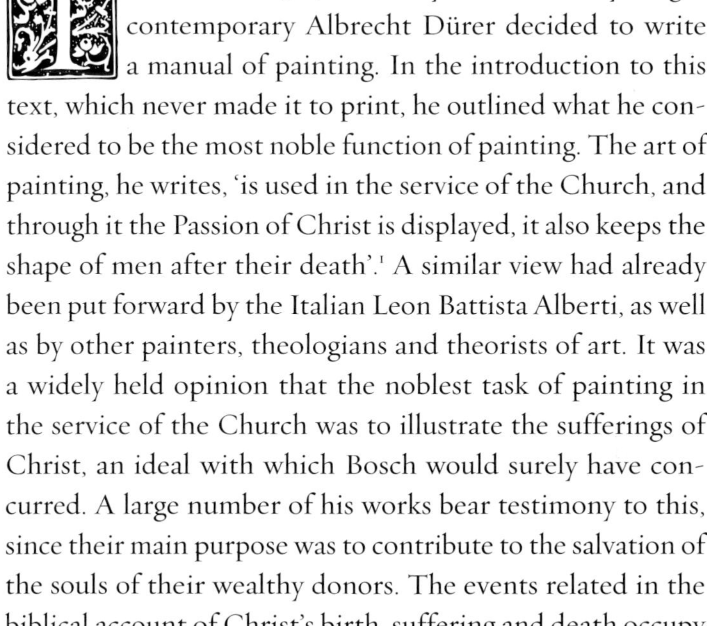

13 Hieronymus Bosch, *Adoration of the Magi*, 1485–1500, oil on panel.

conceived as an altarpiece, is shaped like the prow of a ship. The two wings continue the same graceful outline, which was then starting to become the favourite shape for altarpieces. Despite the clear tripartite division, the space is occupied by a single unified landscape, the raised horizon overlooked by a bright sky. In the centre we see the Adoration of the Magi and on the wings the donors, whose patron saints make supplications in their favour. The donors can be identified by the added coats of arms.[3] St Peter, with the keys in his hand, stands behind Peeter Scheyfve, shown kneeling on the left wing. Scheyfve had been a member of the linen weavers' guild since 1494, later becoming their deacon. In the following year he became the receiver of taxes for the city of Antwerp, a position that he possibly obtained through the influence of his father-in-law Peeter de Gramme, who had previously occupied this office. Scheyfve's second wife was Agnes de Gramme, who died around 1497 and is depicted on the right wing of Bosch's altarpiece. As Scheyfve remarried fairly soon, the date of the work is fairly reliable. Unfortunately, however, it is still not possible to say in which church in Antwerp the altarpiece was originally located, or when and how it came to be in Spain. For a long time it was presumed that the 1567 version now in Spain belonged to the secretary of the count of Egmont, who was involved in the uprising against the Habsburgs. However, confiscated by Jan Casembroot, this 'picture of the Three Magi, painted by Hieronymus Bosch, with two movable sides' showed 'on the outside the coats of arms of Bronchorst and Bosschuyse'.[4] It is difficult to accept an incorrect identification of arms in a period that was so precise about heraldic details, particularly since these differed so completely from the ones shown. Instead, one must conclude that the picture in Madrid of the 'Birth of Our Lord by the hand of Hieronymus Bosch', also with two wings, is the same one brought to the Escorial by Philip II in 1575.[5] What is certain is that neither this picture given to the Escorial nor the version confiscated in 1568 is the same as the *Adoration of the Magi* which, according to Gramaye, was to be found in the cathedral in 's-Hertogenbosch in 1610.[6] Consequently, we know that at some time there were in existence at least three triptychs by Bosch using similar iconography. A large number of works by other painters also bear witness to the popularity of the subject-matter closely associated with the Holy Mass. Indeed, just as Christ had appeared physically to the shepherds and the Magi, he was also present in the form of bread and wine at every celebration of Mass.

Bosch shows the Adoration in front of a stable placed centre stage in the picture and taking up almost the whole width of the middle panel, while the landscape is viewed from a lower perspective. The structure of the stable is not placed so prominently in the picture for its own sake but so as to rank the figures in a hierarchy in relation to the event. Mary is therefore seated with the tiny child on her lap, the projecting roof above her open to the sky. She is separated from the group of Magi by a column, supporting the suggestion of a baldachin, familiar from religious pictures. With their reverent solemnity, the Magi come across as priests carrying out a religious ceremony. Here Bosch makes use of a whole range of suggestions within the picture, linking the act of worship of the Son of God made flesh, represented in the picture, to the depiction of Mass being held in a real church. The kneeling king, for example, has placed an object before Mary, recalling the sacrifice of Isaac as related in the Old Testament. This scene is traditionally seen as a premonition of the death of Christ on the Cross, re-enacted in the celebration of Mass. The second kneeling king is presenting small white discs on a golden dish, a reference to the Host that is transformed into the body of Our Lord in the Holy Mass. Depicted on this king's blue mantle we can make out the Queen of Sheba's visit to Solomon described in the Bible, which at that time often served as a type in pictorial cycles for the Adoration of the Magi. The Moorish king, his face shown almost as an individual portrait, is bringing a silver orb, an ancient symbol of worldly power on which is seated a reddish-golden shining bird with its head bowed (illus. 14). It is reminiscent of the pelican depicted by Bosch elsewhere (see illus. 8), which saves its progeny through its blood offering. Alternatively, it may be a symbolic reference to the phoenix rising from the ashes. Either way, it is clearly intended to be read as a symbol of the Eucharist, since the picture on the silver orb shows the meeting between Abraham and Melchisedech, which was generally taken to be the Old Testament equivalent of the Last Supper.

The art-historical term 'disguised symbolism' has become the one most commonly used to sum up the range of symbolic associations of the motifs in early Dutch painting.[7] It is rather an unfortunate term as it wrongly suggests that the paintings contain secret and mysterious meanings. There was a widespread tendency in the Middle Ages to think in analogies, in figurative imagery and symbolic terms. There is no question that to understand the symbolic content of a picture one had

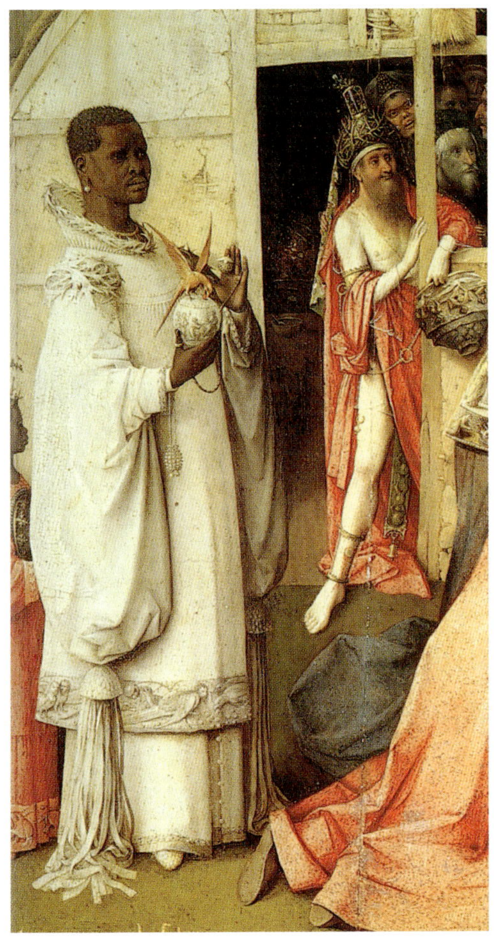

to possess a certain knowledge, but the symbolism was by
no means concealed. Many such pictures were, after all, on
public view, either in town halls or in churches. Particularly
in relation to Christian subject-matter, a distinct vocabulary
of imagery and motifs had been established, repeated over
and over again with variations. In the murals and altarpieces

14 Detail from Hieronymus Bosch, *Adoration of the Magi*.

that richly decorated churches, Christ and the salvation He brought to the world were regularly depicted. Repeatedly, His life and death, along with the legends associated with Him, were represented in pictures. The same goes for those narratives in which salvation was proclaimed, or in which the lives of the saints and martyrs who had spread the Gospel or died in His name were depicted. For example, Bosch portrays St Agnes, whose name is a reference to the lamb (Latin *agnus*), as well as St Joseph, who, according to legend, was so caring. He is shown on the left wing by a fire, where he is drying Jesus's swaddling clothes, made from his trousers.

It is due to the fact that the picture follows the pictorial tradition in such detail that the differences in iconography strike one all the more. Other painters have of course shown the shepherds as witnesses to the Adoration of the Magi, since they were also there. But mostly these peasant figures are depicted as displaying more dignity than Bosch's rather unconcerned-looking shepherds. The manner in which they are portrayed may be explained theologically by the fact that the shepherds were at that time identified with the Jews who had not recognized Christ and had denied Him, whereas the Magi represented the Gentiles who were prepared to worship the Messiah. As in the case of the earlier *Ecce Homo* in Frankfurt (see illus. 9), the small-scale motifs in the background suggest the presence of evil. The bear shown on the right attacking a lonely traveller and the woman threatened by the wolf recall the ever-present nearness of death. In light of the very dangers of earthly existence, it is incredible that the foolish people dancing to the bagpipes in the distance on the left wing are ignoring Christ's message of salvation, heralded by the brightly shining star.

One figure who is particularly out of place is standing in the darkness at the entrance to the dilapidated stable traditionally identified with the synagogue that has fallen into ruin with Christ's birth. The man is practically naked apart from a crimson robe and a number of curious accessories. In Bosch's use of symbolism this strikingly exotic appearance does not bode well in relation to the religious scene. He is carrying in his hands a three-tiered crown decorated with monkeys standing on their heads and wearing on his head a crown of thorns, the golden spikes of which seem not to bother him as they are not in contact with his forehead. A sore on his leg is encased in a transparent cylinder, like a holy relic. As he moves, a belt with a small bell is revealed, decorated with a pattern of figures standing on their heads, suggesting the world turned upside down. The heathen and alien quality summed up in this figure, with its blasphemous parody of Christian symbolism, serves as a convincing caricature of a redeemer figure. To a contemporary observer this could only be the Antichrist. For the theologians of the time the world was full of such false prophets, whom the Bible frequently warned against. Even a critical and educated contemporary such as Sebastian Brant, the author of *Ship of Fools*, was totally convinced that the appearance of the Antichrist preceding the Apocalypse was nigh.[8] Others believed for certain that the Antichrist had already appeared and the time was at hand when the scriptures would be fulfilled.

The belief that the Antichrist belonged to the tribe of Dan and that his earthly mother was a Jewish whore was part and

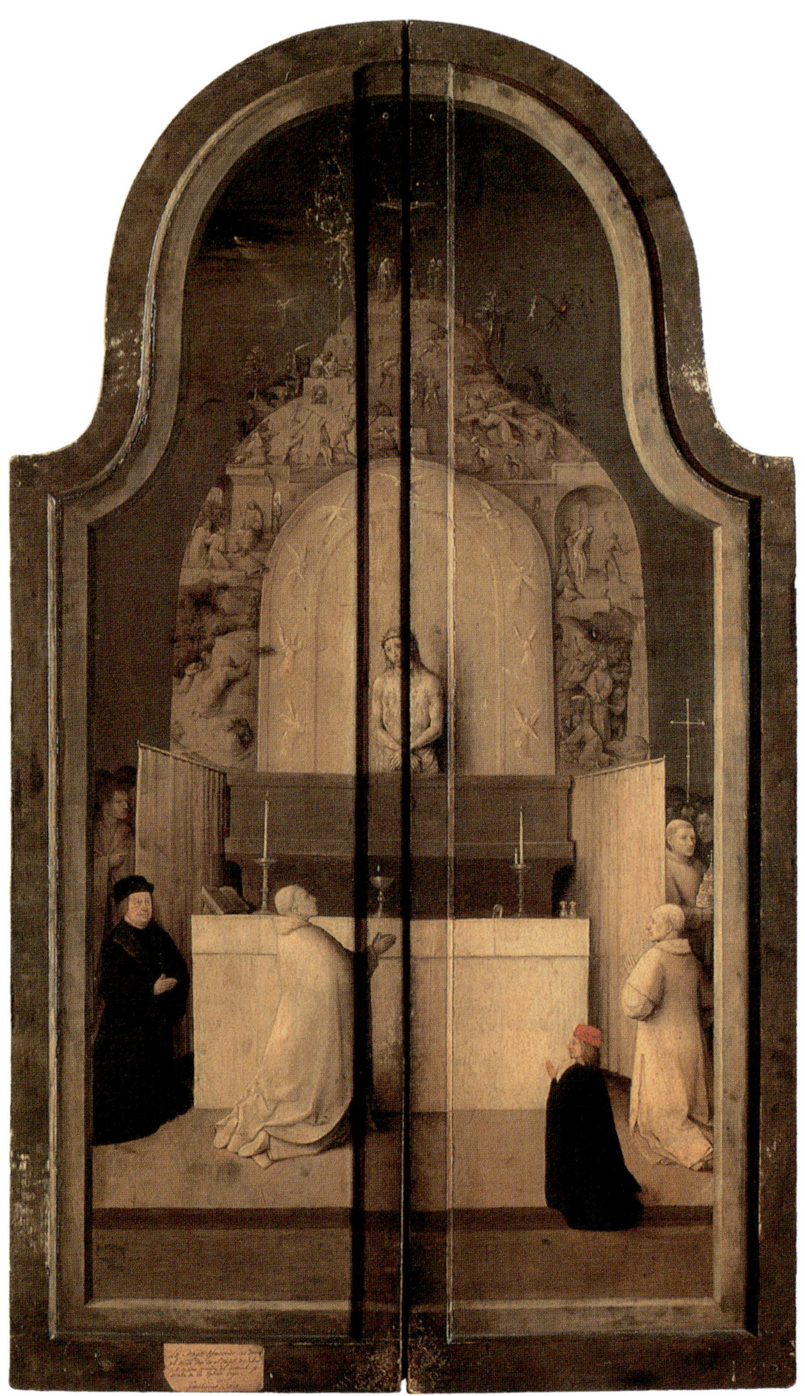

parcel of the anti-Semitic legends current throughout the whole of Christendom. It was thought that just as the people of Israel had once denied and tormented the Messiah, they now refused to accept the Eucharist. What was worse, a rumour was abroad of cases of sacrilege involving the Host turning into flesh and blood.[9] Pogroms and persecution followed in reply to what was seen as a threat.[10] Others linked the concept of the Antichrist to the Turks, who were threatening the gates of Europe. They were seen as the peoples of Gog and Magog mentioned in Revelation who would be present at the last battle at the end of time.[11] The final great battle prophesied in the Bible may be suggested by the two enemy armies Bosch shows riding towards one another behind the stable, though Bosch does not focus on the threat, but on the hope represented by Christ. His appearance celebrated at each Mass signifies the hope of salvation made real by receiving Holy Communion. Thus it is surely no coincidence that when the altarpiece is closed, the figure of Pope Gregory celebrating Mass covers the figure of the Antichrist exactly (illus. 15). On the outer wings when the altarpiece is closed is shown the legendary celebration of Mass at which Christ physically appeared after a server had doubted the act of transubstantiation, by which Christ is truly present in the bread and wine. Where normally the figure of the Redeemer and the instruments of torture are shown, Bosch frames Christ naked and shackled with a series of extremely realistic images showing his Passion, in which the shape of the altarpiece is made use of. The high point of this is Christ on the Cross, painted directly on the central join between the

15 Hieronymus Bosch, closed outer wings of the *Adoration of the Magi*, c. 1496–7.

wings and exactly in the place on the outside where on the
inside the Star of Bethlehem is shining.

The representation of the Mass of St Gregory, by conven-
tion arranged centrally in contemporary print illustrations,
is notably reflected in Bosch's version by keeping the usual
central figure of the Man of Sorrows, but having him painted
on the frame of the shutters.[12] When the altarpiece is opened
up, the body of Christ and the Man of Sorrows also open
up, revealing to all the Incarnation shown on the inside and
enacted in the celebration of Mass at the altarpiece. The
scene is depicted almost entirely in greyish-brown monochrome, except for two donor figures added a few years after
the completion of the altarpiece. They suggest that there was
a second sacred use for it before it was incorporated into the
collection of Philip II. As there are no additional coats of
arms and those existing were not removed, we may be dealing with relatives of the original donors, but who they were
has not yet been satisfactorily identified. Nevertheless, we
can at least say that the iconography points to it as having
been destined at one time for an altar at which the sacrificial
offering of Mass was enacted in the belief that it was identical to the sacrifice of Christ on the Cross. For Bosch, the
altarpiece served a further purpose: he was now represented
by an exquisite piece of painting in the up-and-coming city
of Antwerp, which was at the time in the process of overtak-
ing the mercantile centres of Bruges and Ghent and building
itself up into a metropolis.[13]

Given its greater significance in the Gospels, the depiction
of the Passion plays a more important role in Bosch's oeuvre
than the birth of the Saviour. After all, Christ redeemed the

sins of mankind through his suffering and death on the Cross. The suffering of Jesus is also illustrated in the surviving fragment of an altarpiece now in Vienna (illus. 16).[14] Also in the composition of this small triptych, of which only the left wing, cut off at the top, survives, we find the attempt to create a correspondence between the outside and the inside image, a practice which was unusual elsewhere.[15] A naked child is shown on the reverse outer wing in a dark roundel against a red background (illus. 17), carrying a toy windmill and supported by a walking frame. Even though the Bible does not mention children in an entirely positive way (1 Corinthians 13:11), this figure has been interpreted as an allegorical symbol of foolish ignorance.[16] It is more appropriate, however, to see it as the Christ Child starting out in all innocence on what is a premonition of the Way of the Cross. The way the angle of the Cross and position of Jesus's legs on the inside panel are displayed show a remarkable correspondence. His suffering is brutally illustrated in a similar way to the Frankfurt *Ecce Homo*. Spike-studded wooden blocks dangling from His belt add to his suffering. His physical agony cries out in an appeal for pity. Once again we find the clearly instructive contrast between the face of Christ and the largely brutal faces of His tormentors, one of whom again is carrying the shield with a toad on it. An instructive juxtaposition is also being staged in the foreground, where two soldiers are tormenting the bad thief while the good thief is busy confessing his sins to another thief dressed as a priest. The attempt illustrated by this motif to link the biblical events to the present goes hand in hand with the composition of the picture, which was designed to be easily grasped, using two overlapping spatial

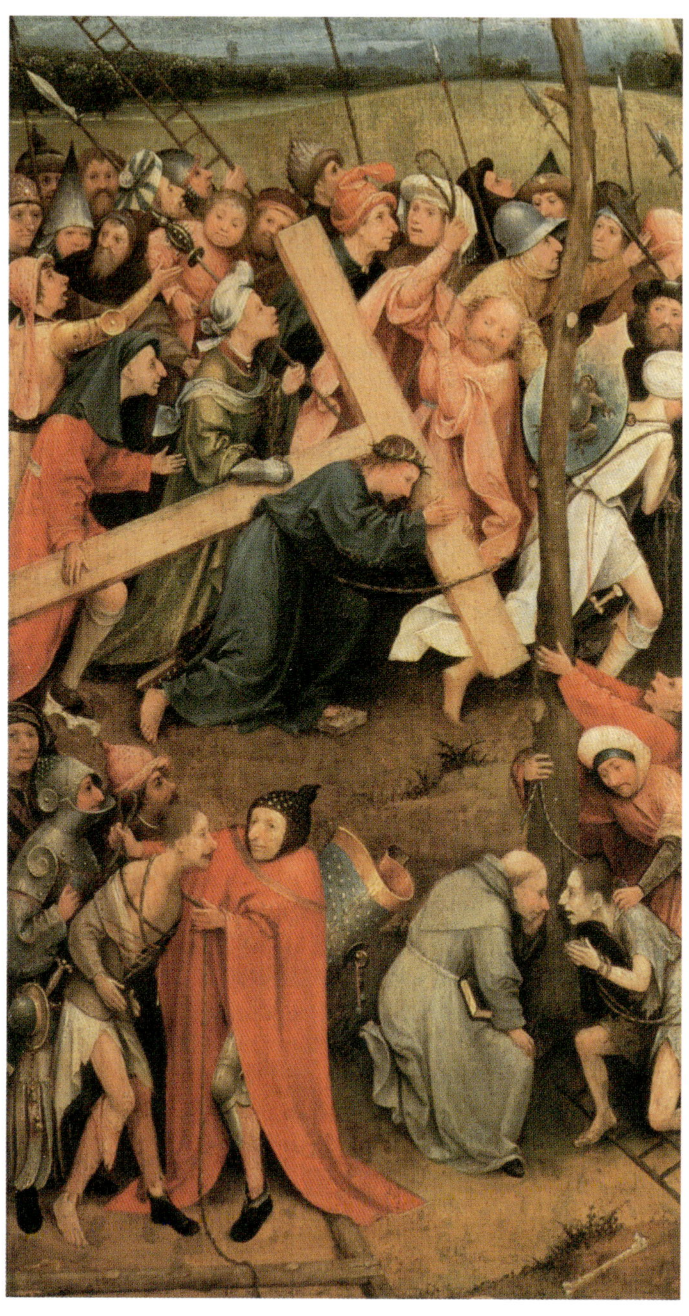

16 Hieronymus Bosch, *Christ Carrying the Cross*, c. 1500–10, oil on panel.

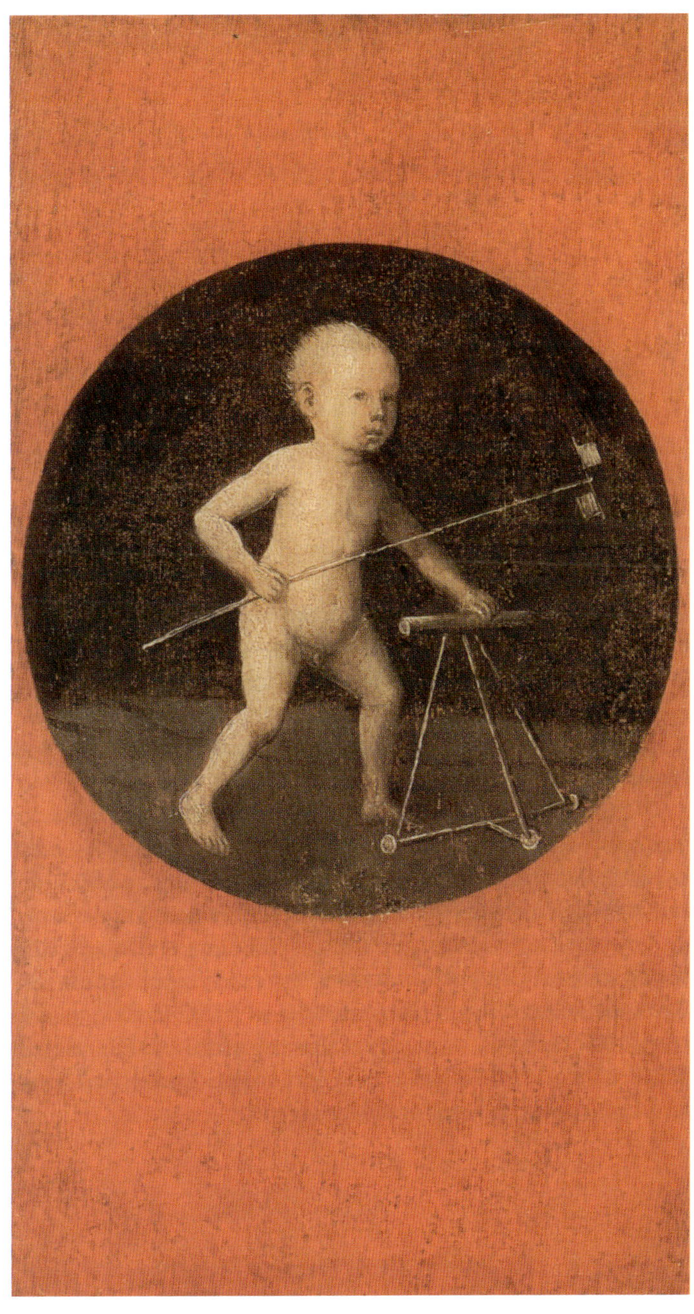

17 Hieronymus Bosch, reverse side of *Christ Carrying the Cross: Christ Child with a Walking Frame, c.* 1500–1510.

zones and an absence of any spatial recession in the middle distance. Both these tendencies have equivalents in other late Gothic pictures, particularly in book illuminations.

A few years earlier, Bosch had painted a similarly conventional *Christ Carrying the Cross* (illus. 18), though it was nearly seven times the size of the picture in Vienna (see illus. 16).[17] The painting shows Christ crushed under the weight of the Cross, helped by the elderly Simon of Cyrene. Behind him on the left the ugly faces of the executioners are visible while on

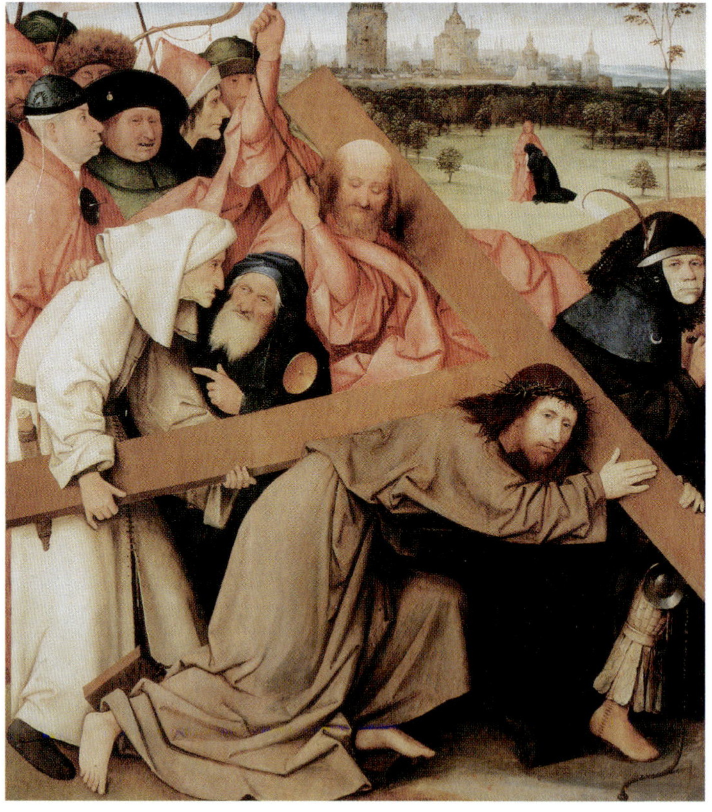

18 Hieronymus Bosch, *Christ Carrying the Cross*, c. 1495–1500, oil on panel.

the right the weeping Mary is collapsing at the feet of John the Evangelist. Again Bosch draws from the familiar gallery of figures to give character to the faces. Something that strikes one is the facial similarity between the man shown brandishing a rope in front of the Cross and the almost identical features on the painting *Ecce Homo*. Presumably the intention behind this characterization was to make the executioners seem real, as examples of sinful mankind throughout the ages, and to present the executioners who did not recognize Christ as representatives of those who have not yet set out on the road to follow Christ. The sufferings of Christ for the sake of mankind are again graphically illustrated here by the spiked wooden blocks under His feet. The narrative of the picture, however, comes over as more concentrated in comparison to the narrative composition of *Christ Carrying the Cross* in Vienna, and Jesus's gaze looking directly out of the picture calls for a heightening of devotion and reflection on the Passion. The original purpose of the picture must remain an open question, but one thing is sure: the painting was catalogued as an individual piece of work as early as 1574 when it was handed over to the Escorial, even though it was unusually large for a devotional picture.

More representative of this type of picture is *Christ Crowned with Thorns*, dating from around 1495 (illus. 19).[18] It is the earliest of Bosch's depictions of the Passion in a half-length format, in which he interprets and develops a type of picture current in Flanders at this period. The large, firmly modelled figures are crowded together with the utmost simplicity, set against a plain grey background. Christ is standing calmly in the middle and is looking almost thoughtfully at the viewer

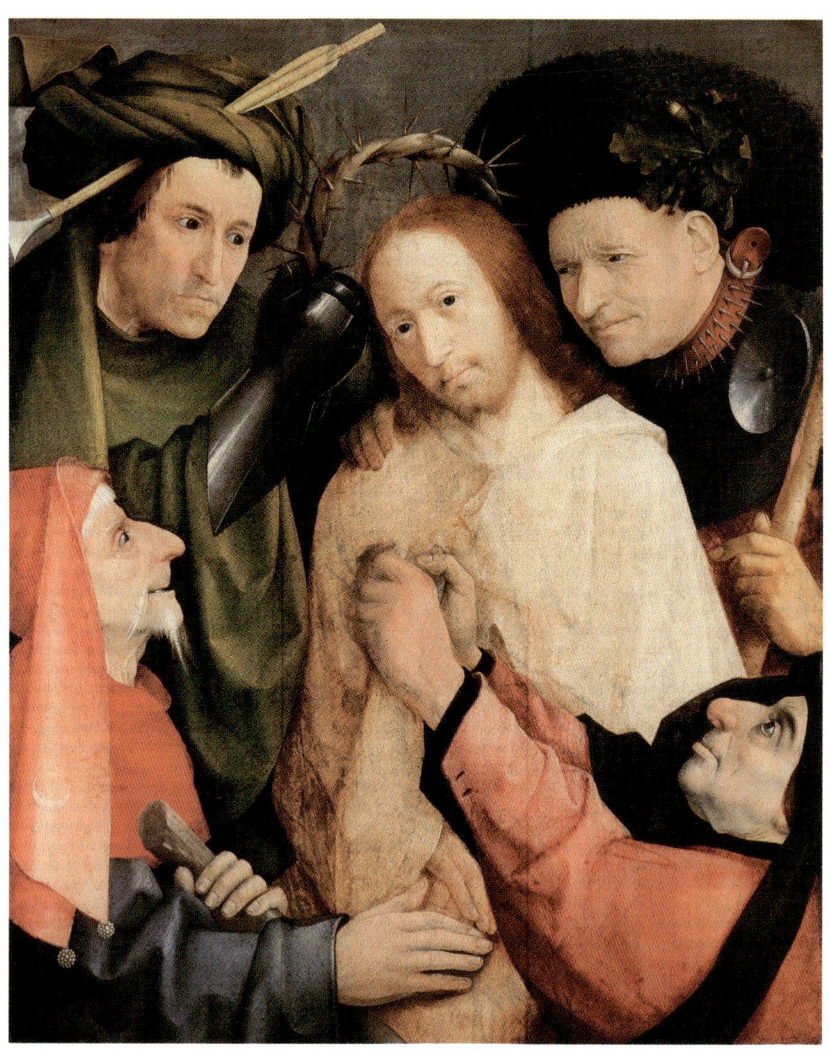

19 Hieronymus Bosch, *Christ Crowned with Thorns*, c. 1495, oil on panel.

while the four tormentors attempt, seemingly ineffectually, to scourge him. Bosch is not just appealing for sympathy but depicts Christ, still totally unharmed, as the ideal human being and as a model of virtue whose suffering is presented as an example of the correct conduct of a Christian in the face of danger and misfortune. Apart from the dog collar, a reference to the Psalms (22:17) included in order to characterize the figure, Bosch uses the faces simply as an illustration of sinfulness and moral corruption.

The climax of this religious instruction through a visual contrast of good and evil is reached in another picture attributed to Bosch, probably dating from some time after 1510 (illus. 20).[19] In this case the hideous faces stand out almost as in a poster against the black background of the picture. The impressive arrangement attempted on the wing showing Hell in *The Garden of Earthly Delights* seems to be carried out here on a larger scale (see illus. 10).[20] Right in the middle of the picture, emphasized by the diagonal upright of the Cross, Christ's face, full of suffering, shines out. The picture is crowded out with seemingly menacing faces of grotesque ugliness, the characters of *Christ Carrying the Cross* in Vienna (see illus. 16) all being represented. The repentant thief is shown at the top right, while the bad one is placed bottom left and is arguing with one of the executioners. The cast is even swelled by the figure of St Veronica, thoughtfully smiling as she holds the veil with the image of Christ's face imprinted on it, looking out of the picture.

The iconic nature of the Ghent *Christ Carrying the Cross* (see illus. 20) has never been in question, but the attribution to Bosch has been a subject of great dispute.[21] There is no comparable pictorial work of Christian devotion in the art of the early sixteenth century on such a large scale, in the way it groups together nineteen almost wholly grotesque caricatures of heads within such a small space. It is nevertheless, for that very reason, possibly a late work by Bosch, though this classification immediately raises another problematic question. Given the fragmentary nature of what has survived of Bosch's oeuvre and the patchy nature of the written records, it is hardly surprising that there has been so little agreement about the chronology of his works.[22] It is no easy matter to identify a stylistic development within the surviving works, particularly since none of them is dated or can be definitively linked to any datable commission. Scientific analysis, particularly dendrochronology, has come up with a good deal of data in the last few years. Thus all the panels that were made of wood from trees felled after Bosch's death can be ruled out as works painted by him. Where it can be proved that Bosch obtained panels that were no longer needed from an old altarpiece, presumably to repaint them, and he would therefore have been painting on old, seasoned panels, dendrochronology can be of no use in establishing the order of the works.

Nevertheless, one can point to stylistic developments, making possible a relative chronology of the works. This can be in relation to surviving sources, the provenance of the pictures, their use and the context of their commission, and visual elements that provide clues for dating such as the style of dress in the pictures. Recently analysis of the pictures by means of infrared reflectography in particular has informed the debate. It has become possible to identify different related groups as regards the style of the underdrawing, as well as differences that stand out as being by another hand and can possibly be explained in terms of the working practices of the workshop.[23] Developments can be identified as well. The *Ecce Homo* in Frankfurt exhibits a wealth of detail and preliminary drawing; *St John the Evangelist on Patmos* is much more restrained, while underneath *Christ Crowned with Thorns* in London there are only sketchy shorthand-like lines done for guidance.[24] In works linked by the style of the underdrawing there are some other common features, such as the representation of the eyes, hands and fingers. The same relationships and a common development can also be seen in the faces. From the masque-like heads that seem to have come out of a pattern book, seen in the Frankfurt *Ecce Homo* and the painting of *Christ Carrying the Cross* in Madrid, the faces develop into the individualized figures of the Prado *Adoration of the Magi* (see illus. 13) or of *Christ Crowned with Thorns* (see illus. 19), and on to the heads of *Christ Carrying the Cross* in Ghent (see illus. 20). It goes without saying that these tendencies are not only attributable to artistic development but to the different pictorial demands, the context of the commission and the intellectual level of the target audience.

The connoisseur focusing chiefly on the individual style of the artist has come in for increasing criticism in recent times. Indeed it is worth carefully analysing basic ways of seeing when tracing the development of an oeuvre. Of course, it is more than questionable to speculate on the evolution from the early period, through maturity and up to the late period, in the case of a painter for whom not a single work survives from before his thirtieth year. Nevertheless such a

development can plausibly be traced on the basis of biography, as it is possible to identify a gulf separating the works
largely by his own hand from those by others of the same
time and place. Among other things, Bosch's characteristic
use of colour is relevant here, such as the unique harmony
between the shades of red and green, the numerous varie-
ties of red mainly brightened with white, and the irrational
play of iridescent shades against a dark background. The
way in which Bosch uses paint as a means of artistic expression is without parallel in his age and makes his pictures
unique. It is true that the imitators and admirers who cop-
ied the products of his graphic invention even in his lifetime
adopted the same subject-matter, manner of composition
and repertoire of motifs, but they did not adopt his formal
language, based as it is on the manner of painting.[25]

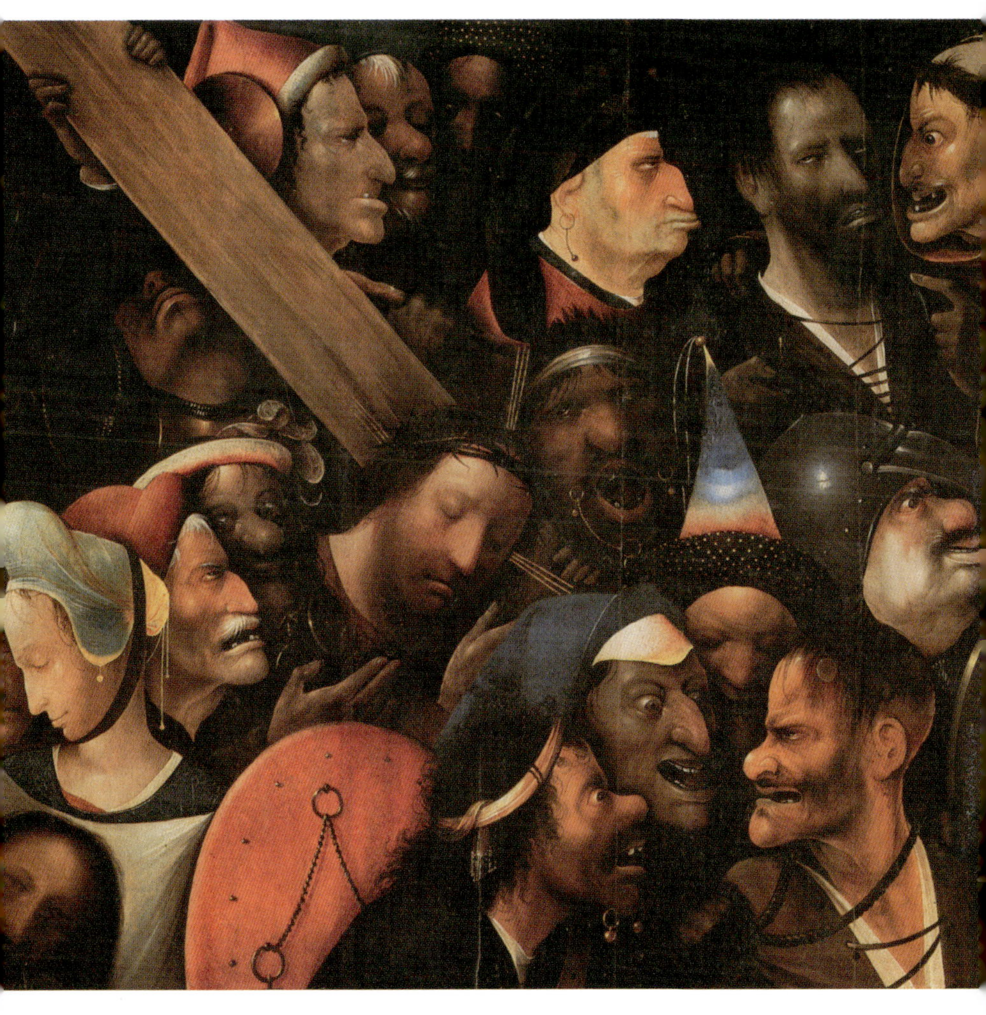

20 Hieronymus Bosch, *Christ Carrying the Cross*, after 1510, oil on panel.

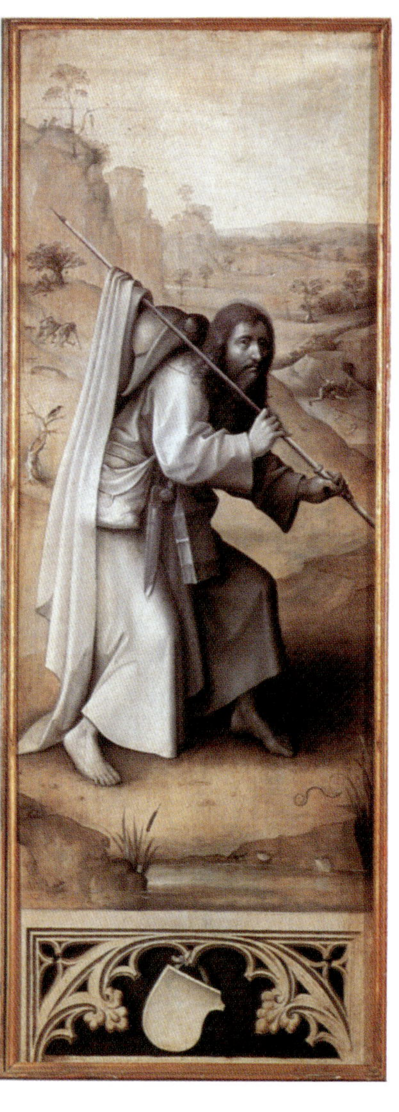
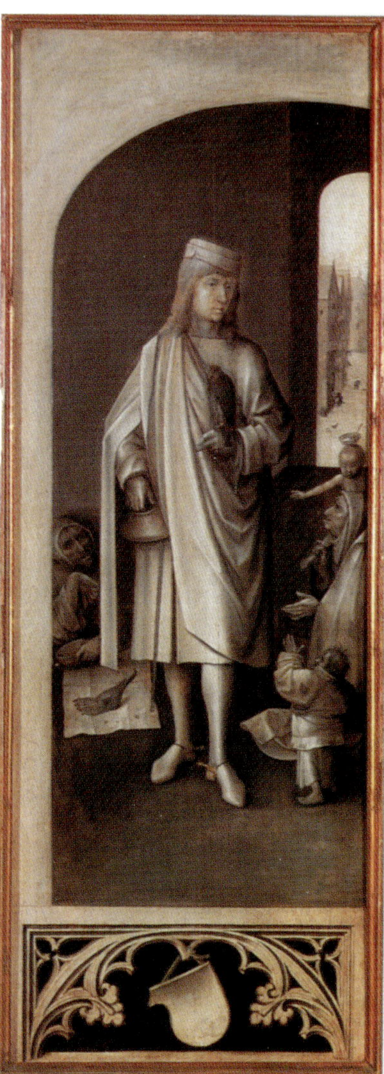

FIVE

Devout Examples

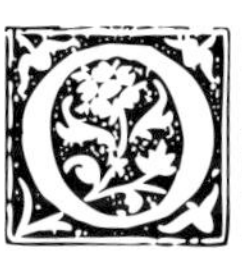O NE OF THE MOST popular and frequently imitated paintings by Bosch is *The Temptation of St Anthony*. Many imitations made during his lifetime can be found in the catalogues of collections and legacies all over Europe. At least two St Anthony pictures, for example, belonged to Isabella of Spain, the mother-in-law of Philip the Handsome, who in addition claimed ownership of two depictions of the penitent Mary Magdalene, also attributed to Bosch.[1] Another picture of St Anthony by Bosch was owned by Margaret of Austria, who ruled over the Netherlands from 1507, after the death of her brother Philip the Handsome, as regent for her son, the future emperor Charles V. In 1516 she had received the picture, described even then as being old, as a gift from Charles's sister Eleanor, and had it hanging in her bedroom.[2] As the name of the painter is given in the court records, the picture was clearly considered not only a work of religious devotion but a work of art. Evidence shows that even in his lifetime Bosch's pictures were seen as works of art, though this does not exclude the possibility of them continuing to be associated with religious practice.

The modern distinction between spirituality and religious practice being perceived as a private matter, on the one hand,

21 Hieronymus Bosch, closed outer wings of the *Last Judgment*, c. 1505, oil on panel.

and as part of the public sphere on the other, was unheard of in Bosch's time. Instead, religiosity as part of communal living – even and especially at court – suffused all aspects of life. In Bosch's depictions of the saints, the figures, familiar from traditional accounts of the lives of the saints and countless illustrations of them, are presented in a totally new manner. His figures are not lifeless pictorial objects of devotion, even when, as he does on occasion, he shows the figures of the saints on the outer sides of an altarpiece just to complete the scene (illus. 21). The pictures of St James the Greater and the other saint on the outer wings of the *Last Judgment* in Vienna are painted in a traditional manner in grisaille on panel. Unlike most of the other painters of his time, however, Bosch does not imitate sculpture through painting but produces visual narratives in simple monochrome. It is therefore not the figure of the saint as an object of veneration that is foregrounded, but a visual narrative illustrating his exemplary life.

This form of representation can be explained in terms of the theological debate that was current at the time around the cult of imagery, which had been gathering momentum through the course of the fifteenth century. Critical theologians of the time demanded that the saints should not be worshipped as patron saints and their images venerated, but that their deeds should be taken as models for guiding people's own lives. In his *Handbook of a Christian Knight*, Erasmus of Rotterdam, the great critic of his age, condemned the sort of idolatry that was focused not so much on Christ as on the veneration of images of the saints. In his *Praise of Folly*, published in Latin in 1511 and circulated around Europe in

numerous editions and pirated copies, Erasmus drew attention to the 'superstitious cult of images' and the mindless
veneration of saints.[3] Bosch painted the lives and sufferings
of the saints in keeping with the demand – which Erasmus
was not the only one to make – to improve one's life and not
to hope for material advantage simply by gazing at images of
saints. His depiction of *St Christopher Carrying the Christ Child*
(illus. 22), dating from some time before 1500, does not
show the broad-shouldered friend in need who, according
to popular superstition satirized by Erasmus, had the power
of protecting people against 'sudden death' without being
given the last rites simply by looking at him. At the same time
Bosch's painting is different from all those pictures where the
depiction of the figures and the landscape has the quality of
heightened mimesis in order to render atmospheric effects
in a picturesque fashion or to imitate the world of things
just as they appear. Bosch's Christopher, leaning heavily on
his stick, carrying the burden of the world, embodied in the
Christ Child, over the river, is surrounded by motifs of dis-
aster and decay. A small figure on the bank is the hermit who
converted Christopher. Christopher had wanted to serve the
most powerful master and had been prepared to dedicate
himself to the Devil until he saw the Devil terrified at the
sight of a crucifix.

Bosch's picture can be interpreted as a painted exegesis
of the legend of the saint in the tradition of the *Legenda aurea*
and theological writings of the time. All the alien and darker
motifs are to be seen in relation to the figure of the Redeemer
and the saint shown in the middle, and are included by Bosch
in a world as he imagined it possessed by evil. On the left in

the foreground, the mast sticking out of the water and the rigging suggest a shipwreck; in the background a tiny naked figure has torn its clothes off, fleeing from a monster. What appears to be the hermit's treehouse is particularly puzzling. From it a jug is suspended whose shape and colour are rendered naturalistically, but which has been blown up out of all proportion. From the Christian perspective merely the exaggerated size of the object is enough to hint that something not in keeping with Christianity is going on. It may indicate that even the hermit's home is not without its sins and temptations. The larger-than-life jug, along with the roast chicken above on the pole, may suggest the deadly sin of gluttony. The broken jug may also refer to lost innocence or unchastity. Bosch's contemporaries might have understood his visual references to the ever-present power of evil in exactly the same way as the public nowadays might react to a reference to Osama bin Laden in a music video by the rapper Eminem.

In the contemporary notion of pictures, everything that Bosch had included in his depiction of St Christopher could therefore be interpreted. Likewise, every single motif was individually interpretable in relation to the fourfold meaning of scripture in biblical exegesis. This medieval practice of interpretation is based on the idea that every word – that is, the *vox* or the *significans* – has only one meaning: the thing signified. The meaning of words was here said to have originated with human beings – with Adam's naming of things. On the other hand, according to St Thomas Aquinas in his *Summa theologiae* (1, qu. 1, a. 10), the thing itself – the *res* or the *significatum* – was said to have many different meanings. The meaning of things was held to be God-given because God had

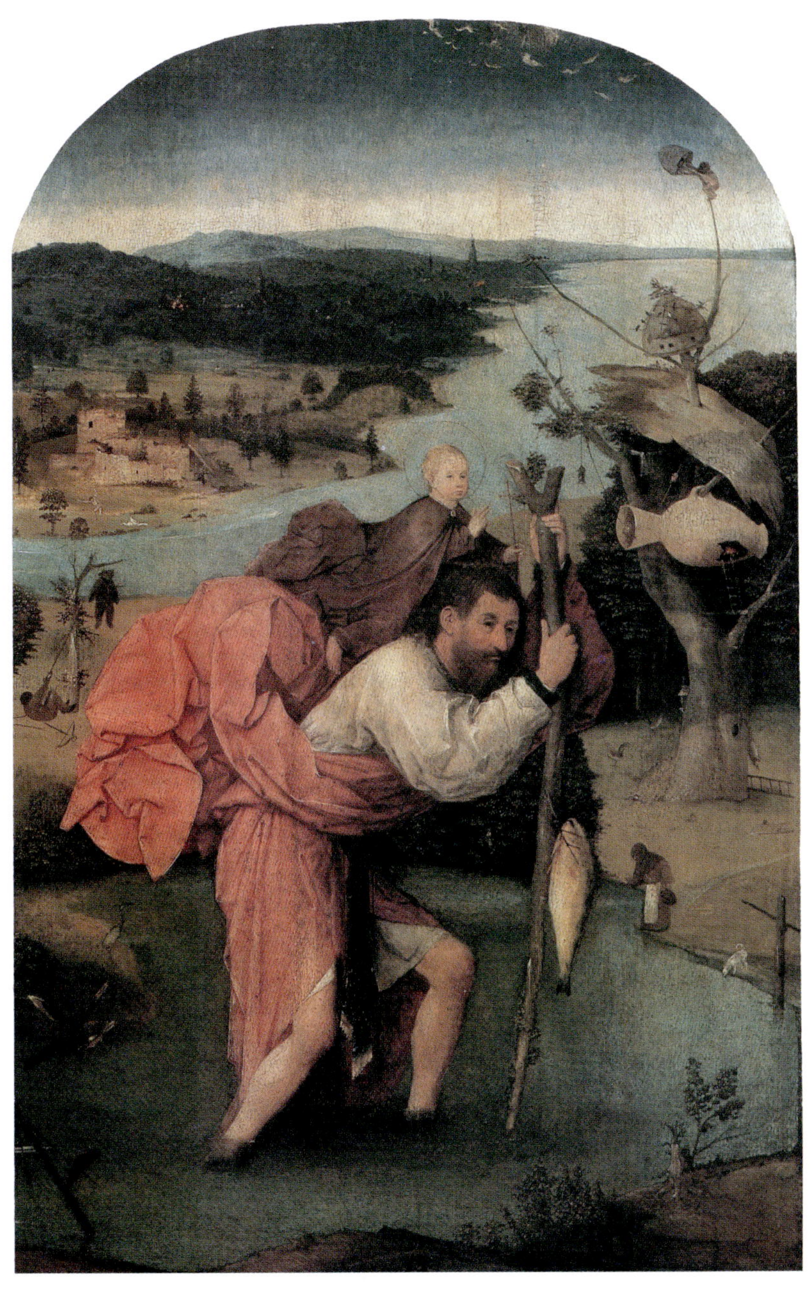

22 Hieronymus Bosch, *St Christopher Carrying the Christ Child*, before 1500, oil on panel.

himself written the book of Creation. Based on this premise, Western theology had very early on developed the doctrine of the dual or multiple meaning of scripture, culminating in the much-quoted principle of the fourfold meaning of scripture: 'The letter teaches of deeds, allegory of what is believed, morality of what is done, anagogy of things to come.'[4]

According to this doctrine of the fourfold meaning of scripture propagated by St Augustine, one of the Fathers of the Church, a word in the historical sense signifies the thing named in each case, which according to the Latin term *res* means both the thing and the prevailing conditions. The second, allegorical meaning is derived from these conditions, including its relevance to the Gospel story. The third level is the moral and tropological meaning, from the Greek *tropos* – turn or way – focused on the significance of the thing for the individual soul in the world. Finally, the fourth or anagogical meaning, from the Greek word *anago* – ascent – is focused on the promise of a world beyond. This model of interpretation was widespread in Bosch's day, eventually even becoming the basis of new religious or secular texts. Thus allegory took on the role of a universal model of interpretation, a *hermeneutica universalis*. This included in particular depictions of St Christopher, to which it was applied so automatically that even Protestant theologians recommended it. Martin Luther saw in the thoroughly laudable pictures of this saint an 'example and a likeness of the Christian life'.[5] And it was in fact a picture of St Christopher that Philip Melanchthon in 1531, in his *Apology of Augustine's Confessions* and in *Elementa rhetorices*, also took as an example of his concept of useful instruction through pictures:[6]

In my opinion the picture of St Christopher is what originally came to mind for the purpose of giving an example of a preacher of the Gospel as he is carrying Christ to show him to other people. Such a man must be capable of enormous spiritual power and that is why he is painted with a big, strong body. And just as those who preach the Gospel are faced with endless danger, this hero is stepping out through a sea or right through the waves . . . You see how cleverly this picture illustrates the nature of Christ and in particular what a preacher of the Gospel must be made of and what he will have to bear. This picture therefore deserves praise and it is displayed in all the churches – not to feed superstition thereby but to remind us of the dangers facing us.[7]

Even if Catholic theologians did not go along with all the details of this method of interpretation,[8] there was nevertheless a widely shared consensus that depictions of the Gospel story and of the lives of the saints should convey messages of moral teaching, speaking directly to the interested observer, both entertaining and educating him.

This is also true in the case of the picture painted around 1495 of the saint after whom Bosch is named (illus. 23).[9] Here, St Jerome is anything but an object of idolatry calling for veneration. The life of the great teacher of the Church whom we have to thank for the standard Latin translation of the Bible, the Vulgate, was not just familiar to educated people in Bosch's day; the legend of the lion that had a thorn removed from its paw by Jerome and so became a tame and

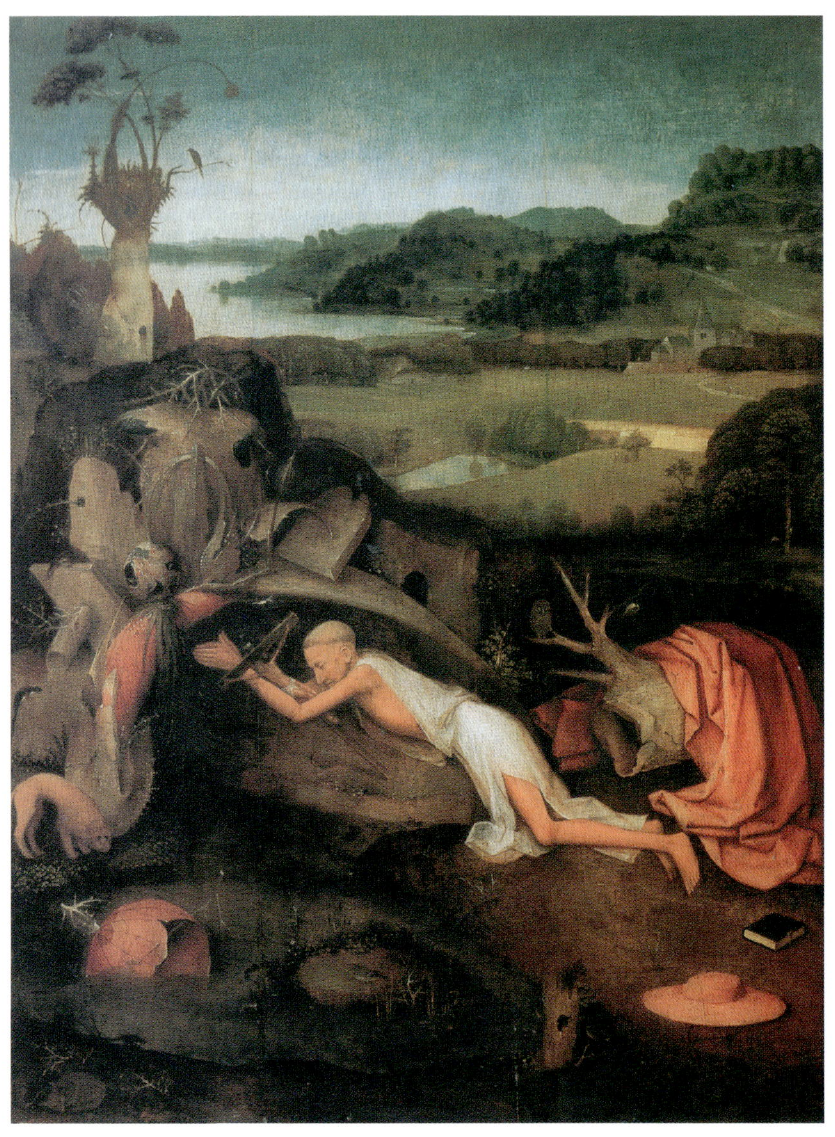

23 Hieronymus Bosch, *St Jerome at Prayer, c.* 1495, oil on panel.

faithful companion was widely known. Unlike the arrangement in traditional representations, Bosch shows the thin
and haggard-looking saint prostrate, fervently cradling the
crucifix in his arms, against an open landscape. Starting out
as a dark, uniformly brown foreground, it then stretches away
into a green middle distance in which a farm becomes visible
towards the soft blue hills of the background. Jerome's cardinal's hat is lying on the ground behind him and the splendid
red robe is abandoned, thrown over a dead tree trunk. His
prayer book is also abandoned, along with his companion the
lion, shown tiny and emaciated on the left-hand side of the
picture. The weird plants and vegetation growing rank and
decaying around him, as well as all the animals surrounding
him, are seemingly ignored by the hermit lost in meditation.
He takes as much notice of the lizard as he does of the little
birds, or the owl sitting on the branch of the dead tree, or for
that matter the fox, curled up asleep at the front edge of the
picture, right next to a pecking cockerel.

For the observer unfamiliar with the theological ideas
and texts, a lot of what is in this picture may come across
as alien. This is not, however, entirely the fault of Bosch's
manner of visual narration and his nature symbolism, but is
mainly due to the fact that knowledge about the themes and
motifs of Christian art and the narratives based on them is not
nowadays as widespread as it was then. The observer with a
thorough knowledge of the Bible may be reminded, looking at
the fox, of the passage in St Matthew's Gospel in which Jesus
describes His place in the world: 'The foxes have holes, and the
birds of the air have nests; but the Son of Man hath not where
to lay his head' (Matthew 8:20). For the observer familiar

with St Jerome's letters, the landscape shown by Bosch calls to mind Jerome's description of that 'wilderness' into which he had withdrawn. In his call for people to rise up and follow Christ, in his letter to Eustochium Jerome had told of the time when he 'had no companions but scorpions and wild beasts . . . there I made my oratory, there the house of correction for my unhappy flesh.'[10] Based on this text, a collection of lives of the saints called the *Vaderboek* relates that he stayed there day and night, 'lying on his face – not daring to raise his eyes to Heaven'.[11] Like Jerome's letter, Bosch's painting should be interpreted as a call to follow Christ. This central message is a guide to the interpretation of details that at first glance seem alien. This is exactly what the hybrid plants stand for, for example, with their rank, part-hollow, part-thorny growth; a gardener would perhaps refer to them as 'nature running riot'. They embody the sins and temptations of the world, as it were, present since the world began, which St Jerome sought to overcome through prayer and fasting.

This might be a key to interpreting all the details in the picture within an interpretative framework based on the Gospel. In Bosch's day, when people looked at pictures as allegories, their multiple layers of reference were not decoded according to a system of fixed meanings. Various ways of interpreting the same picture were therefore possible, and desirable. The only thing that was beyond question for contemporaries was that the saints, regarded as examples illustrating the way to follow Christ, were not associated with heresy or some arcane doctrine.

Bosch's pictures of saints were designed to be thought-provoking and an encouragement to follow Christ. Take for example a small triptych with an image of a crucified female saint (see illus. 12):[12] this work again had its origin in the context of private religious devotion, but the figures of the donors once portrayed on the insides of the wings were painted over at quite an early date. The damaged central panel has also been considerably reworked. That is why, in 1771, Antonio Maria Zanetti was not sure whether the picture showed a male or a female saint. Even now art historians cannot agree on the identity of the beautifully dressed girl depicted. It was thought to be St Julia, although her legend makes no mention of a crucifixion. The picture painted by Bosch is presumed to be of St Wilgefortis, who was revered equally in Germany and the Netherlands, and also known as Sint Ontcomer (St Uncumber). She had asked God to mutilate her appearance so she would not have to marry. After she had grown a beard, her father had her nailed on a cross, from which she preached for three whole days, converting a lot of people, including her father, who was full of remorse. The scenes once depicted on the inside wings, which have disappeared along with the donors, fitted this legend. Where you can now see St Anthony, there was once another scene from the life of St Wilgefortis. The scene on the right, which can no longer be properly interpreted and, like *The Temptation of St Anthony*, has nothing to do with the central panel, once illustrated a storm that God visited upon the unbelievers after he found out that the saint had been crucified.

Some other pictures by Bosch only became difficult to understand after they were mutilated, including two panels now in Rotterdam that once served as the wings of a triptych (illus. 24–7).[13] As both the inside and the outside were done

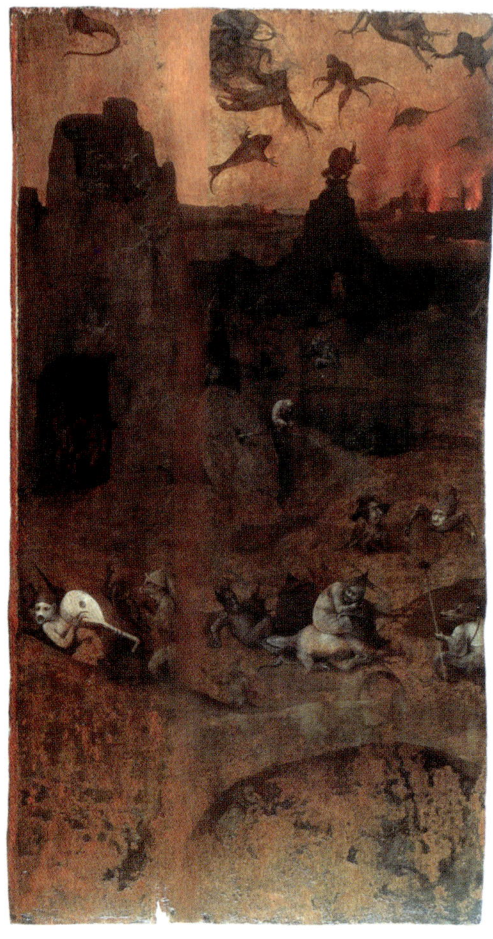

in grisaille, the now lost corpus was presumably a carved centre shrine. By reference to other works of art, as well as to
texts from the Bible and exegesis, the surviving pictures can
be decoded as dealing with the themes of sin and redemption.
While the left wing illustrates the Fall of the rebel angels on
the third day of creation when evil came into the world, the

24, 25 Hieronymus Bosch, lost triptych: *Fall of the Rebel Angels, Noah's Ark on
Mount Ararat*, 1510–15, oil on panel.

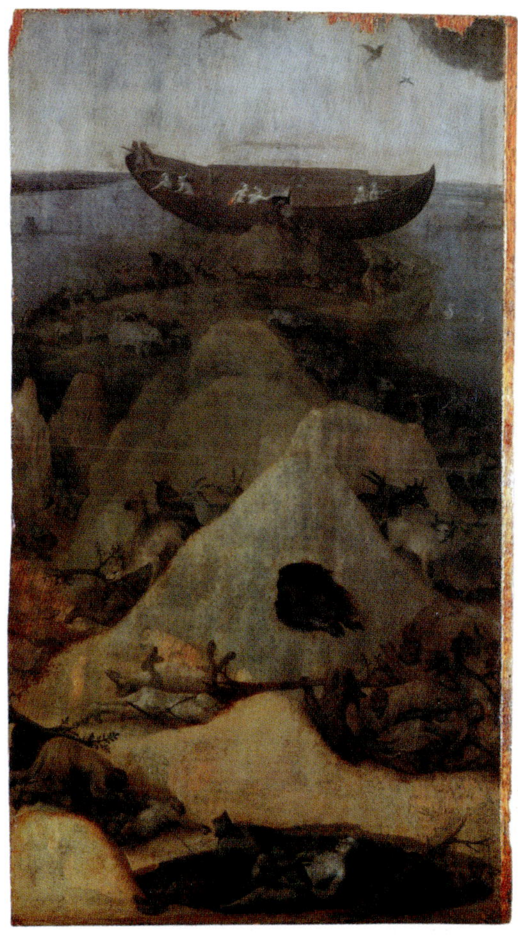

right-hand inside wing shows the Ark high and dry after the Flood with its cargo of living beings spreading out over the devastated earth. The four allegorical medallions of the outer wings refer to the events of the Book of Job. Here Bosch makes use of the Old Testament narratives to illustrate Job's devoted suffering as exemplary conduct in the face of evil, depicting

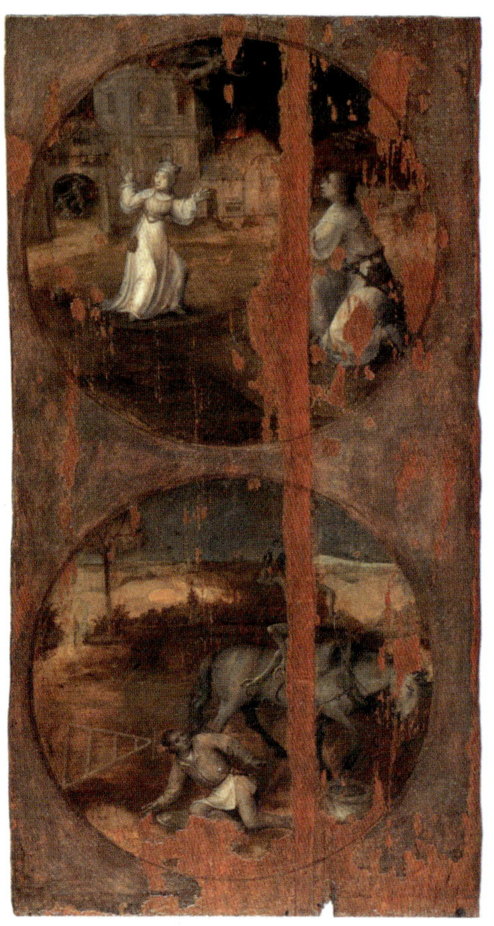

him as prophet of the Resurrection. Even someone not able to interpret the biblical references from the literary point of view will easily identify the human being tormented by the powers of evil in three of the four roundels and recognize him as being a man of religion who, his earthly sufferings now over, is being aided by an angel in the direction of eternal life.

26, 27 Hieronymus Bosch, *Mankind Beset by Devils*, c. 1510–15, oil on panel, outer wings of lost triptych.

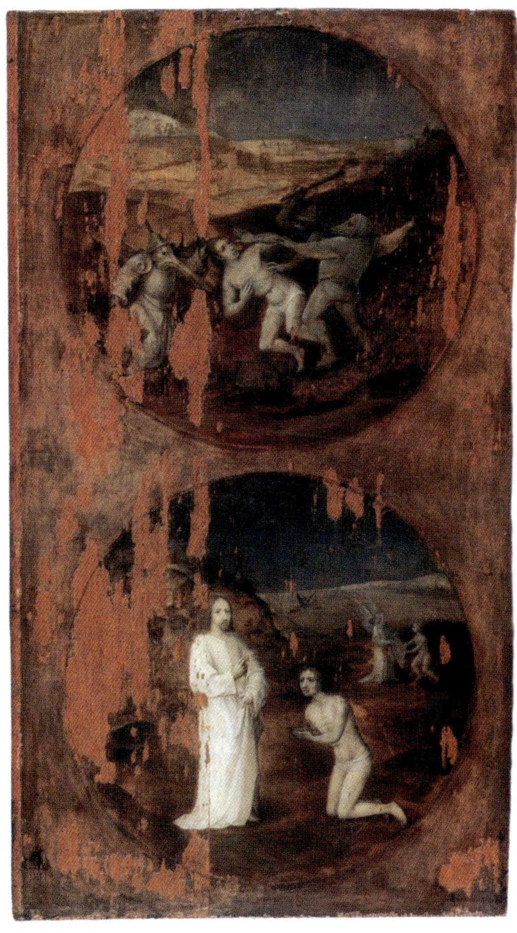

While he was satisfied with faint suggestions in the four roundels on the panels from Rotterdam, Bosch makes use of a wealth of detail to communicate a visual message aimed at teaching a moral lesson in most of his pictures. One example is the triptych dating from around 1504 that was later badly damaged (illus. 28).[14] The painting on the outside has

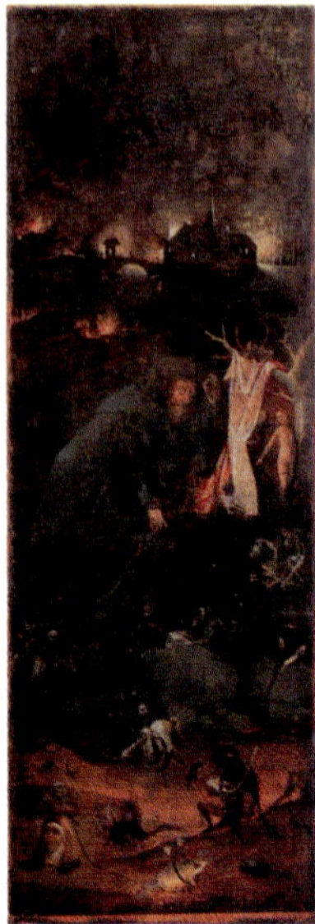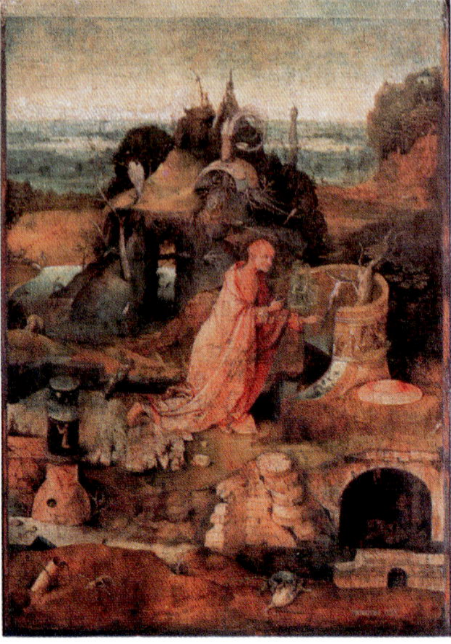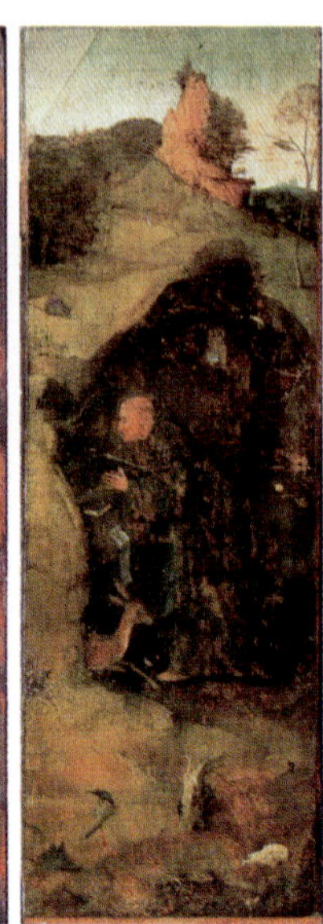

not survived and the inside, showing three hermit saints, has
been extensively restored. On the left wing, the temptation
of St Anthony is portrayed, on the right wing St Giles, and
on the central panel St Jerome is mortifying the flesh with a
stone in his hand. In addition to the already familiar motifs
characteristic of the attitudes and actions of the saints, the
painting is enriched by a number of pictures within the picture, given as reliefs (illus. 29). It is easy to interpret the
portrayal of Judith who, with her chaste virtue, triumphed
over the lust of Holofernes, the chief of the army whose
head she is holding in her hand. While this motif is taken
from traditional Christian iconography, in the case of the
other images in the picture Bosch strays onto less familiar
ground, even though one can find parallels in illustrations
painted in the margins of books. Opposite the relief of Judith

28, 29 Hieronymus Bosch, *Hermit Saints Triptych, c.* 1504, oil on panel, and detail.

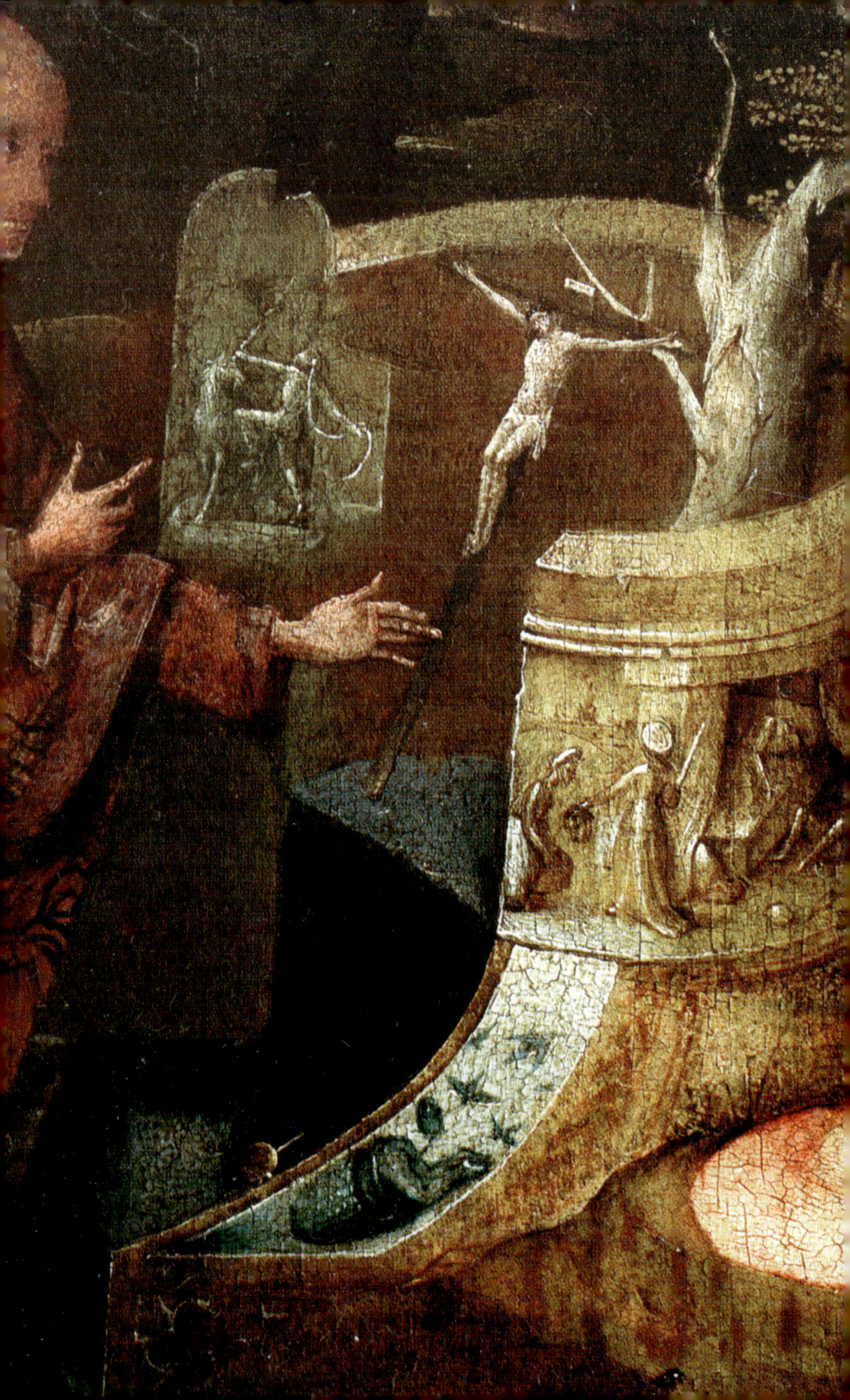

a man with a unicorn is shown, a Marian symbol of chastity.
Contrary to the statement by 'Physiologus' that only a virgin
could capture a unicorn, here it is the figure of an acrobat that
embodies the efforts of the saint to overcome his instincts.
Of greater mystery is the motif of a man who is halfway into
an upturned bee hive. Bosch also used this in the picture of
St Christopher, where it is to be found at the top of a tree.
This remarkable motif also occurs in a drawing (illus. 30).[15] In
the *Hermit Saints* triptych it is finally turned into a scatological
motif; the naked bottom – for which there is no more room
in the hive – has the branch of a tree sticking out of it with
an owl sitting on it, surrounded by flapping daytime birds.
The man in the hive who has been driven into it by his foolish
greed for honey could be interpreted as an image of gluttony
and boundless excess. His bare behind is an expression of

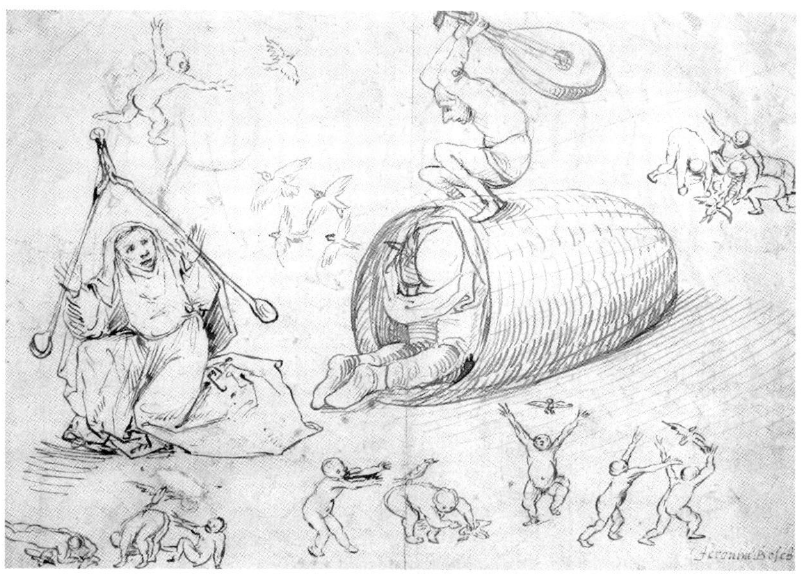

30 Hieronymus Bosch, *Beehive and Witches*, c. 1500–1515, pen and iron-gall ink.

his impurity, further highlighting the sinfulness of what he is doing, something also emphasized in the triptych by the presence of the owl, which here has little to do with the now familiar symbol of wisdom. Bosch's contemporaries attributed negative associations to this bird purely on account of its avoiding the light; they saw in the owl the embodiment of intellectual blindness, sloth and sin.[16]

References to ever-newer meanings in relation to the subject of a picture, and in relation to one's own life, seem to have been popular, particularly among the nobility. Depictions of the temptation of St Anthony were especially appreciated in this way. Proof of this can be found in the extremely high number of copies of the triptych – over thirty – the original of which is now in Lisbon (illus. 31).[17] The triptych may be identical to a work mentioned in the records and acquired by Philip the Handsome towards the end of 1505 as a gift for his father.[18] The written document gives not only the purpose of the acquisition and the high price of 312 guilders paid to the aldermen of the free council of Bruges, but details of the composition. The work is described as showing 'several stories' on the side panels that were 'abundantly illustrated in other places'. This description may refer to the grisaille panels of the outer wings (illus. 32), which, unlike the *Last Judgment* in Vienna, for example, are richly composed with a large number of figures. On the left is the arrest of Christ, on the right Christ carrying the Cross. With a directness of painting unusual for its time, the events of the Passion are illustrated, just as they are on the back of the *St John* panel (see illus. 8) and the outer wings of the *Adoration of the Magi* (see illus. 15).

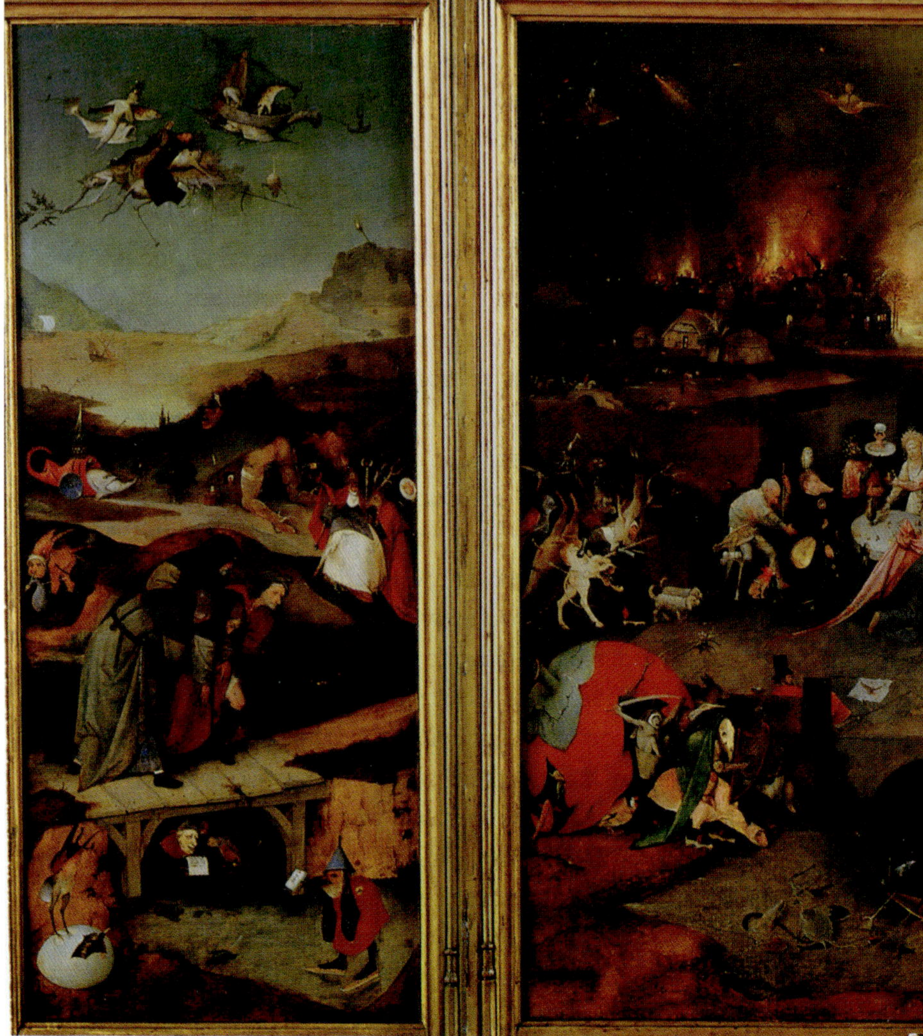

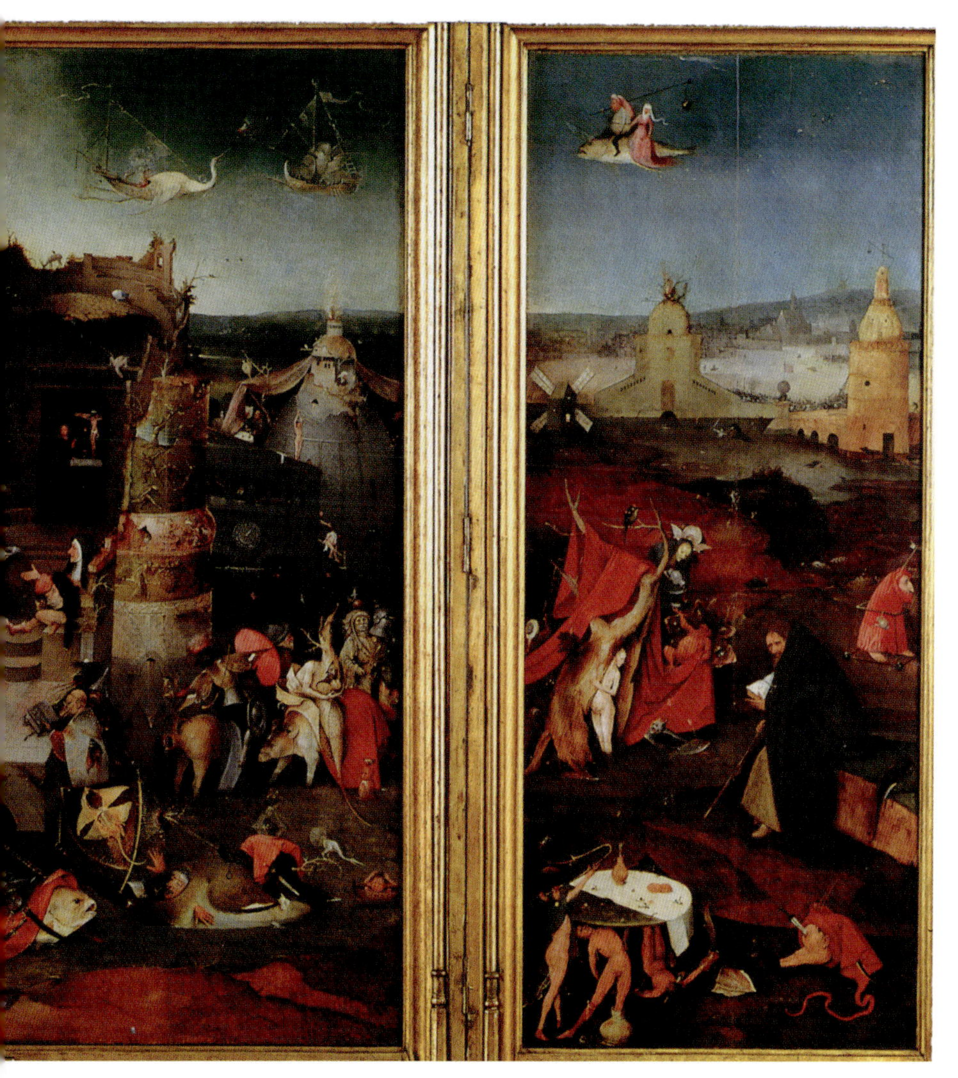

31 Hieronymus Bosch, *The Temptation of St Anthony*, 1502–3, oil on panel.

In all Bosch's representations of the Passion the focus of the narrative is on the juxtaposition of Christ with mankind hostile to Him. The idea of Redemption embodied in Christ, which was immediately expressed in the Ascension, something never depicted by Bosch, becomes secondary.[19] Instead, the narrative of the Passion is concentrated on the guilt of mankind, sinning against Christ and showing no gratitude for God's grace. The association of human sinfulness and the Passion of Christ, and the lack of respect, identified by many theologians in Bosch's day, for His task of redemption, explain the contemporary quality of the subject-matter and the link to the life of St Anthony related within. Thomas à Kempis and other representatives of the *devotio moderna*, along with theologians such as Dionysius van Rijkel, had called upon sinful humanity to take the hermit saints – the 'holy fathers' – as a model. Just as often, their lives were the subject of sermons, writings and images. And yet it was a new idea to portray the life of St Anthony on the three panels of an altarpiece. The circumstances may possibly be explained by the context of the commission, but it is no longer possible for us to piece this together. The fact that the triptych in Lisbon was the product of graphic invention never before attempted in such detail is proved by the drawing that is partly visible under the layer of paint, and by various pentimenti showing where the design was altered in the course of painting.[20]

On the middle panel of the triptych when open, the central figure of St Anthony dominates the centre of the composition and the focus of attention. His head is shown at the centre of the constellation of images around him, and all the scenes and motifs are focused on him. Looking out of

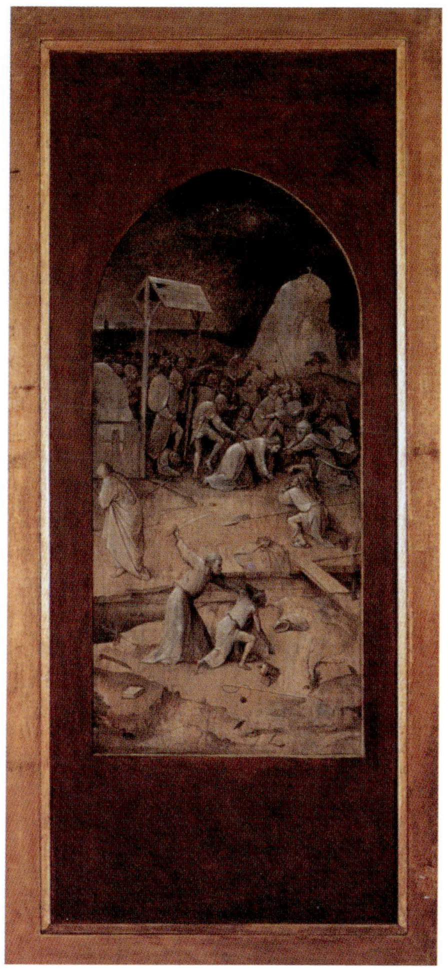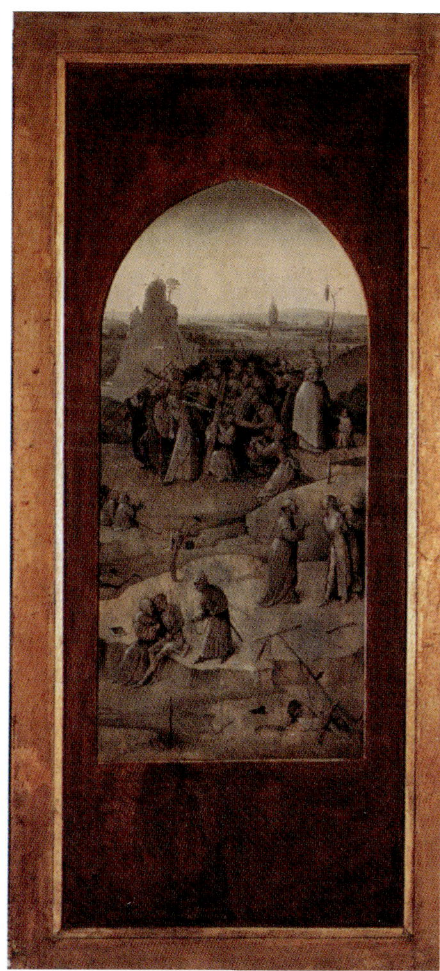

32 Hieronymus Bosch, closed outer wings of *The Temptation of St Anthony*.

the picture and offering a blessing with a gesture of his hand, which at the same time indicates the appearance of Christ, he reminds us of the familiar call to follow Christ. We are not told how to read it. This is also made clear by the images on the inner wings, on the left side of which the well-known temptation of the saint is illustrated. Caught by demons, he is tossed into the air and falls to earth, where he is found by companions and carried off. The scene on the right-hand panel, where a naked woman appears to the reading saint in a hollow tree, suggests the usual temptation by sexual desire. The *Legenda aurea* and the *Vaderboek*, a collection of lives of the saints likewise widely known in Bosch's day, describe the life and sufferings of St Anthony. Born the son of rich parents, he gave away half his inherited fortune to lead the life of a hermit. In various guises the Devil attempted to torment him and lead him into temptation in a number of different ways, but he remained steadfast. The central panel in particular tells of his steadfastness, showing that the saint falls for none of them in the end as the fiends of Hell, the monsters and hybrid creatures are enough to terrify him simply by their presence. Around the figure kneeling in silence, Bosch ranges all the visions that Anthony has to struggle against. The artist invents an appropriate gallery of graphic images depicting what is going on within. The mass of details in the picture do not just illustrate the temptations of the saint; they are also designed to be a direct enticement to the observer's fantasy. We may be intrigued by the bird-like creature with the conical hat, identified as a messenger by a sign around its neck; or wonder what the three characters facing him under the bridge are reading. They draw attention to themselves in

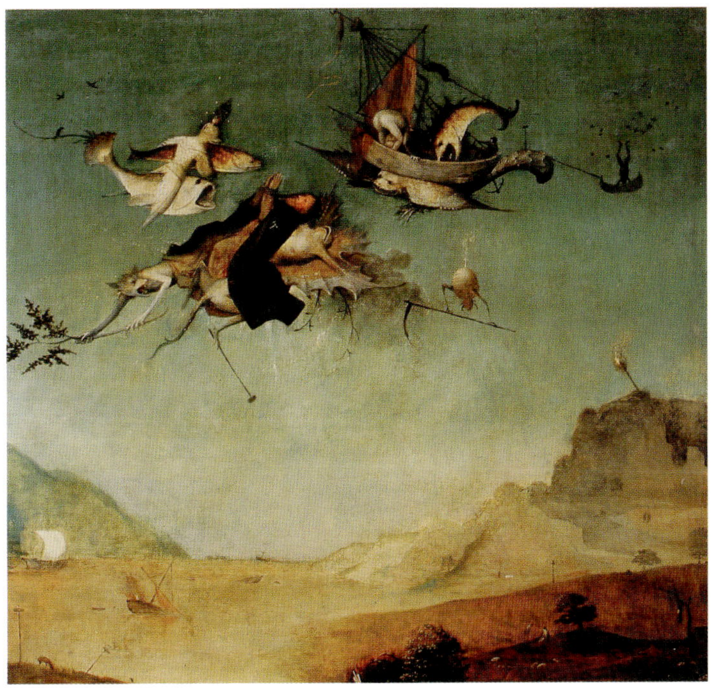

the same way as the airship-like vessels, made up of fish and birds, sailing across the sky or the ominous landscape with the fire in the central panel (illus. 33).

It is easy to get carried away interpreting the details and it is therefore not surprising that art history has had a problem with the interpretation of this painting. Admittedly, there has been little doubt that we are dealing here with some moral example of virtuous steadfastness, but the details can be interpreted in a multitude of different ways. What we can say is that the general consensus has been that all attempts to do so lead us into the trap of seeing the images as evidence of the painter's heretical ideas. Feel free to find references to

33 Detail from Hieronymus Bosch, *The Temptation of St Anthony*.

astrology or alchemy, if you so wish; after all, the mystical and religious writings of the time are full of such references, none of them incompatible with the interpretation of events in the world in terms of the Gospel. The fact that Bosch's pictures became so widely known and highly popular shows that his contemporaries did not consider them heretical. His works were so well known to the public that not just the painter, but even the often high-ranking owners of the better-known pictures would have come in for some suspicion from the Inquisition. But there is no indication that this was the case.[21] The large number of partly faithful copies of the *Temptation of St Anthony* in Lisbon suggests that the public did not just see in them a model of religious virtue for devout people to examine their own consciences by; any other picture of St Anthony would probably have done for this. It must therefore have been the narrative richness of these remarkable works of fantasy, the products of Bosch's endless pictorial imagination, that very soon made his works into objects highly sought after by collectors.

SIX

The Art of Invention and the Invention of Art

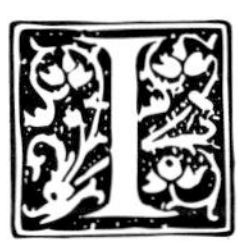N THE CENTRE of any study of Bosch's oeuvre has been, and remains, the question of the meaning of his paintings. It needs to be specified what meaning is sought and for whom it is meaningful. Many art historians have looked for *the* definitive meaning by asking what message Bosch was aiming to convey through his work. The answer to this question comes up against the difficulty that we now know for certain that not all the pictures talked about until recently as being works by Bosch were actually painted by him. The fact that other painters produced pictures in the manner of Bosch, however, indicates that this visual language was capable of being learnt and was aimed at a public that understood what it was all about. In fact, it is possible, using a large number of different sources, pictures and writings, to piece together fairly reliably what a contemporary observer would have been able to make of these pictures according to his or her existing knowledge and educational background. This is because Bosch's pictures were part of a visual culture that was not just comprehensible in theory for his contemporaries, but one with which they were thoroughly at home. In Bosch's day, particularly in the institutions of the court and Church, there was discussion about the use and

abuse of images. This at least throws a light on the terms of the debate within which the meaning of the images and the subject-matter of the pictures were a focus of negotiation.

Whenever one comes across statements about the production of pictures, going beyond methods of creating paint and how to achieve pictorial effects, they are usually directly equated to the production and reception of written texts. This was most clearly expressed by the Italian Leon Battista Alberti, whose writings on the theory of art were read north of the Alps in Bosch's day. Following the example of antiquity, he had systematically applied to the visual arts the rules of rhetoric familiar to every educated person from classical writings. By the use of rhetoric propagated and practised everywhere in Europe, in this period pictures came to be regarded as a means of communication, of equal standing to words and with a direct correspondence to writing. 'Ut pictura poesis' – 'as is painting so is poetry' – is how the Roman poet Horace put it in his *Ars poetica*.[1] This statement, which actually called for writers to be more graphic, gave rise to the doctrine that pictures should be as valid as poetry: paintings should not just be created artistically but should be considered art. Alberti saw the various forms of the visual arts as subject to a common goal in relation to the theory of art, by classifying all public images as means of aesthetic education in the service of the common good. Here, too, he was following the principle of rhetoric that all speech acts are governed by a common purpose. Their aim should be to please, educate and emotionally affect in order to persuade the audience as effectively as possible and direct them towards moral attitudes and actions.

The theologians of the age also made use of the doctrine of communication based on rhetoric that was generally accepted as the norm, and called for it also to be applied to pictures. They saw the main task of the visual arts as contributing to the salvation of souls. This could come about by works of visual art being employed as a means of religious instruction, as Pope Gregory the Great had recommended. His famous dictum that pictures should be useful for the illiterate, 'who could at least read by looking at the walls what they cannot read in books', was to hold sway throughout the Middle Ages.[2] But pictures were not just reserved for the illiterate, and in book illustration, for example, a complex pictorial imagery that went far beyond illustrating the words of the text developed very early on.

Take as an example of expression equal to that of a communication through words, or even surpassing them, a drawing by Bosch now in Berlin (illus. 34).[3] The drawing, apparently without any preliminary sketching, was done with 'iron-gall' ink, which now appears slightly brown due to the ageing process.[4] It shows a small wood in front of which is a dead tree with a gaping hollow in the middle, out of which an owl is peering. This is causing the three long-tailed birds sitting on the bare branches to screech – these can be identified as the proverbial chattering magpies. The trunk of the tree below is also broken and hollow. In this opening, a fox is sitting with a cockerel running towards it. These two are a familiar pair of adversaries, in whose example eating and being eaten (the latter to be avoided by cunning) are thematized.[5] They also serve to symbolize the classical recognition that silence is golden: only because it starts to speak does the

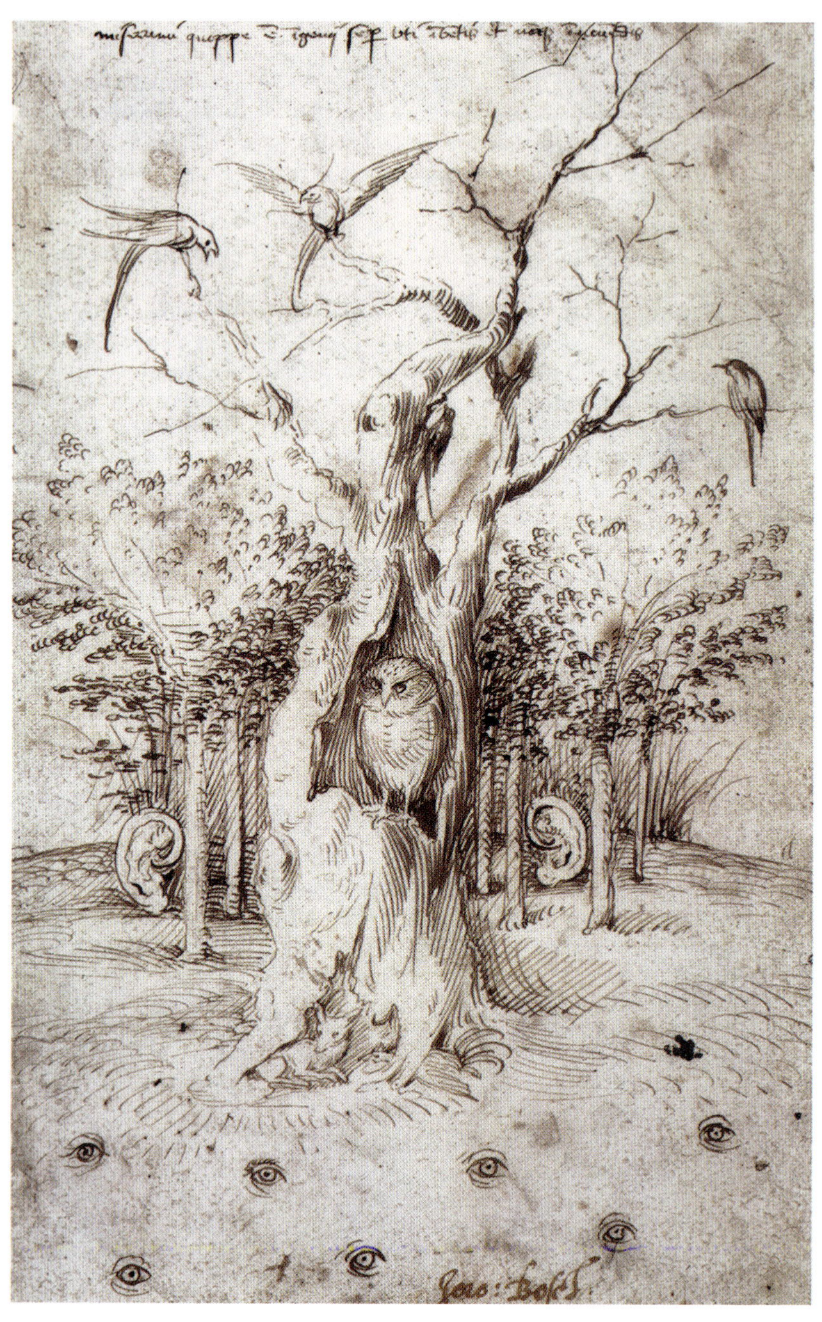

34 Hieronymus Bosch, *The Hearing Forest and the Seeing Field*, c. 1500–1505, pen and brown ink.

fox lose its prey from its mouth. A commentary from the sixteenth century sums the message up with 'the fable teaches the lesson that talkativeness is always harmful.'[6]

The human ears intriguingly positioned in the wood and the seven eyes shown on the ground can also be interpreted as appeals for silence and warnings to people to be careful. Woods with ears and fields with eyes were not peculiar to Dutch proverbs in Bosch's day. Heinrich Bebel, for example, in 1508 quotes from the *Proverbia germanica*, a collection of proverbs published in Latin: 'Campus habet oculos; silva aures' – 'the field has eyes, the wood ears' – explaining that 'by this is meant that we should do nothing in the woods and open fields (where people might be) that should be kept secret.'[7] Anyone who thinks this message is too simplistic is recommended to take a look at the extensive literature on Bosch's drawing. This graphically illustrates the proverb that a picture can say more than a thousand words. Depending on the author, the motifs shown are interpreted more or less persuasively and on occasion given a new interpretation, prompting ever more opinions on the imagery.[8] The Latin saying included at the top of the drawing has added to the multiplicity of different interpretations: 'It is the characteristic of an unhappy spirit always to seek the company of animals and never friendly ones', as it translates in English.[9] This is a quotation from the work *De disciplina scholarium* – on the nature of education – attributed to Boethius, the philosopher of late antiquity, much reprinted in Bosch's day.[10] It is by all appearances written with the same ink as the drawing. Whether this is by the draughtsman himself we cannot say, since there are very few examples of Bosch's handwriting. Because the wood shown in the picture is called *bosch* in Dutch – the same as the painter and the town he came from – for the majority of interpreters it was obvious that the drawing had to be interpreted as a reference to Bosch himself, carrying a very personal message. The Latin saying is therefore taken to be either a sceptical acknowledgement of the limitations of his own creativity or the opposite: an expression of the pride of the artist in what he is doing.[11]

Irrespective of whether Bosch himself used the Latin saying – and one would not put it past him – the statement could nevertheless be applied to his art. The words must therefore be read in the context of a theory of poetry and art for which the new, something that has never existed before, was not the absolute ideal. 'It is difficult to write with propriety', Horace had written in his *Ars poetica*, 'and you with more prudence will reduce the *Iliad* into acts, than if you first introduce arguments unknown and never treated of before.'[12] This was in no way opposed to the pursuit of fantasy promoted by both artists and poets. The *phantasia* of art was to the medieval mind a kind of gift, making it possible to select from the God-given repertoire of natural forms and constantly come up with new combinations. In a similar way, Bosch's combination of different visual references to both talking and keeping silent can stand as an exemplary illustration of the process of artistic invention.

The origin of every work of art, as far as contemporaries understood it, was *inventio*, the invention or discovery of subject-matter. According to the principles of classical rhetoric, this was the basis of every process of artistic production. The next stage in this act of creation was, according to this theory, *dispositio*: the selection, assessment, classification and structuring of the material discovered. The climax of the process of production was *elecutio*, giving the formal and material aspects a suitable form. At the same time the desired aim of the work had to be taken into account, along with the conditions for its reception. This regularly formulated requirement of the theory of art and of rhetoric is well demonstrated by Bosch's works. Nevertheless, however much people have speculated on the subject-matter expressed in the imagery, for example in the case of his drawings, up until now they have rarely considered the function of these pictures. The pictorial composition and the wealth of motifs indicate that *The Hearing Forest and the Seeing Field* was more than a preparatory drawing for his assistants in the workshop intended to be used as a basis for a later painting. That there existed drawings in which individual motifs and pictorial ideas were jotted down as source material for his assistants to use stands to reason. A small sheet with sketches on both sides, now in Berlin, points to this purpose (illus. 35).[13] On the front there is a drawing of two monsters – one a bird monster grinning contemptuously and the other a small hissing dragon. A few lines of shadow procure a spatial illusion. It is a sketch capturing a pictorial idea with a free but assured stroke of the pen that could be employed later in painted works. We find, for example, a hideous creature related to the bird monster on the left wing of *The Garden of Earthly Delights* (illus. 36).

Nevertheless, the fact that a pictorial idea captured by a sketch is repeated in a painting is not necessarily an indication that a preliminary drawing was used as a model. A drawing such as *Tree-Man*, from between 1500 and 1510

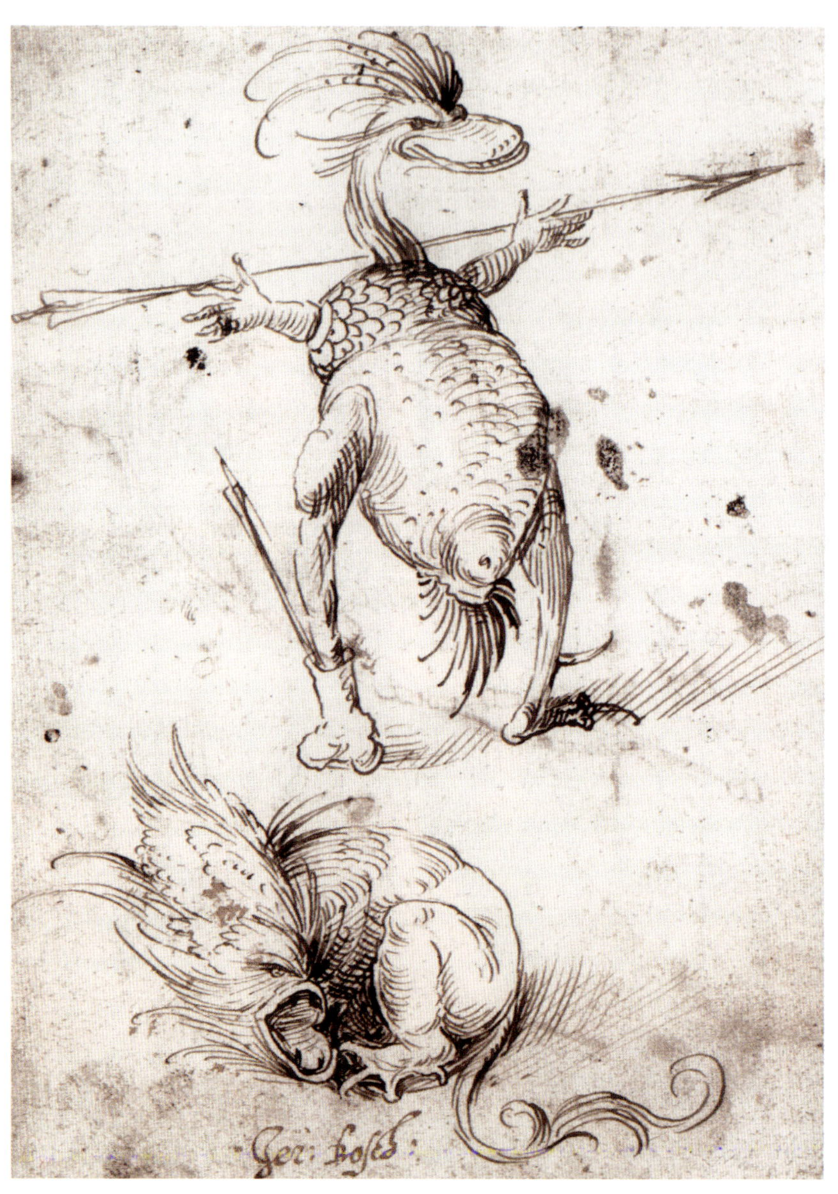

35 Hieronymus Bosch, *Two Monsters*, c. 1505, pen and brown ink.

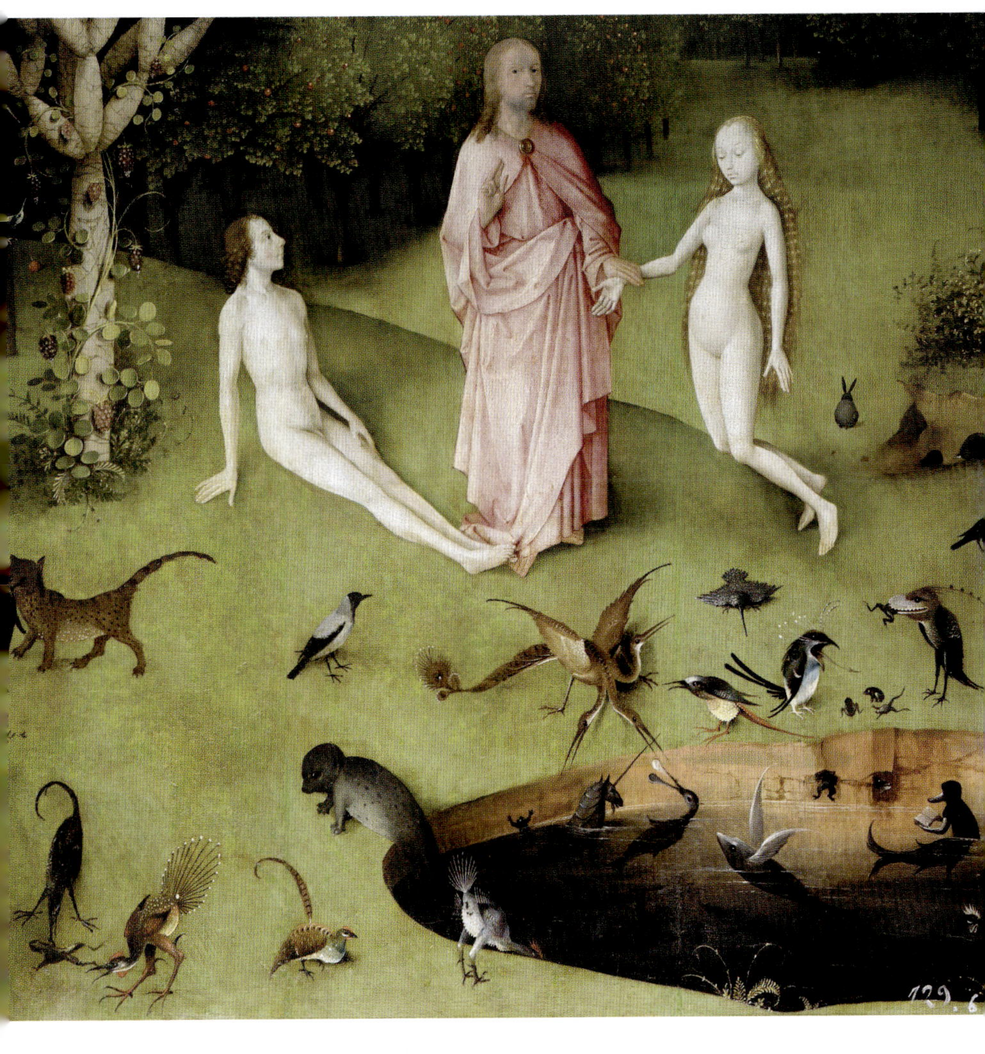

36 Detail from Hieronymus Bosch, *The Garden of Earthly Delights* (see illus. 4).

(illus. 37), was presumably not intended as a preparatory
study for the motif in the panel showing Hell in *The Garden of
Earthly Delights* (see illus. 2).[14] As a picture, the drawing works
as a complete whole. The monstrous creature with boats
growing out of its legs is placed within an open landscape
representing the world seemingly stretching into infinity. In
a way unique for the art of his time, Bosch manages to render
his imagination with such depth and aerial perspective by
using the strokes of his pen almost impressionistically, with
nothing but extremely fine hatching and minute stippling.
The centre of the drawing is occupied by the menacing-
looking Tree-Man, with sinister dinner guests assembled in
his hollow rear end. What we are to make of the figures in this
den of vice, not placed in the rear end of the tree creature
simply by chance, is made clear by the flag with the Turkish
crescent and the owl being scorned by a bird in the branches.
Another owl being attacked by birds on a little island on the
right, the magpies in the tree on the left or, as counter images
indicating something more positive, the deer and the heron
in the foreground, all add to the possibility that the scene
can be read allegorically. Just on its own, the unnatural combination of flora and fauna embodied by the Tree-Man has
been interpreted as an indication of sin. The use of hybrid
creatures carried to a fine art by Bosch, combining things
drawn from nature to create monsters never seen before,
was a well-known way of characterizing evil. Even the much-
read introduction to Horace's *Ars poetica*, condemning such
monstrosities, contributed to this growing tendency to use
and interpret grotesque creatures as visual symbols of evil.
The Tree-Man, with his body symbolizing an 'ark of evil',

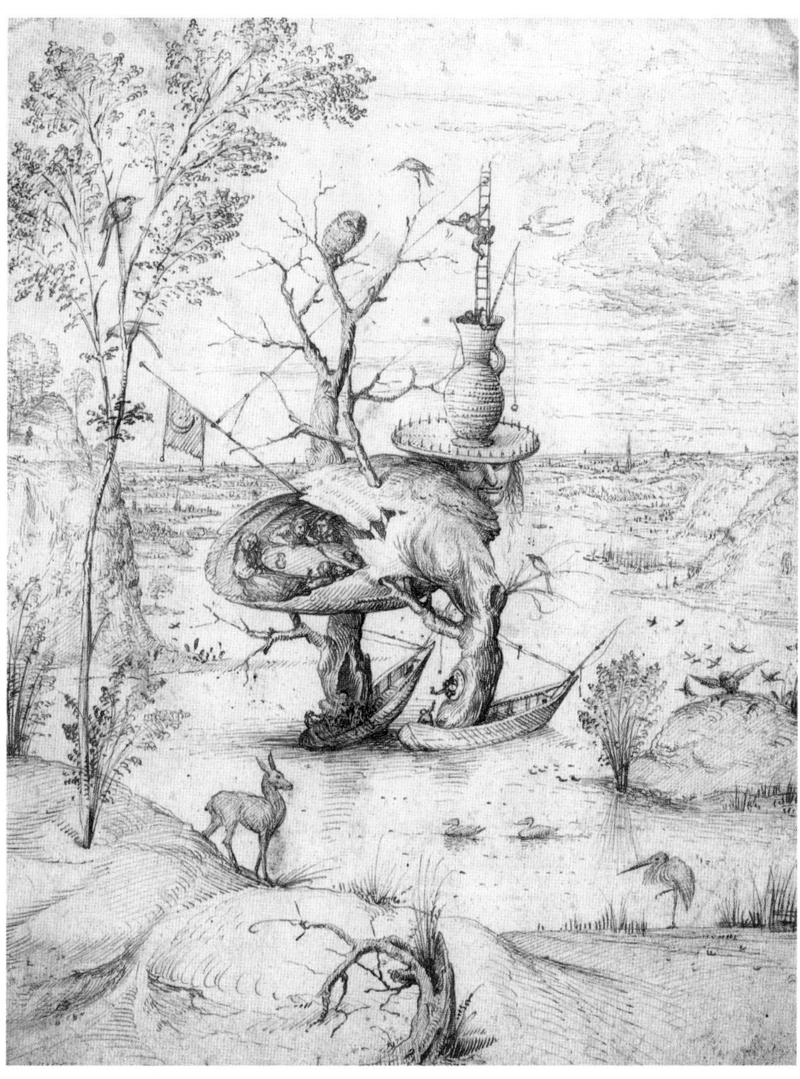

37 Hieronymus Bosch, *Tree-Man*, 1505–10, pen and brown ink.

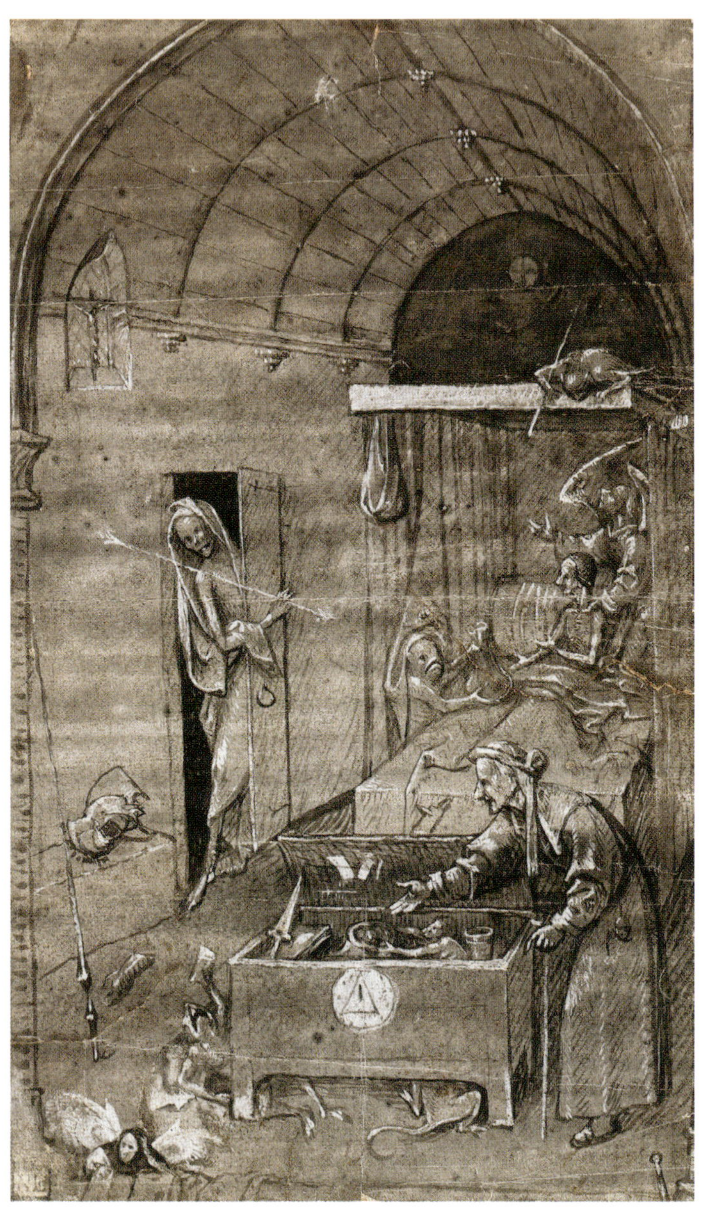

38 Hieronymus Bosch, *Death and the Miser*, c. 1500–1510, brush with grey and black ink, heightened with white, on grey paper.

along with the many individual motifs in the drawing, can have multiple interpretations, and we can but wonder at the virtuosity displayed in the drawing.

Just like *The Hearing Forest and the Seeing Field*, *Tree-Man* embodies a type of graphic art that was new in this period.[15] Preparing for a painted composition by means of a preliminary drawing was largely unheard of in Bosch's day. As a rule, even in Bosch's case, one began by applying charcoal or brush and ink directly onto the surface of the picture. Unsatisfactory results were simply wiped off or, as is often the case with Bosch, simply ignored. What one might call isolated visualizations have survived as preparatory drawings for paintings, to show clients or those commissioning expensive altarpieces what they would look like later. Such drawings might have formed part of the contract made between painter and client.

We have every reason to believe that the drawing of *Death and the Miser* (illus. 38) started life in the form of visualizations.[16] The drawings done on dark-backed paper using dark grey ink, with their raised white sections, correspond to the type of drawing whose pictorial composition was popular in Bosch's day. Their style is to a large extent in harmony with the underdrawing of the painting of the same subject (illus. 39), visible to the naked eye.[17] The composition appears more concentrated in the painting: the left-hand wall, which is shown in the foreground in the drawing, is left out, allowing more of a focus on the relation between the crucifix in the window at the top and Death, who is coming to fetch the old miser. Thus not only the composition of the subject but the expression of the idea behind the picture is more successful in the painted version. This clearly suggests that we should not take the drawing to be a copy of the painting.

Quite apart from the question of attribution that remains unsettled even now, it is obvious that this drawing served a different purpose in respect to form and composition from that of the small sketch in Berlin (see illus. 35). The way it is drawn links it in terms of pictorial composition to *Tree-Man* and other drawings attributed to Bosch, occupying a unique position in the art of their time, quite apart from the use of motifs. Up until now no precursors have been identified for Bosch's loose, free style of drawing, or anyone who immediately followed on from where he left off. His followers drew monsters and hybrid creatures, as is shown by the sketch in Berlin, but the loose hatching and the barely rounded contours that suggest they were done in haste clearly differentiate this drawing from the work of imitators and admirers who are focused more on the visual taxonomy of his formal language. With them the individual motifs look as though they are put together painstakingly but without spatial awareness, like the arrangement of a butterfly collection.

Despite the shorthand at work in the drawings, the small sketch highlights a remarkable peculiarity of Bosch's hybrid creatures. They are, after all, intended to fulfil a function, unlike the *disjecta membra* they are always likened to – the apparently dismembered assorted monsters from illustrations painted in the margins of medieval manuscripts. Nobody before Bosch ever depicted monsters in such detail, making them so believable yet at the same time totally improbable. It is the imaginative vitality of his grotesque creatures of Hell that to a large extent make for the charm of his pictorial

39 Hieronymus Bosch, *Death and the Miser*, c. 1500–1510, oil on panel.

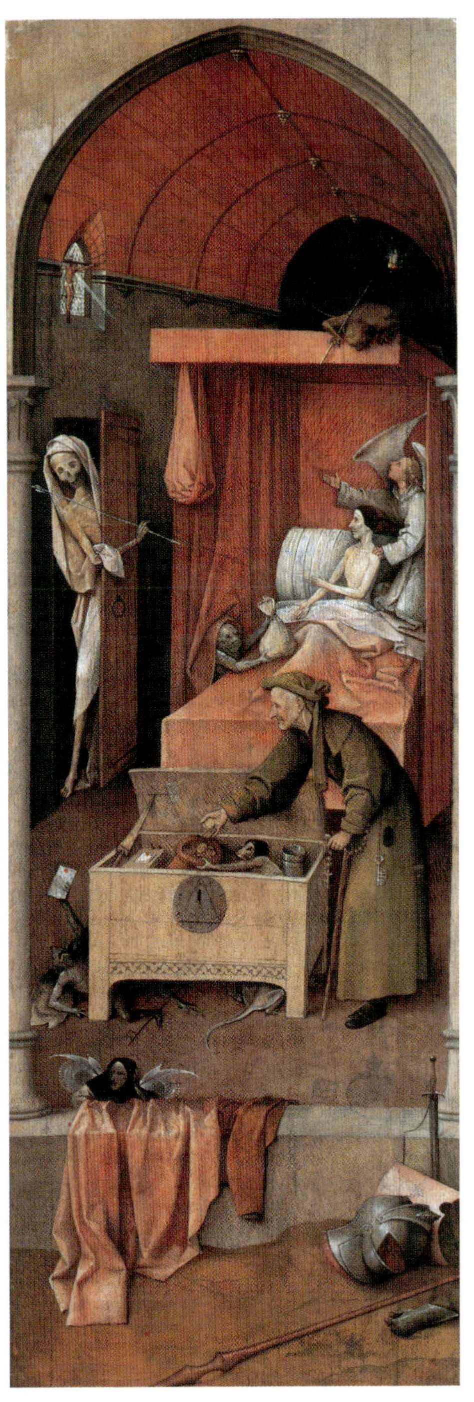

world and which from early on earned him the nickname 'devil maker'.[18] The charm of this fantasy world is also found in other drawings by Bosch, such as *The Hearing Forest and the Seeing Field*, *Tree-Man* and *Death and the Miser*. In these cases, the drawings were definitely aimed at buyers who valued pictures as examples of a particular artist's work. Proof that this awareness was growing in the period around 1500 is provided by Albrecht Dürer, who added a handwritten note to a drawing by Raphael saying that Raphael had sent him the drawing to 'show him his hand'.[19] The first art collections, providing a record of a similarly motivated interest in collecting, came into existence in this period. The discovery of the value of art in the case of such pictures was at the same time to bring about an acknowledgement of the special value of artistic invention. The pictorial composition of Bosch's drawings and some of his paintings, such as *The Garden of Earthly Delights*, were aimed at the type of collectors then beginning to appear for the first time, drawn for the most part from the nobility and the urban elite.[20]

With their motifs that could be interpreted in many different ways and their free compositional form, Bosch's pictures appealed to a public that was increasingly sensitive to artistic invention and innovation. In his day, people were not just receptive to the messages carried by the subject-matter of the pictures but to their particular form as well. There is a theoretical reason for this: the contemporary theory of art based on rhetoric identified a close association between form and content rather than a dichotomy, as study of the arts became associated with the growth of the Kantian concept of beauty. For a public applying the rules of rhetoric to pictures, the motivic lexis of these paintings was just as indistinguishable from their artistic grammar and syntax as from considerations of style and its appropriateness. This *aptum* or *decorum* was a basic requirement of rhetoric. The main thing was to consider carefully all the elements and aspects that were important for the work of art, and the context in which it was to be shown, so as to create a harmonious and hopefully an effective whole. The ancient theory of rhetoric in Bosch's day gave to discussion about art a considerable repertoire of ideas and concepts, focusing on both the subject-matter and the formal aspects of pictures. The newly awakened interest in the way pictures were made was, however, not just a theoretical idea based on classical models, but had a thoroughly practical side. Training in the techniques of art, after all, was part and parcel of the education of nobles. Art collecting took off hand in hand with the spread of this new ideal of culture, which was also being advanced by literature. Hieronymus Bosch is one of those artists who responded to the need that was newly developing and who produced pictures that were at the same time artistically conceived and created. Bosch's contemporaries must have recognized that too.

The world Bosch painted, in which objects that do not belong to each other mix and supposedly lifeless objects awaken, is analogous to a world-view in which mythical creatures, like antipodes and akephaloi, served as proof of the endless creative power of the Maker. Even in an age of discovery and in Bosch's lifetime, people had not abandoned their belief in this marvellous bestiary. Maps of the time show that creatures from the realms of fantasy, once confined to the periphery of the globe, were now to be found in the newly discovered lands. It may therefore be supposed that Bosch's grotesque creatures were imitated so much because they confirmed the worst fears of his contemporaries. The fact that there were marvellous creatures was just as much beyond question as the permanent presence of evil in the world. It was not just the margins of books and maps that were home to all sorts of grotesquery in the art of the period, and we certainly cannot write off Bosch's references to devilry as simply a fashion of the time.[21] In the popular illustrated prints of this period such images are totally absent, apart from a few exceptions, such as the engravings of Alart du Hameel, an artist within Bosch's own circle (illus. 40).[22] Only in the middle of the sixteenth century did the grotesque references to devilry turn into a truly mass phenomenon, at the time considered highly entertaining and comical.[23] This is one more reason why it is not enough to reduce Bosch's artistic inventions to the sphere of theological and moral instruction.

The fascinating uniqueness of Bosch's paintings is certainly due to his endlessly creative fantasy. 'Creating was always inventing for him', Max J. Friedländer wrote in 1927, describing the vocabulary of Bosch's imagery as 'direct artistic expression'.[24] In this context his financial situation plays a role that should not be underestimated. In an age when art was almost exclusively dependent on commission, he was in a position to produce pictures totally in accord with his own ideas and to draw without having to be worried in advance about the drawings having a definite purpose. Unlike most of the other painters of his age, he was in a financial position that allowed free rein to his pictorial imagination. The outpouring of compositions made possible by this, though, is

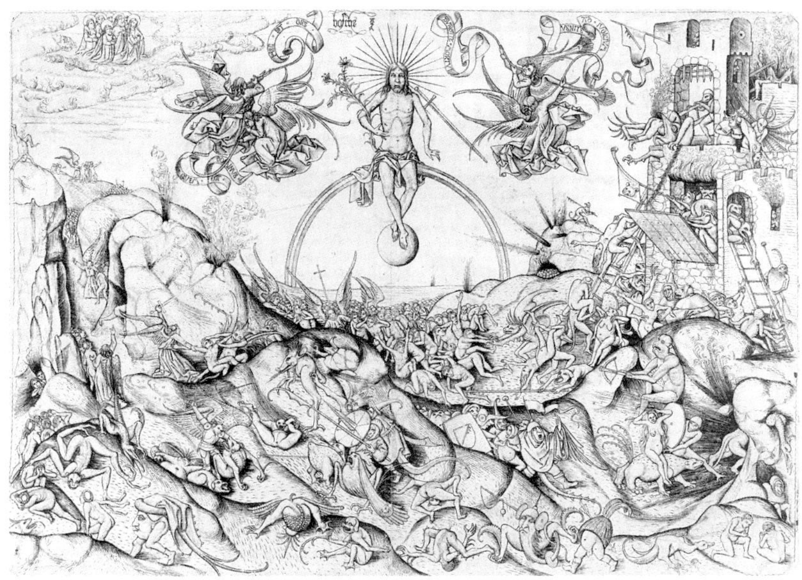

no explanation for the phenomenal spread and large-scale imitation of Bosch's world of imagery. The fact that he soon became famous and that his pictures were sought after all over Europe even in his lifetime is largely due to the public appreciation of these works as artefacts and the admiration they attracted. The unique pictorial composition of his drawings as works of art was greatly admired (see illus. 34, 37); even when these drawings can be shown not to have been produced on commission, they soon managed to find an audience. This is clearly demonstrated by the fact that they have withstood the test of time and have survived. Anyone wishing to understand Bosch's pictures has to take into account the dependence on the court and courtly ideals of the public who purchased these works. In fact, it was not long before the innovative and inventive products of Bosch's imagination

40 Alart du Hameel, *Last Judgment, c.* 1478–94, engraving.

were to be found in the collections of the nobility and the prosperous upper classes of the up-and-coming Dutch cities, aspiring to the ideals of aristocratic life in favour since antiquity. This was the public that provided a favourable breeding ground for the rapid spread of the products of Bosch's graphic invention. After 1500 in particular, the world of the European courts was increasingly to become the sounding board of Bosch's art.

The *Seven Deadly Sins* and the *Last Judgment*

'SOME TIME AGO there was a genre of painting called *Grillo*', Felipe de Guevara wrote in around 1560. For pictures of this sort, he continues, 'we praise Hieronymus Bosch, or Bosco as we call him.'[1] The term goes back to Pliny the Elder, who also wrote about art and artists in volume 35 of his *Natural History*, published in AD 77. In his description of painters of 'minoris picturae' – small pictures or bare subject-matter – Pliny also mentions Antiphilus, who had painted a man with a ridiculous appearance and the name Gryllos, 'and hence it is that pictures of this class are generally known as "Grylli"'.[2] Guevara goes on to say that Bosch 'painted strange figures, but he did so only because he wanted to portray scenes of Hell, and for that subject matter it was necessary to depict devils and imagine them in unusual compositions'.[3] Bosch's art, of course, was about a lot more than painting monsters and chimeras: 'It is certain, and anyone who has carefully looked at Bosch's works must realize this, that he paid much attention to propriety and always most assiduously stayed within the limits of naturalness, as much as and even more so than any fellow artist.'[4] At the end of these comments, Guevara cites as a typical example of Bosch's art, not a picture on a panel, but 'a table in the possession of

Your Majesty' (illus. 41).[5] It is not recorded how this work from the period 1505–10 came into the collection of Philip II. It is, however, known that 'a Tabletop on which the seven Deadly Sins are painted' was brought to the Escorial at the king's behest in 1574. The catalogue entry very precisely describes the pictorial object. It says that it shows the subject 'in a circle and Christ Our Lord in the middle; and in the four corners of the Tabletop another four circles, in which are painted the following: In one, death, in the others, Judgment, Hell and Paradise.'[6] The pictures of the sins of mankind are arranged in the round, signifying the eye of God, in the pupil of which the wounded Christ is displaying his wounds to the observer.[7] Around the pupil are the words 'cave cave deus videt' – 'Beware, beware, God is watching.' What God sees is reflected in the outer circle of the eye. They are the Seven Deadly Sins of which mankind, having forsaken God, has become guilty: envy, anger, pride, lust, sloth, gluttony and avarice. The last of these is represented by the corrupt judge accepting bribes from both parties. In the next picture the envious are pointing the finger at one another, and in the next, drunken revellers are attacking one another. The Devil is holding up a mirror to the vain woman, as the painter does with the lustful courtiers by giving them a fool as a companion who is having his naked bottom thrashed. The slothful one is neglecting his spiritual duties and the glutton is begrudging the hungry one even a sip from the water jug. The Latin name of the Seven Deadly Sins is given at the bottom of the each of the tableaux. The words affirmed by the white banderoles unfolding above and below the sins mirrored in God's eye ring out rather like a proclamation: 'For they are a nation void of counsel, neither is there any understanding

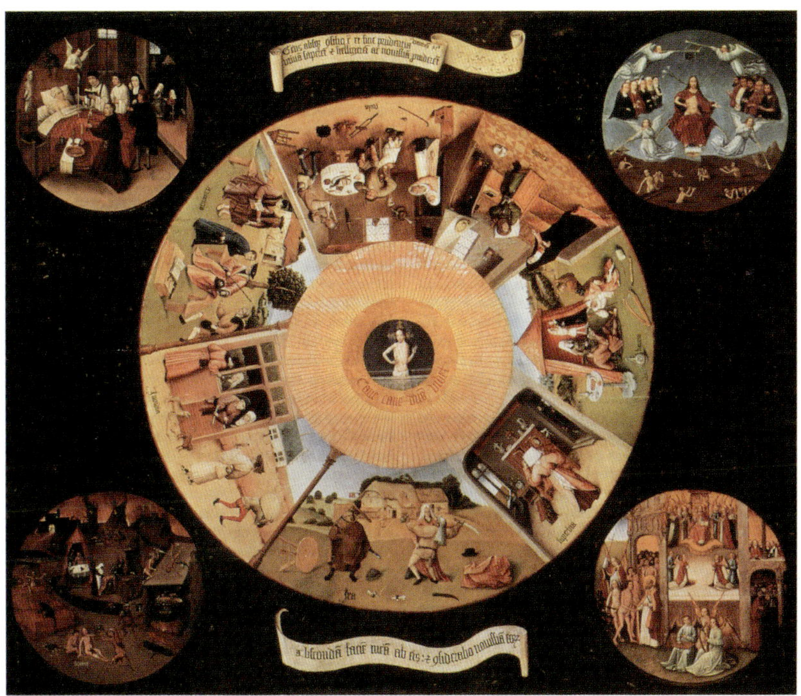

in them', the upper one reads, and the lower one: 'O that they were wise, that they understood this, that they would consider their latter end!' (Deuteronomy 32:28–9).

The subject, even without the warning captions, leaves little room for doubt. Sinful mankind, having offended Christ by their conduct, was in Bosch's day a favourite topic of sermons and religious literature all over the Christian world. If we can believe Dionysius van Rijkel, no stratum of society was exempt from having generally forsaken God. Kings and princes no more fulfilled their most sacred duties than did the clergy; 'Even the Pope, his curia and all stations of society both high and low' had sinned. Dionysius focused

41 Hieronymus Bosch, table with the *Seven Deadly Sins*, c. 1505–10, oil on panel.

his attention on the Seven Deadly Sins and the Four Last Things, portraying a detailed picture of the awaited punishments.[8] Bosch's figures embody sinful mankind threatened with the fires of Hell by a merciful God. Their conduct makes a depressing contrast to the Man of Sorrows, whose Passion is forgotten amid the goings on of the world. The same is true of the *Last Judgment*, another small round picture, facing a sinful world. In a roundel, the evil ways of the world are confronted with Hell. Every sin has its own punishment, again indicated by captions: the lustful one ends up in bed with toads, the angry one is beaten, and someone who has spent a lifetime devoted to gluttony is served with slithering snakes. In Bosch's version of Hell, there is a perverse rule of like for like. Just as in the law where the punishment should fit the crime, so the torment of Hell fits every sin. It is a view common to all devotional literature that everyone must suffer in equal measure to their sins.[9]

The warning was heeded for a long time after Bosch's death. The tabletop with the *Seven Deadly Sins* was hanging in the Escorial from 1574. Siguença saw it there in 1605:

in the chamber of His Majesty, where he has a bookcase like those of the monks, there is another excellent piece. In the centre, in a circle of light and glory, he placed our Saviour; around Him are seven circles in which are seen the Seven Deadly Sins [illus. 41], in which all the creatures that He redeemed offend Him without realizing that He is watching them and sees everything.[10]

Sigüença describes the tabletop as 'a mirror in which the truth of Christianity is reflected so we might all see ourselves in it', and in general Bosch's pictures are said to be 'books of great wisdom and artistic value'.[11] It is surely no coincidence that this was the only work that was praised so highly and so soon by Guevara, even though he knew many of Bosch's works and owned six himself. He calls this work 'admirable in its entirety'.[12] He was particularly impressed by the depiction of envy. In fact, Bosch had turned the traditional iconography into a street scene. The dog with two bones in front of it is after the one in the hands of the man who is jealously eyeing the noble with the falcon, and next to him a servant is carrying off a bulging sack. Social distinction indicated by the clothing does not permit any contact between the young man and the woman shown inside the house who are exchanging carnations, the traditional symbol of a vow, through the bars of the window. 'The allegory of Envy', Guevara wrote, 'in my opinion is so excellent and ingenious and its meaning so well expressed that it can vie with the works of Aristides, the inventor of the paintings that the Greeks called Ethike.'[13] Here he is making a reference that his educated readers would have easily understood; it is to Pliny the Elder, who in his *Natural History* informs us not just that Aristides was the first to give expression to the conditions of man's soul and the stirring of his emotions, but of the incredibly high prices that his pictures fetched, which was likewise true of Bosch's works in Guevara's day.[14]

The tabletop of the *Seven Deadly Sins*, it is presumed, had come about as a superior piece of decoration for a noble residence or the home of a wealthy collector. Quite early on, the painted tabletop became a pictorial panel, something that happened to a number of similar pieces of furniture. The surviving examples, often decorated with coats of arms, prove that painted tables were valued pieces of furniture in court collections. Such tables were to be found in patrician houses too, where the lifestyle and domestic trappings of the nobility set the tone. This can be seen from the wealth of surviving Dutch legacy lists. They also record different versions of Bosch's tabletop. One version, for example, was in the possession of Nicolas Jonghelinck in Antwerp until 1565.[15] From Philip II he had leased three of the most lucrative customs posts in Brabant and earned a fortune through banking and insurance that enabled him to acquire an estate along with its title, making him a noble. 'A painting by Hieronymus Bosch of the VII Deadly Sins' is also found in the inventory recorded in 1574 of Margaretha Boghe, who likewise belonged to the upper class of Antwerp with aristocratic pretensions. She was the widow of the master of the Mint of Brabant, Joris Vezelaer.[16] He was not just the governor of the Antwerp Mint but a dealer in luxury goods on the side. From 1528 he supplied jewels, gold artefacts, luxury furniture and tapestries to the court of the French kings. Even in Bosch's day, the *Seven Deadly Sins* was displayed alongside the highly valued pictorial medium of tapestry, giving a further clue as to where the public for the products of Bosch's graphic invention were to be found.[17]

These various pieces of documentary evidence for Bosch's *Seven Deadly Sins* can hardly refer to one and the same painting and have thus given rise to doubts that the example in Madrid was the work of his own hand. Indeed, the difference between the visible painting and the underdrawing showing through the layer of paint in many places seems to indicate that we are dealing with an original design. Without question some of the parts, particularly the roundels with the Four Last Things, are done less expertly.[18] It has therefore been supposed that the tabletop was among Bosch's earliest works. That would also explain some of the archaic touches in the appearance of the clothing. However, the majority of critics now assume that workshop assistants were involved in the production of the painting, which by no means needs to be an early work. There are also signs of a number of hands being involved in the production of other works by Bosch, who can doubtless be credited with the pictorial composition, the design and the overall appearance of the finished picture. Focusing exclusively on the artist, art historians have interpreted the eschatological message of the imagery in the tabletop as a programmatic depiction of Bosch's world-view. There is something to be said in fact for the argument that the painter shared the ideas included in the picture about the individual and the collective fate of mankind.

Nevertheless, it is also important to keep in mind the aristocratic public for these pictures and to remember that it was a triptych of the Last Judgment that Philip the Handsome commissioned from Bosch in 1504. The 'large picture 9 foot high and 11 foot wide', which Philip had commissioned 'for his most select delectation', was to show 'the Lord's judgment over Heaven and Hell'.[19] This painting, costing 36 guilders, was more than 2.5 m tall and more than 3 m wide, making it far larger than the triptych of the same subject now in Vienna (illus. 42).[20] Unfortunately the figure of the donor, which was at one time portrayed on the bottom left of the central panel, can no longer be identified, his coat and a caption being only faintly visible to the naked eye through the layer of paint.[21] We must be dealing here with an individual noble. As Philip was married after 1496, there is some doubt concerning the accepted date of the surviving work and its being in agreement with the date given in the records. Unfortunately there is no clue as to the coat of arms, and the shields shown on the outside at the feet of the figures of the saints were left blank (see illus. 21). It has also been accepted that there existed a connection between Philip's commission and the triptych in Vienna, the reason being that a facial similarity could be made out between Philip the Handsome and the saint shown on the right outer wing.[22] Did Bosch actually paint a secret portrait? A likely explanation for the unquestionable likeness may be that the painters of Philip's official state portraits sought to adapt his facial features to those of St Bavo, as he was widely portrayed, a practice also followed by Bosch. However, even if one has doubts about the secret portrait and does not accept that Philip's commission bears any relation to the altarpiece in Vienna, the saints shown on the outer wings painted in grisaille nevertheless suggest a commission from either the nobility of Flanders or the Habsburgs. St James the Greater, shown on the left outer wing, was revered as the national saint of Spain and might represent the Spanish branch of the House of Habsburg, while the saint shown on the right can be identified as St Bavo, representing his Dutch roots. Bavo was in addition the patron saint of the city of Ghent, where on 24 February 1500 Philip's son and heir, Charles, later to become emperor, was born. Such references, however, remain obscure, particularly since the saint with the falcon can also be interpreted as St Hippolytus.[23]

As regards the date of the triptych in Vienna, it was for a long time based on the commission made to Bosch in 1505. By comparison, however, with the triptych dating from before 1497 with the *Adoration of the Magi* (see illus. 13), giving it an earlier date would seem to be appropriate on stylistic grounds. Dating the wooden panel of the triptych of the *Last Judgment* by dendrochronology would also allow for a much earlier date.[24] As in the case of the *Seven Deadly Sins*, a number of differences visible to the naked eye between the finished picture and the underdrawing clearly indicate that we are dealing with an original design and not just a copy or a repetition.[25] The free strokes of the pen of the underdrawing are to be found in other works by Bosch, such as in the two depictions of St John the Baptist and St John the Evangelist (see illus. 6, 7) and the *St Christopher* in Rotterdam (see illus. 22). It is just as likely, however, that it was the work of several hands. The left inner wing, for example, is painted much more thickly than most of the other areas of the picture. This phenomenon can be shown to exist in the other triptychs by Bosch where it is presumed different assistants were involved. The iconographic programme for the picture will however have been worked out by Hieronymus Bosch, subject to the agreement of the person who, considering the size of the painting, had probably commissioned it.

While there is still a question about the date and the attribution of the painting, there is no doubt as to the focus: the end of time as prophesied in the Bible – the Last Judgment (see illus. 42). 'When the Son of Man shall come in his glory,

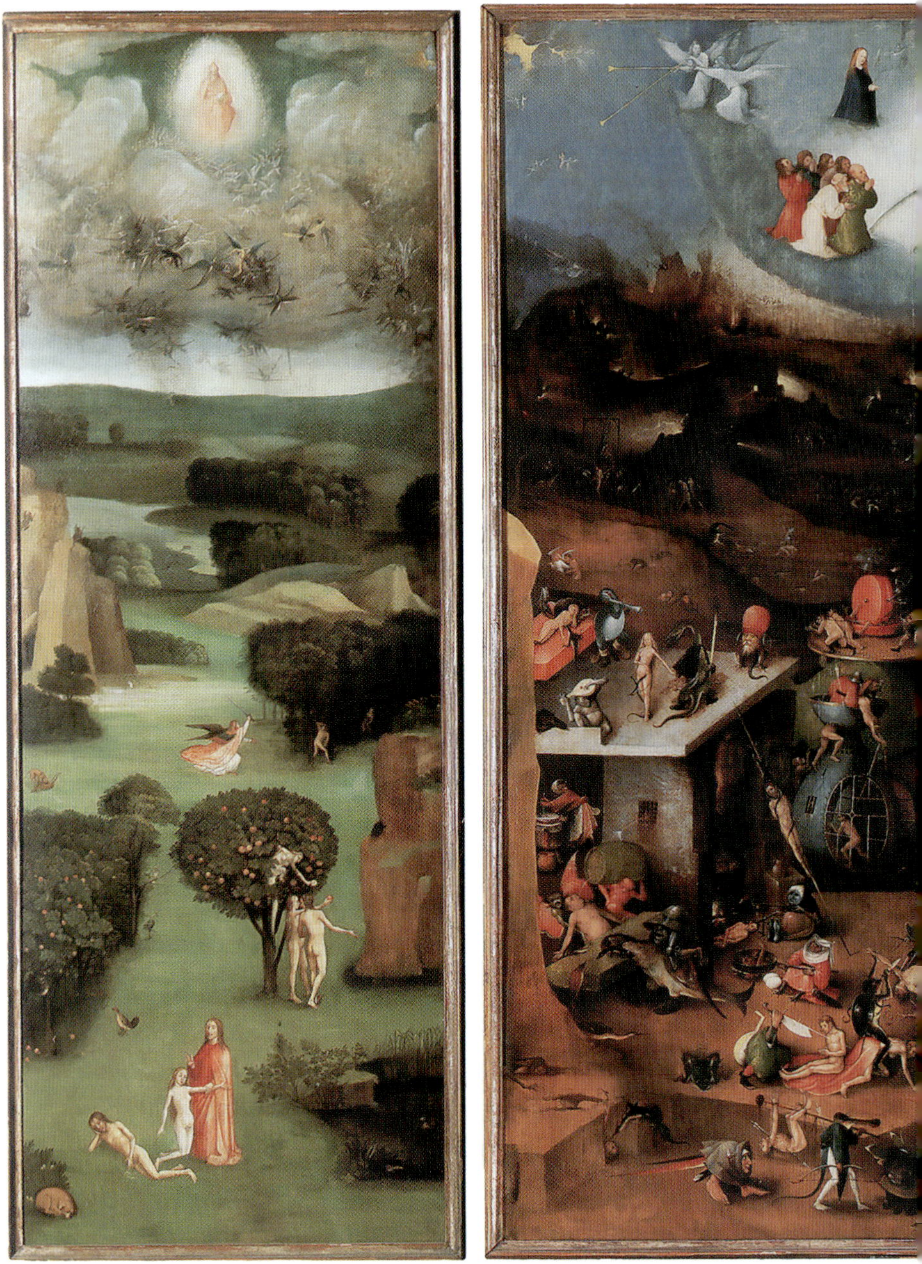

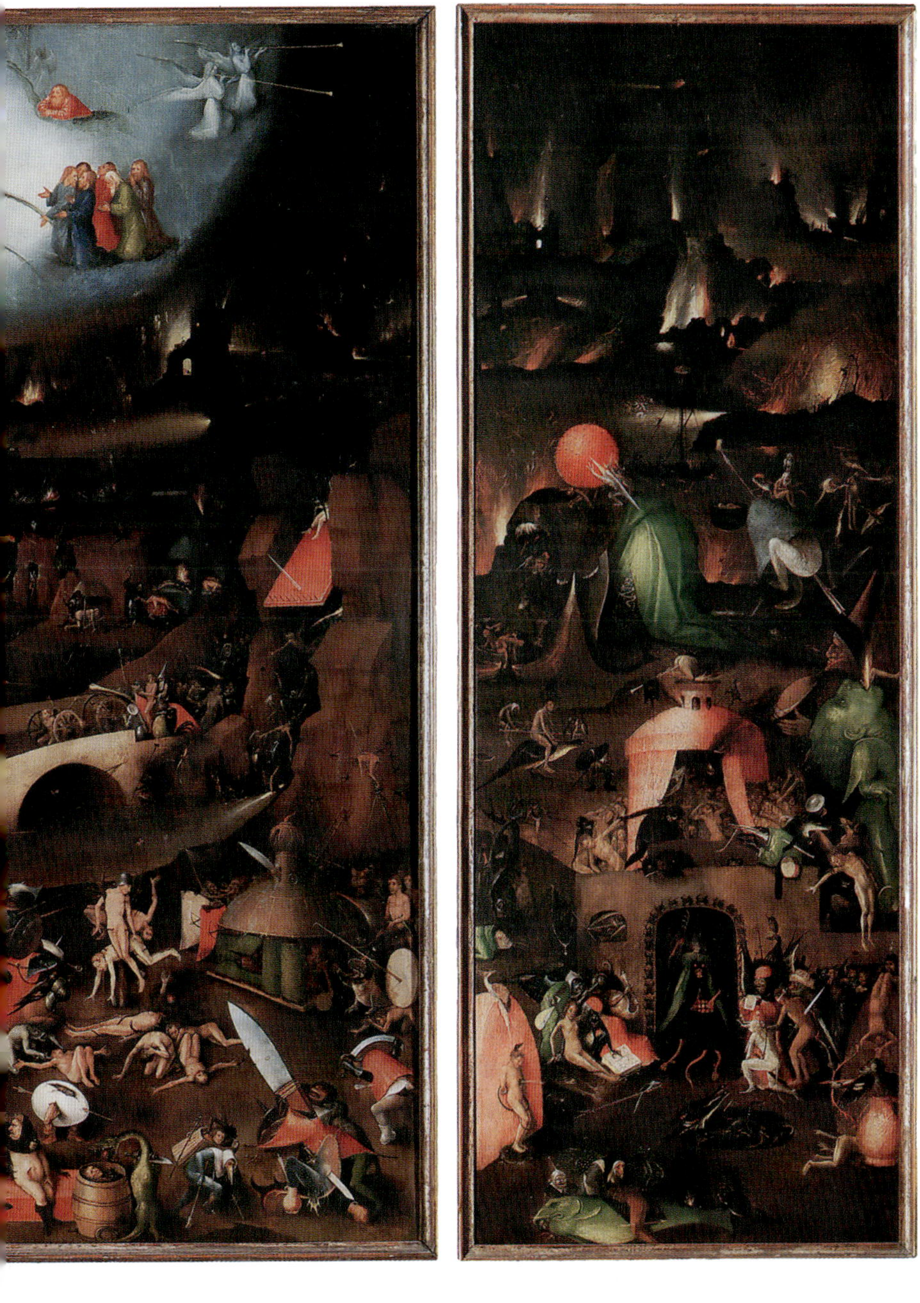

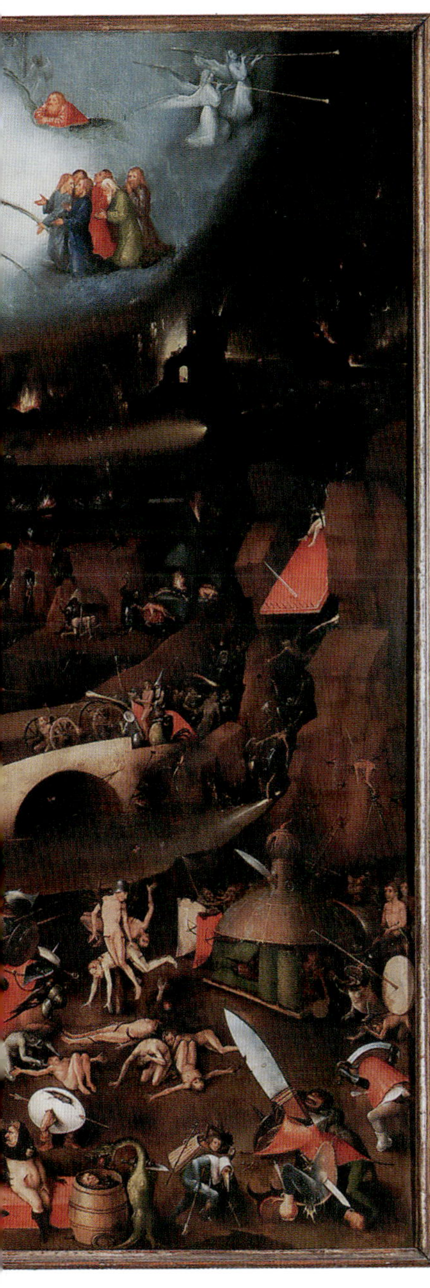

42 Hieronymus Bosch, *Last Judgment*, c. 1505, oil on panel.

and all the holy angels with him, then shall he sit upon the throne of his glory', as it says in St Matthew's Gospel, 'and before him shall be gathered all nations: and he shall separate them one from another, as a shepherd divideth his sheep from the goats: And he shall set the sheep on his right hand, but the goats on the left' (Matthew 25:31–3). This biblical reference provides the basis for the pictorial composition of the event, Hell being situated to the left of the Judge of the World, on the right-hand side for the observer. The left-hand side of the picture is accordingly given over to Heaven, on Christ's right-hand side. This is the composition of most depictions of the Last Judgment and Bosch's version at first seems to follow this pattern. In place of the usual temporal symmetry, however, according to which the awakened dead are being judged, before going up to Heaven or being plunged into Hell, Bosch gives us a sweeping panorama of the biblical narrative from the Creation to the end of the world. The depiction begins on the left wing, first with the creation of Eve, the Fall of Man in the middle distance and on to the expulsion from Paradise in the background. The background shows evil coming into the world in the shape of the tempting serpent, depicting the Fall of the Rebel Angels recounted in the Bible. Assisted by the Archangel Michael, dressed in golden armour, God the Father casts them out of the heavenly realm. This is where the human story of salvation and damnation takes off. Following the prediction after the Fall that mankind, having been cast out of Paradise, is to eat bread in the sweat of their face and woman in sorrow will bring forth children, life on earth has been an almost uninterrupted series of travails. On the central panel, where other triptychs

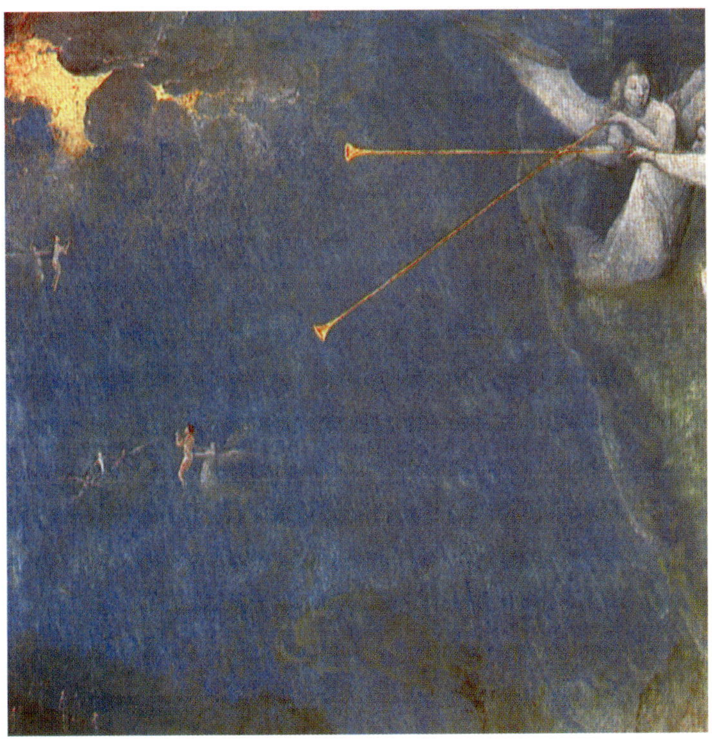

of the Last Judgment from the period show the Resurrection of the Dead, in Bosch's version a hellish universal cataclysm is being staged, extending onto the right wing. In Bosch's triptych in Vienna, salvation is to be found only on the edge (illus. 43). The sum total of five souls – hardly visible – in the left-hand top corner of the central panel are being led into Heaven. The fact, however, that mankind can find salvation through God even in the nethermost depths of Hell is illustrated by an angel on the left who is leading an individual soul up the mountain, despite a toad-like monster who is already aiming its crossbow at them.

43 Detail from Hieronymus Bosch, *Last Judgment* (see illus. 42).

This generally rather unpromising version of the biblical narrative has been taken as an indication of a pessimistic attitude on the part of the painter. Nevertheless, his picture is a reflection of a range of widely held theological views: this includes everything from St Augustine's doctrine of predestination through to religious writings containing moral teachings that were in Bosch's day among the most widely distributed printed material. Middle Dutch literature is rich in descriptions of eternal fire, Hell and the punishments awaiting sinners there. These are usually based on the biblical accounts of a subterranean fiery furnace, a yawning chasm full of sulphur (Revelation 9:2 and 20:10). Besides purely theological treatises, there are a large number of popular writings dealing with this kind of subject-matter. Exact descriptions of the terrors of Hell and the sins giving rise to them can be found, for example, in the writings of Jan van Ruysbroeck and Dionysius van Rijkel and in the much-read *Visio Tnugdali*, or *The Vision of Tnugdalus*,[26] which describes a journey in a dream by the eponymous knight through Purgatory and Hell. A multitude of sins and the most varied punishments are described in it, though not all of the Seven Deadly Sins are mentioned.[27] Ruysbroeck neglects to describe, for example, the punishment for unchastity. He would surely have known an example of this, 'but I shall leave that out, as it is not seemly to hear about it', he writes.[28] Bosch does not shrink from also showing in the central panel the familiar naked people from the *Seven Deadly Sins* who have to share their beds with monsters. Using all the means available to a rhetoric of imagery that is not always subtle, Bosch invites the eyes of the observer to wander through the panorama of guilt and atonement he has created. Quite apart from any theological problems over viewing such imagery, it must have been the sheer inexhaustible variety of the scenes and motifs in Bosch's works that intrigued the courtly public. But this does not mean that there was no theological lesson being taught along with the enjoyment of the spectacle.

Looking at Bosch's art from the rhetorical point of view, Guevara makes a comparison to Aristides, the classical painter, praising the depiction of emotions aimed at appealing to the observer's passions. The theory of art based on the laws of rhetoric had dealt in detail with the stirring of the emotions through images, and considered whether it was possible for pictorial representations to have the same emotional effect required of good speech. Earlier, Thomas Aquinas had demanded of images with Christian subject-matter not just that they should instruct the public, but in addition that they should contribute 'to the stirring of devout passion'.[29] Images of evil in particular were consequently recognized as having a directly visceral impact on the observer and indeed even on those who were still strangers to the awareness of God's grace. The fear of evil created by means of images might awaken in them the still dormant desire for good, so the details of the Devil's abominations could not be portrayed too graphically. The engagement of the emotions, achieving the desired effect based on the model of classical rhetoric, is in line with the overall goal of medieval Christian ethics, which was to encourage disgust at evil and admiration of and desire for good. A long religious tradition considered images to be superior as a medium for the promotion of belief in the Gospel. As William Durandus had written in his *Rationale divinorum officiorum*, the spirit was moved far more by viewing an image than through scripture.[30] There was, admittedly, an awareness of the limits of what could be depicted since it was the most elevated spiritual feelings that were difficult to convey in images. What was acceptable as regards visions of Hell was not automatically the case, according to the theory of art, when it came to imagining Heaven.[31] This justified any lack of detail in the composition of paintings of the joys of Heaven. In place of excessive narrative accuracy in depicting the visions of a heavenly Paradise, the observer was visually encouraged to make use of his imaginative faculties, leading the way to religious experience and spiritual insight. It was a given in rhetoric that something not really present could be made intelligible to the imagination of the public simply by the use of a straightforward, clear image, and that allowing fantasy free rein was at the root of the strongest possible emotional effects. In this respect, the theory of rhetoric went hand in hand with the theological idea that the other world ruled over by God was impossible to describe.

However fantastical his visions of Hell were, when suggesting the heavenly realm Hieronymus Bosch mainly limited himself in his paintings to depicting a heavenly light emanating from God. In a painting in Venice, the vision of the eternal hope of redemption has been captured in what comes over as a surprisingly modern form (illus. 44–7).[32] It belonged to an iconographic programme whose extant parts circle around the familiar theme of damnation and salvation. The original connection between the four pictures is admittedly unclear; nevertheless, the message of what remains is largely comprehensible. The Fall of the damned and Hell are depicted along with both the heavenly and the terrestrial

Paradise. This last one in particular has led to speculation that can perhaps be dispelled by ascribing different meanings to the picture, according to the doctrine of the fourfold meaning of the scriptures. Taken literally, the picture would seem to designate the concrete, historically verifiable place that was regularly indicated on seventeenth-century maps. Taken allegorically, this could mean Paradise, no less. At the same time the garden-like landscape with the fountain could be a reference, based on the Song of Songs, to Mary, Mother of God.[33] The garden could even be taken as an allegory of the Church. Tropologically — that is, relating to the life of the individual — the motif could refer to the soul of a believer; anagogically, it could refer to the paradise of kingdom come and allude to the ascent which is also implied by the tunnel of light. Perhaps for contemporary observers these very allusions to possible interpretations, encouraged by Bosch's generous use of motifs, amounted to part of the attraction of his pictures. Even for modern interpreters there is a considerable fascination, which few of those writing about Bosch have been able to avoid. Whatever the case, we can accept that Bosch was valued by the collectors of his time not just as a moralist. A collector such as the connoisseur Cardinal Domenico Grimani must have been equally fascinated by the unusual nature of the way the pictures were painted, and by Bosch's pictorial narratives. In 1521, according to Marcantonio Michiel, there hung in his palace 'the painting of the Inferno with a large assortment of monsters', a picture referred to as *Dreams* (*Sogni*), and another painting also attributed to Bosch, showing Jonah and the Whale.[34] Cardinal Grimani was an ambitious collector and lover of Dutch painting, which was coming to be

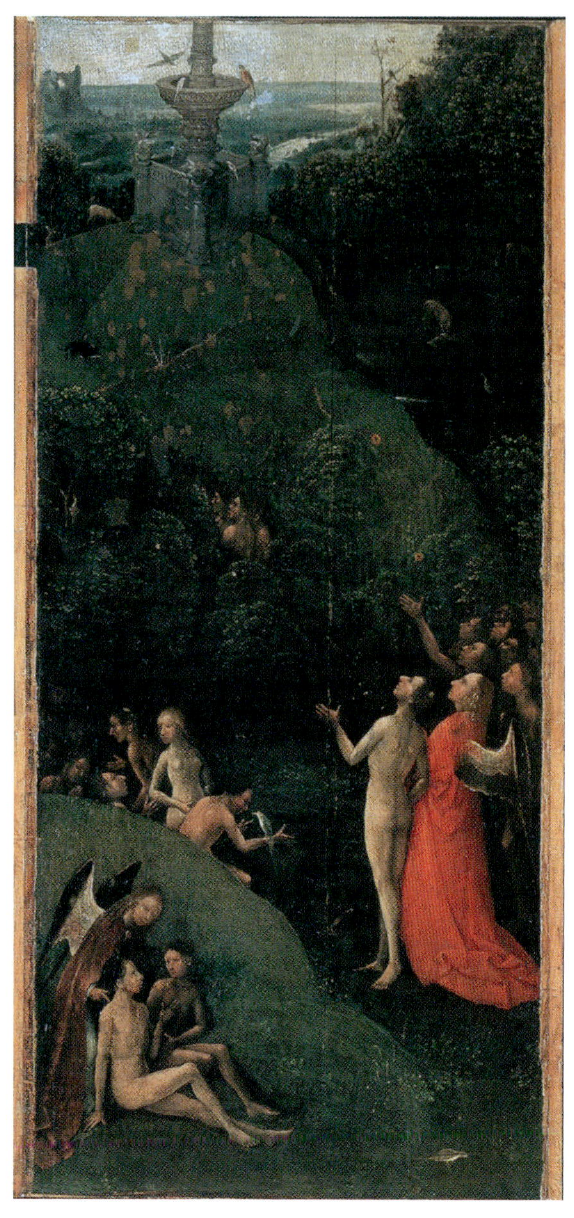

44–7 Hieronymus Bosch, wings of a lost triptych: *Terrestrial Paradise, Ascent of the Blessed, Fall of the Damned, Hell*, c. 1505–10, oil on panel.

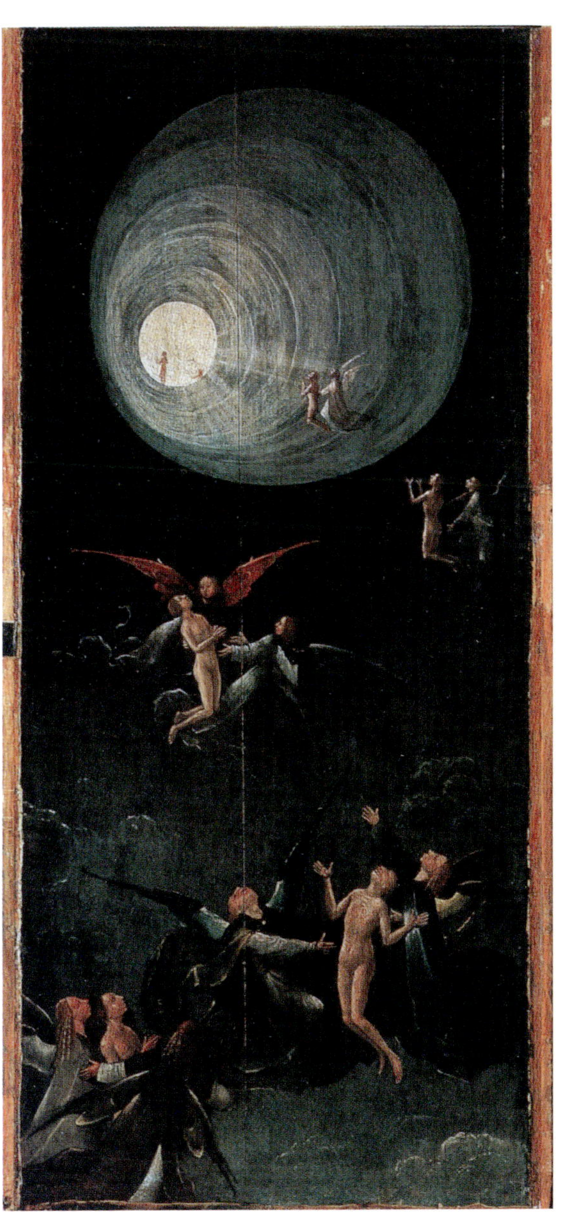

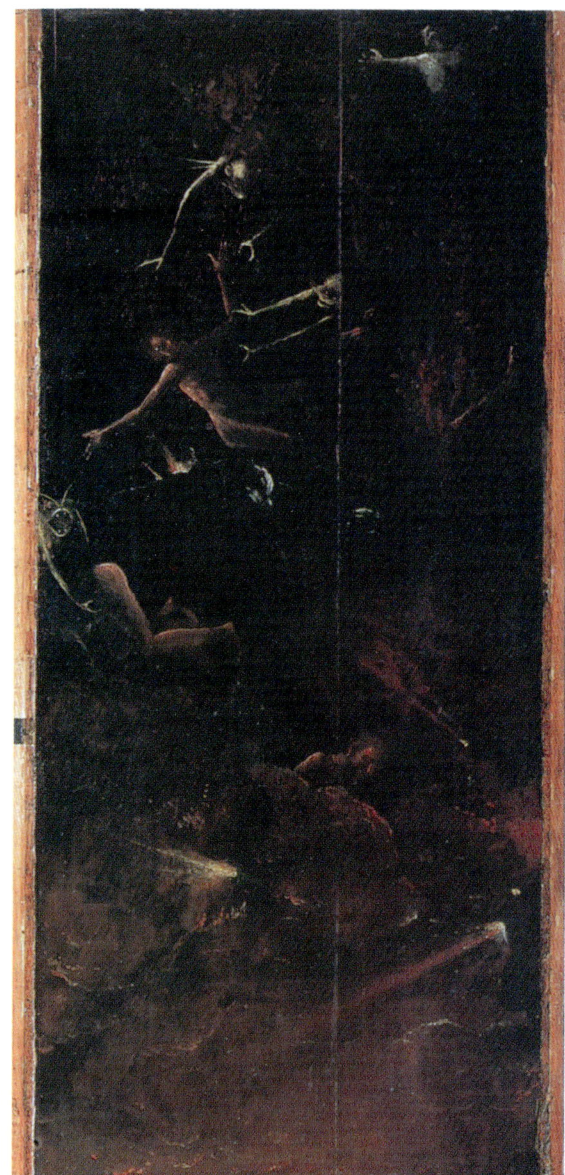

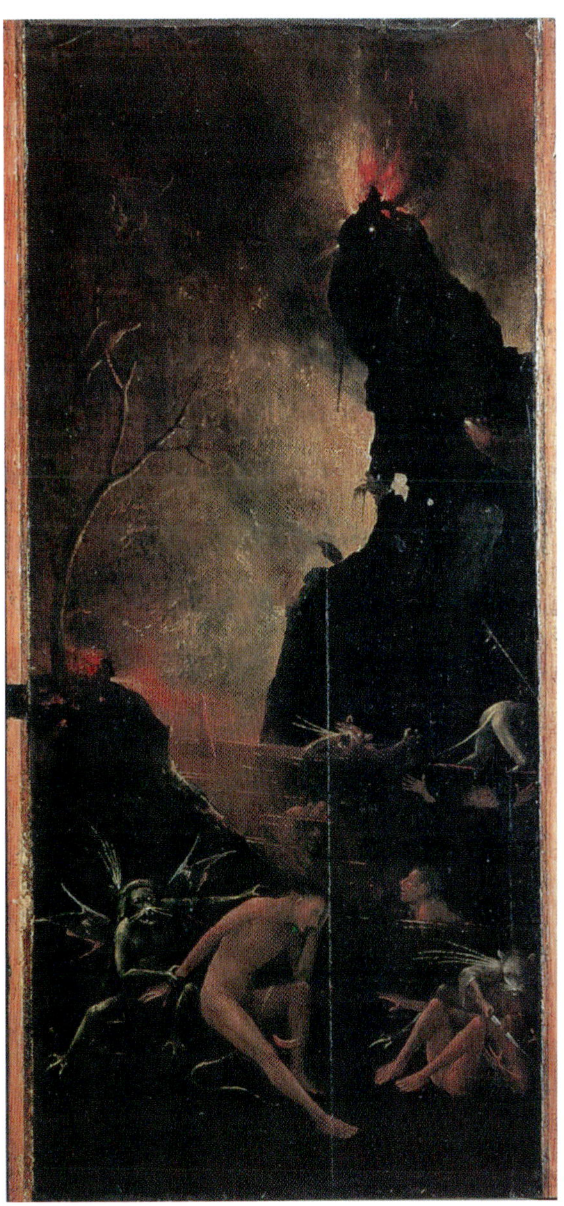

appreciated more and more, even in the Italian courts. He was also a representative of those in the aristocratic elite of Europe who were particularly enthusiastic about Bosch's eschatological pictures. The panels in Venice lost their original context and what happened to the central part, perhaps a carved depiction of the Last Judgment, is not known. Damage or even the total loss of unique works was a risk in the art market of the time.

EIGHT

The Haywain and The Garden of Earthly Delights

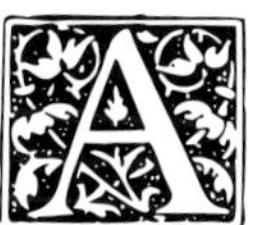 FEW SURVIVING SOURCES offer an insight into the tremendous difficulties surrounding the transporting of art in Bosch's day. Often these are just passing comments in letters, catalogues and inventories that suggest tragic losses during transportation. For example, Mencia de Mendoza, the widow of Hendrick III of Nassau-Breda, contacted her Flemish agent Arnão del Plano in 1539. On her commission he had acquired a representation of *The Haywain* by Hieronymus Bosch and sent her the bill. Unfortunately, however, the work got lost, and in return she tasked him with searching for a replacement *Haywain*.[1] It appears that the picture first ordered never arrived in Spain, but nothing else can be deduced from the correspondence. Two versions of the picture are now known to be still in existence (illus. 48), one of which was sold in 1570 by the widow of Felipe de Guevara to Philip II.[2] The version now in the Escorial has been dated by dendrochronology to some time after 1496; the other one, now in the Prado, to 1508 at the earliest. The first version mentioned here is more carefully executed so that Bosch's figures, usually resembling silhouettes, are embellished by a modelling of the physical details and folds of the garments that is alien to his style. Bosch's

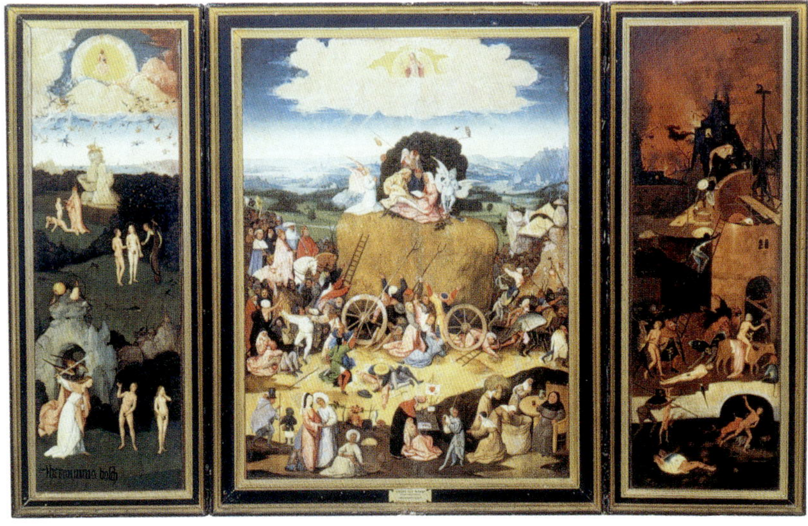

authorship has therefore never seriously been considered in relation to this older version. However, the Prado version is probably not by Bosch either. The figures and the shapes have been done in a totally different way to other pictures attributed to Bosch. It is not just that the visible brushstrokes do not seem right for Bosch, being thickly applied to the layer of paint and making the painted surface appear remarkably rough, so that the outlines of the objects and figures come across as blurred. In addition the painter has left blank spaces for the figures in setting out the background landscape, only for them to be filled in during a second phase of work. Thus this version of *The Haywain*, as with a representation of the Last Judgment in Bruges, can be attributed to one of Bosch's assistants – perhaps to a pupil of Bosch already praised by Guevara, who is identified by many authors as the painter Gielis Panhedel, originally from Brussels, also known as

48 Hieronymus Bosch, *The Haywain*, c. 1515–16, oil on panel.

Gielis van den Bossche.[3] According to the account books of the Brotherhood of Our Lady, he was the one who painted the inner sides of the wings of the altarpiece in the chapel of the Brotherhood, where the outer sides were by Hieronymus Bosch. Even if this identification cannot be proved, the brush marks of *The Haywain* also correspond to those of the over-painting in the picture of St John in Madrid (see illus. 6), providing the only evidence that Bosch and his most faithful imitator worked on the same picture.[4]

Even without the large added signature there would be no doubt about *The Haywain* being a product of Bosch's graphic invention. This work, too, involves the cluster of themes around sin and redemption. This is clearly announced by the brightly coloured outer wings of the triptych (illus. 49). Against a wide-open landscape, showing illustrations of everything being given over to robbery, death and all manner of goings-on without a thought of God, a man identifiable by the basket on his back as a wayfarer is trying to fend off a dog. There has been con-siderable discussion in art-historical circles about whether this prominently displayed worldly figure should be seen as posi-tive or negative. His way through the world would in Bosch's day seem to refer to the popular image of the Pilgrimage of Life depicting man as a traveller, as *homo viator*, on the journey through life. But was the observer really supposed to iden-tify with one who belonged to the generally despised travelling people? Unlike urban beggars, wayfarers had no fixed status in law. Protected solely by the Christian commandment 'love thy neighbour', they were subject to the whims of authority, just as man, burdened by Original Sin, was protected on his journey through life and the sinful world by God's grace alone.

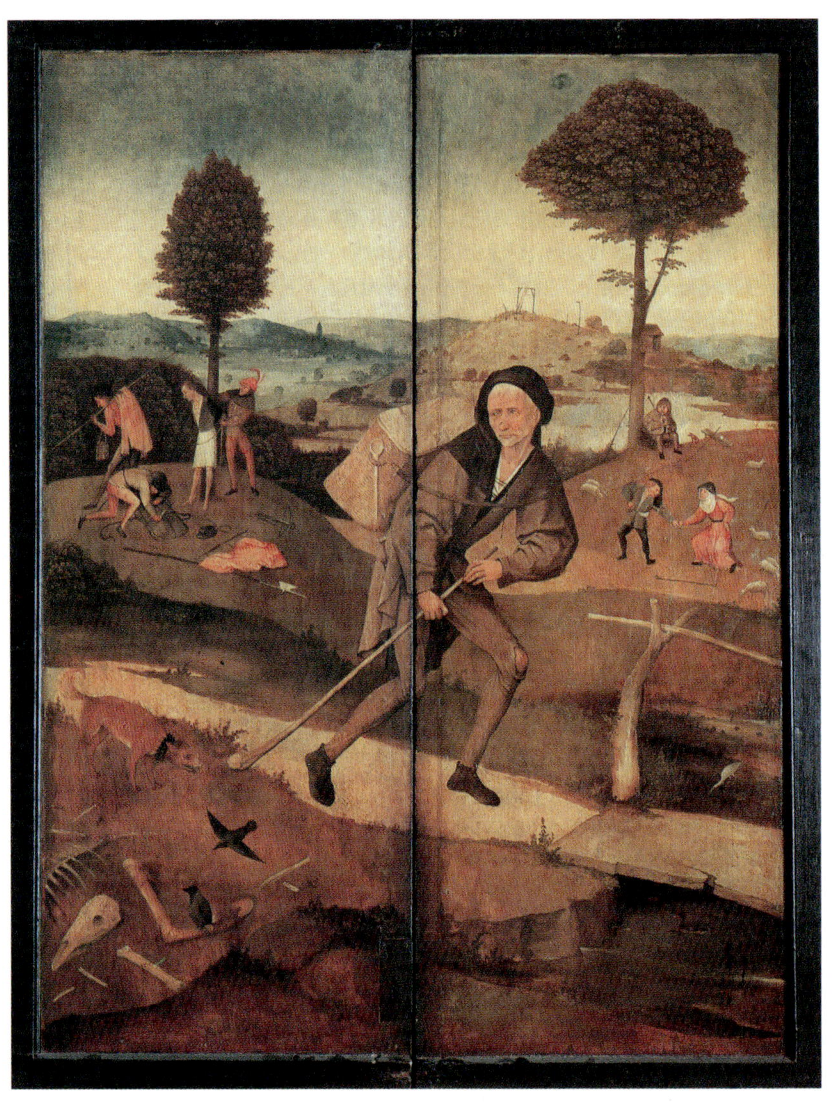

49 Hieronymus Bosch, closed outer wings of *The Haywain*.

Bosch also placed this figure on the outer sides of another altarpiece that survives only in fragments (illus. 50).[5] As a depiction on the outer sides of a triptych, Bosch's figure is unparalleled in inviting reflection on the course of one's life and on fate, along with *The Haywain* on the central panel. Apart from the image of the heavily laden cart, the interior of the triptych shows a tableau familiar from the *Last Judgment* in Vienna (see illus. 42). And just like Bosch's depiction of the Last Judgment, *The Haywain* is also intended to be read from left to right.[6] Beginning with the Fall of Man, Bosch depicts the history of mankind over time, one thing

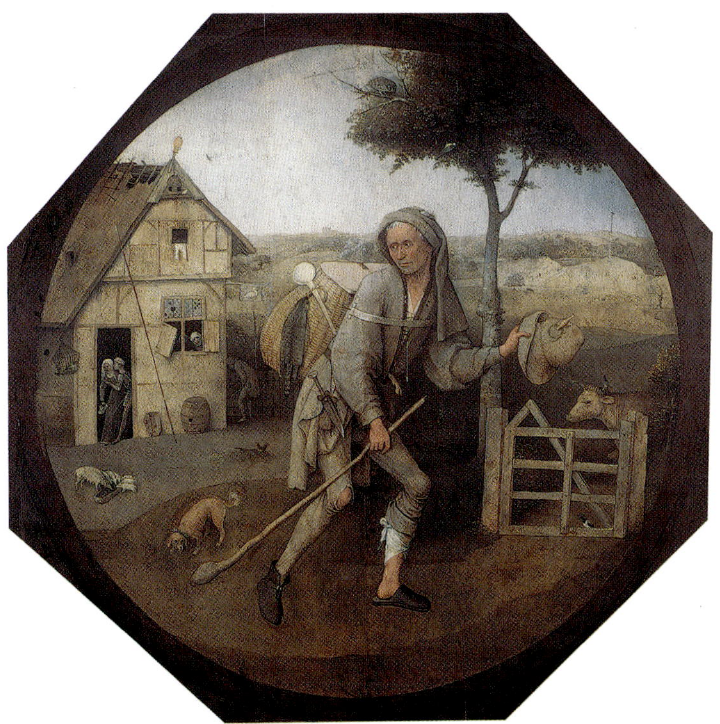

50 Hieronymus Bosch, fragment of the outer wing of a lost triptych: *The Wayfarer*, c. 1515–16, oil on panel.

following another, finally damned as worthless creatures and meeting their just end in the inferno. *The Haywain*, too, starts with a reference to the Paradise lost – a Paradise that was sacrificed to the sinfulness of mankind.[7] In the central panel the abstract concept of the sin of avarice is graphically illustrated by a panorama of every conceivable form of activity. All sections of society are represented in the goings-on around the hay, which turns into a symbol of all earthly, and therefore transitory, goods. Even representatives of spiritual and secular power, the Emperor and the Pope, have joined in the hellish melee. Sitting up on their horses, they are following the procession of vice, leading inexorably to Hell. The shaft of the cart pulled by monsters has already arrived there. Nobody is paying attention to the Man of Sorrows appearing in the clouds, who is raising his hands almost in despair.

The fact that this way of reading it was shared by Bosch's contemporaries is demonstrated in a text by Ambrosio de Morales published in 1585 that the author claims he wrote in his youth.[8] He had presumably come to know the work when he was a private tutor to Felipe de Guevara's son in 1544–5.[9] He had written a description of *The Haywain* as a literary exercise in the spirit of the classical *Tablet of Cebes*, 'with the condition of the human state represented with much sarcasm and insight'.[10] The fact that Bosch's triptych was to be read from left to right was just as clear to Morales as was its moral message: 'In the painting he shows us a panorama of our miserable lives and the great enchantment that we seem to find in its vanities.'[11] 'With subtle detail and skilful execution', Bosch had painted the figures that Morales then lovingly describes and interprets in detail for several pages.[12] His appreciation of the way the painting was done, along with his detailed observation in accordance with all the rules of rhetoric, are an indication of how those members of the public of the time who were connoisseurs and educated saw Bosch's innovative pictures.

Another picture that was intended to be scrutinized in similar detail by an educated, courtly public is what is now Bosch's best-known work (see illus. 4). Interpreters have not felt so challenged by any other of Bosch's creations, and by scarcely any other work in the history of European art, as they have by what is known as *The Garden of Earthly Delights*. This misleading title became standard at the end of the nineteenth century, for lack of any other recorded title.[13] It is true that dendrochronology dates it to some time after 1460–65, but hardly anybody is seriously suggesting that *The Garden of Earthly Delights* is an early effort by Hieronymus Bosch, who was then barely fifteen years of age.[14] This, the greatest of Bosch's surviving works, must instead date from after 1500.[15] There is proof that this, his greatest triptych, was in the palace of Hendrick III of Nassau-Breda in Brussels in 1517, only a year after Bosch's death.[16] He may have inherited it in 1504 from his uncle Engelbrecht II, along with the palace in Brussels. Hendrick, closely associated with the court of Philip the Handsome, may have acquired it himself instead – he was after all one of the best-known patrons and art lovers of his time. No amount of money and no effort were spared over the most sumptuous decor for his residence in Brussels, which became, along with the adjoining park and its animal enclosures, an attraction for foreign travellers. In 1521, Albrecht Dürer thought the palace 'so delightfully built and just as beautifully adorned'.[17] There he was shown 'all the treasures, a meteorite and the large bed in which fifty men can lie'.[18] He does not mention Bosch's *The Garden of Earthly Delights*, perhaps because the artist on his travels was not given access to all the rooms. Canon Antonio de Beatis, accompanying Cardinal Luigi d'Aragona on his journey through Germany, the Netherlands, France and Italy, visited the palace on 30 July 1517. Several months later he still remembered seeing the individual pictures there. Besides the very lifelike naked figures in Jan Gossaert's *Hercules and Deianira* and *Judgment of Paris*, in which the three goddesses were depicted in the most perfect manner, he saw there

> some panel paintings of various bizarre themes where seas, skies, woods, the countryside are simulated, together with figures who emerge from a mussel shell, others who defecate cranes; and men and women, white and black, with different postures and expressions, birds, animals of all kinds rendered with great naturalness, things so pleasing and so fantastic that they could not be properly described in any way to those who do not know them.[19]

The itinerant canon admires the paintings and their curious inventiveness without attempting any descriptive interpretation of what he has seen. Nevertheless, it is clear that the rather brief description refers to none other than Bosch's *The Garden of Earthly Delights* which, after the death of Hendrick iii and his son, passed into the possession of his nephew William of Orange. From there the work was confiscated by the duke of Alba.[20] From the estate of Alba's son it passed into the hands of Philip ii in 1591, under whose ownership it was catalogued two years later as 'a painting of the mutability of the world'.[21] In 1605 José de Sigüença called it 'el quadro del madroño' – 'the picture of the strawberry plant'.[22] This red fruit depicted on the central panel, the dull taste of which does not keep the promise of its delicious appearance, was what he saw as largely embodying the visual message of the picture – not to be led astray by a beautiful appearance.

The outer panels show the state of the world on the evening of the third day of Creation, as described in the Bible (illus. 51): 'At God's bidding, let there be light: and the light was divided from the darkness, likewise the firmament, the waters and the land were made.' Afterwards, according to the Book of Genesis, he created vegetation, 'grass, the herb yielding seed, and the fruit tree yielding fruit after his kind, whose seed is in itself' (Genesis 1:11–13). The fact that the angels had already fallen, bringing evil into the world, is illustrated by the alien-looking plants sprouting all over the place. At the top of the picture there is a quotation from the ninth verse of Psalm 33, which was generally taken to refer to the command to Creation continually repeated in the Book of Genesis: 'Ipse dicit et facta sunt, Ipse mandavit et creata sunt' – 'For he spake, and it was done; he commanded, and it stood fast.' This reference is emphasized by the figure of God the Father on the top left, next to the inscription. The figure was a widely used type and should be seen in terms of a symbolically used pictorial topos, ranging on the same

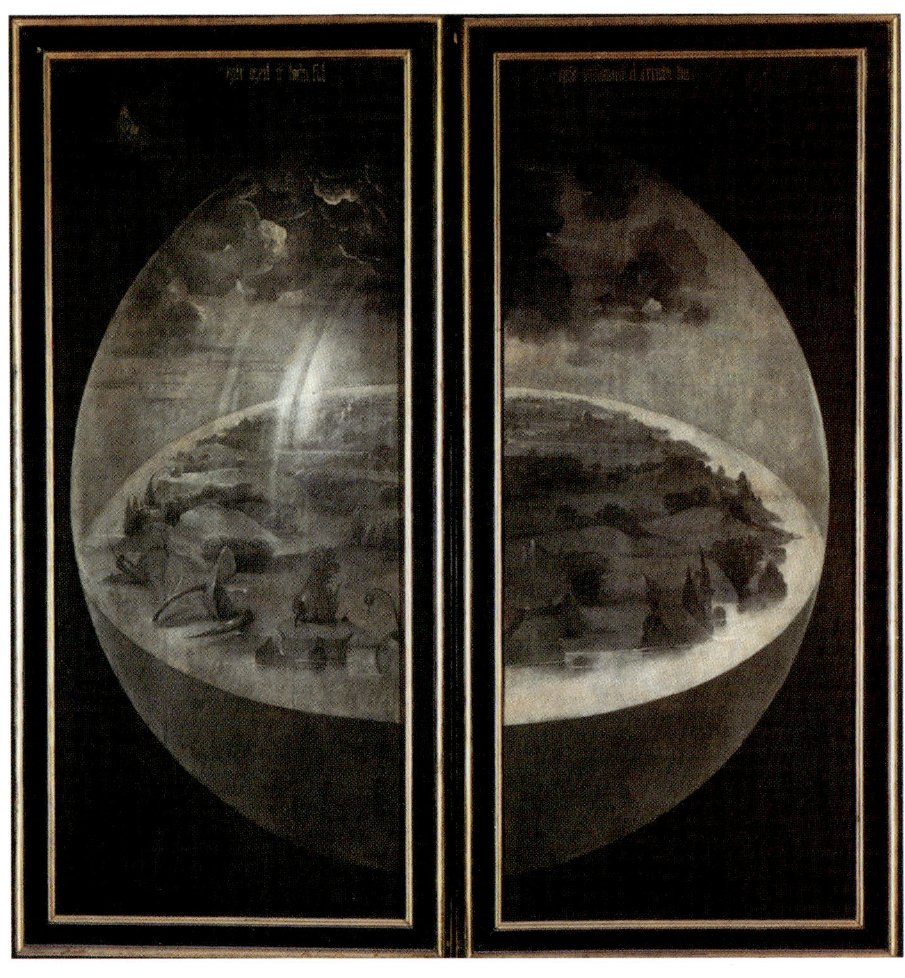

51 Hieronymus Bosch, closed outer wings of *The Garden of Earthly Delights* (illus. 4).

level as the quotation from the Psalms. By contrasting the standard image of God Almighty with the detailed painting of the surface of the earth, Bosch is translating the idea of the opposition of spirit and the material world into the medium of painting.

The inside of the impressive triptych has presented a challenge to modern interpreters. As in the case of *The Haywain*, the central image in particular has given rise to a whole host of conflicting views, notwithstanding any agreement over the details of what is depicted. In studies of art history such depictions have often been described using the German term *Wimmelbild*, which we might gloss as a scene of mayhem, an appropriate description for the almost indescribable riot of all manner of figures and happenings (illus. 52). The figures and groups of naked men and women are clearly differentiated into separate areas of the picture – those at the front, in the middle and at the back (see illus. 10). They seem to be of indeterminate age. There are no children or old people, though there are dark-skinned people, even some with downy fur. Grouped together in silence, they come across as alien, particularly given the unnatural size of the plants and animals in comparison to them. They are devouring the fruit, feeding one another or being fed. Many of them have fish on their heads or fish in their arms. Many of the men and women are touching one another tenderly – one couple sits in a bubble, another couple have withdrawn into a shell. One man has raised a flower to spank someone who is sticking his naked bottom out at him with a bouquet of flowers coming out of it. What is on display here, translated into

the medium of language, strikes one as belonging some-
where between erotic allusions and explicit sexuality.
Bosch's visual language, however, has nothing to do with
pornography. The reason for this is that Bosch reduces the
naked human body to a flat, two-dimensional shape, so that
the slim, fragile silhouettes signifying human beings lose
all resemblance to flesh – though this does not make their
activities any less sinful.

If the central panel had been lost, there would probably
have been no hesitation in expecting in its place a picture of
the Last Judgment. It is all the more surprising that scholars
of art history have spent such a long time debating whether
the scene shown on the central panel should be interpreted
positively or negatively, whether it shows an innocent paradise
or the worst of vices.[23] The reason for this view is due not the
least to the fact that the Fall of Man is not explicitly depicted
on the left wing, unlike Bosch's other representations of the
subject (see illus. 42, 48). Based on this observation, many
scholars read the central picture as something like 'What if' –
a vision of the world if Adam and Eve had not sinned. Bosch,
however, does not depict an idyllic situation. It is a long way
from the Garden of Eden on the left wing, for example, where
suggestions of evil familiar from elsewhere in Bosch's works
are everywhere present. Bright, slimy reptiles are just as sug-
gestive of the presence of evil powers as is the fact that the
cat shown in the foreground has caught a mouse (see illus.
36). The very first human couple will not escape their fate,
following the view held by St Augustine and many medieval
theologians that the Fall of Man took place at precisely the
moment shown by Bosch. It is the moment when Adam turns

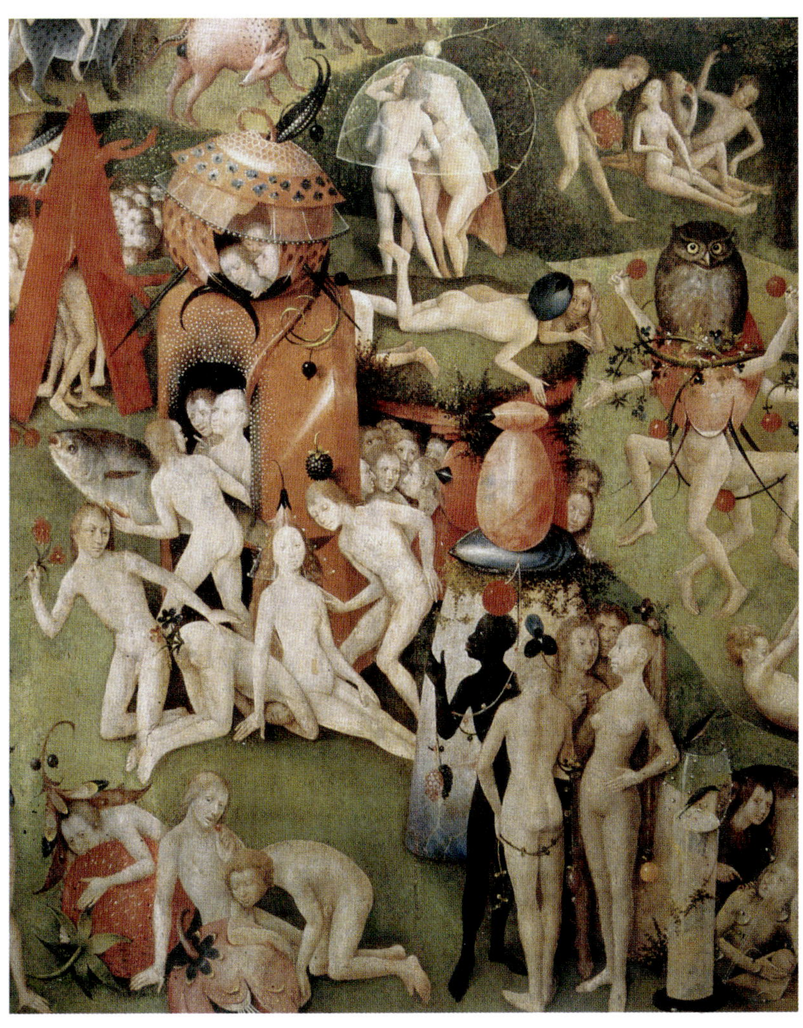

52 Detail from Hieronymus Bosch, *The Garden of Earthly Delights*.

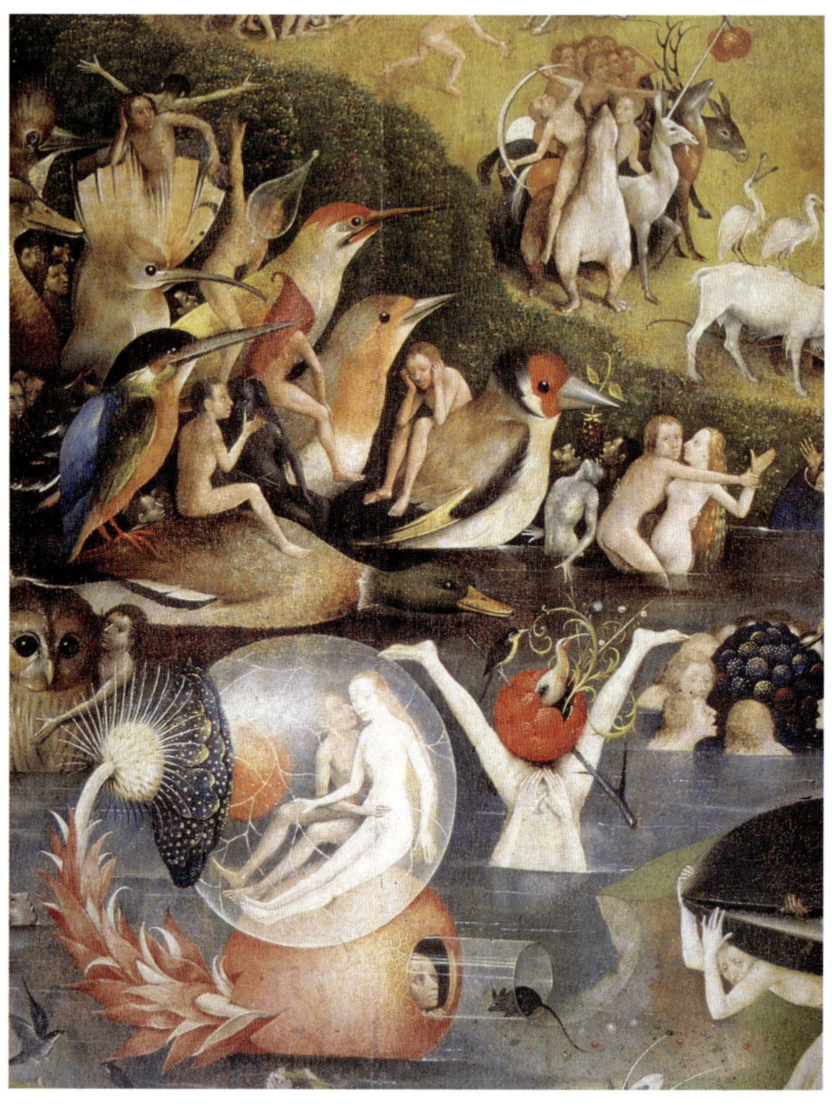

53 Detail from Hieronymus Bosch, *The Garden of Earthly Delights*.

his face from God and towards the woman given to him as a physical companion. It is this turn towards the physical that determines the rest of the biblical story. All the details in the picture should be read against the background of this basic premise common to all theology, even the apparently idyllic central panel.

Dionysius van Rijkel was one of the earliest to come up with the misunderstanding that all evil was ugly for the simple reason that there is 'no more abhorrent cesspool in the world than the unrepentant sinner and vicious man, who however has much natural beauty in his nature and appearance'.[24] If you take seriously the warning that evil can be encountered even in the form of outer beauty, you will also discover the warning indications pictured by Bosch in the central panel (illus. 53). The fact that this is a world turned upside down, as known from proverbs, is shown in graphic detail by the individual motifs, such as the figure standing on its head, also included by Bosch in other places. This can also be seen from the way the composition is put together, with its crazy, topsy-turvy differences in scale. In conjunction with salvific history, the central panel cannot appear as a positive utopia, for what is depicted, despite its entertainment value, disagrees too much with everyday moral thinking and the particular ethics of the social estates. The same courtly audience who understood the three panels of *The Haywain* as a visualization of a temporal sequence would have understood the central panel as an allegory of unchastity and as a drastic depiction of the moral decline of the world.

This series of scenes also stages the great drama of the biblical story, the first act starting with Genesis and the final

one finishing with the Inferno. As in the other great triptychs, Bosch shows foolish mankind forgetting everything
God had foretold. Starting with the background of the wing,
showing Paradise and Satan's Fall from the choir of angels
– a clear indication of the moment when evil came into the
world – there is little room for a positive interpretation of
the events in the central panel. From the point of view of
composition too, everything is directed towards Hell. Thus
the scale of the human figures shown becomes smaller and
smaller from left to right. There can be little doubt about
what is shown on the right wing. Scholars agree that what
we have here is the most impressive vision of Hell in the
history of Western visual art. The dark brown background
gives way to an overwhelming chaos of hellish events, with
individual motifs and groups forcibly standing out. Take
for example the larger than life musical instruments, the blue
bird-headed monster defecating into a transparent chamber
pot and the Tree-Man also familiar from a drawing (see illus.
37). Whereas Hell in the centre of the picture – where the
knife is sticking out between the ears – looks frozen and icy,
the buildings that can be vaguely made out in the distance
are in flames. Guevara had concluded when looking at the
Seven Deadly Sins that Bosch had painted weird things 'because
he wanted to portray scenes of Hell, and for that subject-
matter it was necessary to depict devils and imagine them in
unusual compositions'.[25] This description, which seems to
be so true at first glance, on close inspection, however, proves
not really to be the case; what Bosch paints is not all that
unusual after all (see illus. 2). Not only is the burning landscape, illuminated by the light of the fires, realistically painted,

but he shows accurately reproduced contemporary musical instruments and kitchen utensils being used as instruments of torture. Hell turns into the world turned upside down, a hare dragging a man off impaled on a hunter's pole, or an egg cracking open a man. Elsewhere humans are being eaten, cut up like game, broken on the wheel or put to judgment by the sword.

The range of Hell's executive power is scarcely distinguishable from the normal earthly punishments available in Bosch's day. When you look closely at the details it becomes clear that the impressive thing about Bosch's vision of Hell is not the result of an encounter with the unknown underworld. Instead, much of it comes across as familiar and only becomes uncanny by everyday objects appearing to change their size and having their function perverted. The activities illustrated also emulate familiar ones; of course, they are not carried out by humans but on humans. This Hell is above all uncanny for the very reason that it comes across as so familiar. The 'uncanny', as described by Freud in his famous 1919 essay, does not appear as new or strange, but as something intimately familiar, 'which has become alienated from it only through the process of repression'.[26] A lot of what Bosch shows is derived from the tribulations of everyday experience, and the pains that the fire and the sword inflict on a human being can easily be identified with. Who does not know what cuts and burns feel like? Bosch's pictures and those of his followers come alive by showing the viewer what is admittedly a distant, but nevertheless an uncannily familiar, Hell. The fact that on the right at the front a pig in a nun's habit is coaxing a signature out of a poor sinner is

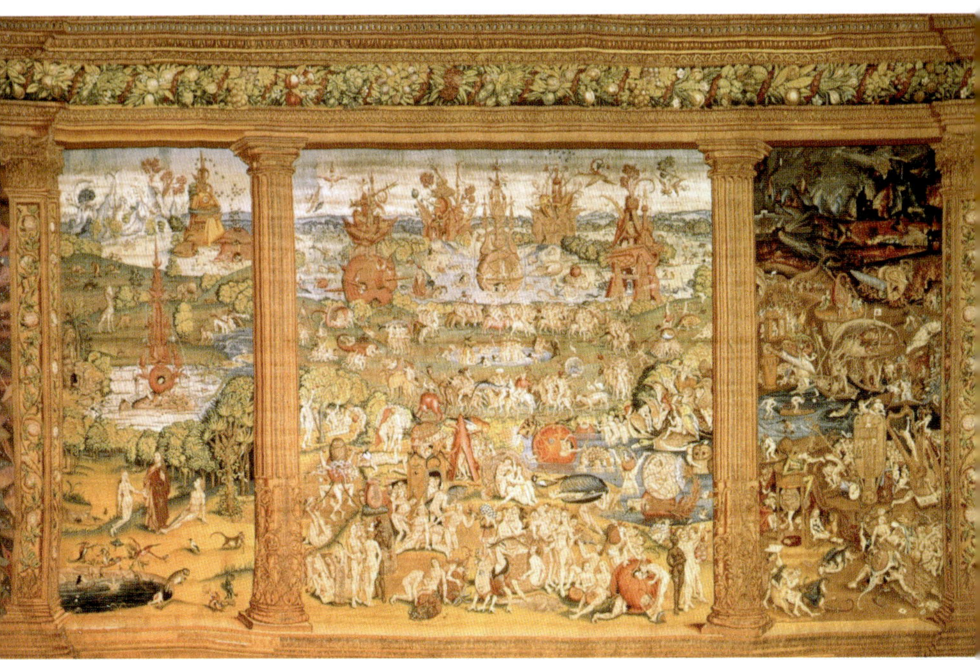

here just as much in line with Dionysius van Rijkel's criticism of the Church as is the unflinching rejection of any form of unchastity, such as that being exhibited in endless variations and combinations in the central panel.

The fantasy world of Bosch's pictures bears looking at very closely, letting one's eyes roam, and interpreting in the same manner. The painter was undoubtedly working towards what theologians questioned as *concupiscentia oculorum* – enjoyment of the eye – that was after all legitimized here as instruction combined with observation.[27] Even the almost emblematic way Bosch portrays the figures is not used so that the abstruse, obscene and pornographic becomes an invitation to the viewer to stare, gloat or be excited, but

54 Brussels workshop, tapestry of *The Garden of Earthly Delights*, c. 1550–70, gold and silver thread, silk and wool.

instead is an invitation to wonder and reflect. In Hendrick III's palace, *The Garden of Earthly Delights* invited the viewer to see his own morality and the canon of courtly values in relation to the subjects of the pictures. This particular context explains a lot of what seems mysterious about Bosch's pictures. *The Garden of Earthly Delights* was hung in one of those castles dedicated to entertainment and pleasure, with a connoisseur owner who clearly had a taste for curiosities. This was where there was a bed for fifty guests provided for use on the occasion of feasts at court. Nevertheless, this extravagant feasting culture was subject to a highly rigid courtly ceremonial and a strict social discipline, and the moral character of these values and norms is reflected in Bosch's pictures. The proof that it was a public of nobles who appreciated the innovative products of Bosch's graphic invention is demonstrated not just by the catalogues of collections belonging to princes and the wide circulation of painted copies, but by the reproduction of *The Haywain* and *The Garden of Earthly Delights* in the courtly medium of tapestry produced over the course of the sixteenth century.

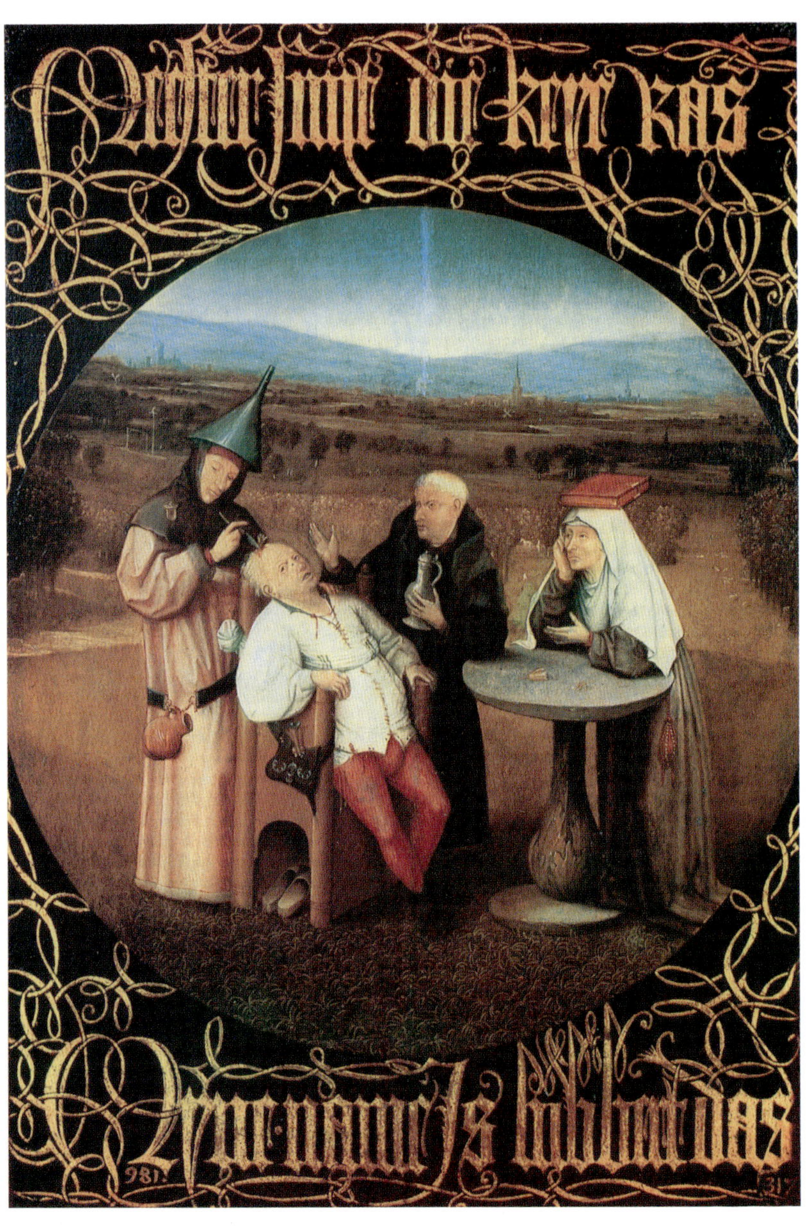
Meester snijt die keye ras

Mijne name is lubbert das

The Folly of the World

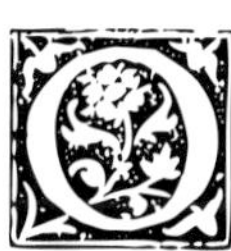

ONE OF THE EIGHT VERSIONS of what is known today as *Cutting the Stone* (illus. 55) was included in the inventory of a Dutch castle.[1] It belonged to Philip of Burgundy, the youngest illegitimate son of Philip the Good. In an inventory made out in 1529 it is noted that in the 'new dining room' of the castle of Duurstede, furnished eight years previously, there hung a picture of 'Lubbertas having the stone cut away'.[2] The title is derived from the rhyming inscription: the golden Gothic letters say 'Meester snijt die keye ras, Mijne name Is lubbert das' – 'Master cut away the stone, my name is Lubbert Das [badger]'. There is no doubt about the subject. According to a Dutch proverb, a stupid person is said to have a stone in his head. The operation, realistically depicted by Bosch, is intended to relieve the person of the stupidity blatantly exhibited by his apparent belief in the success of the operation. Lubbert with his slippers is marked out as a fool by his face; his name is also one that such characters were known by in contemporary folk plays. What we are supposed to make of the surgeon is highlighted by the inverted funnel, suggesting a fool's cap. In Bosch's picture, criticism of blind faith in quackery is linked to an attack on the clergy, abandoning the victim to the consolation of the

55 Hieronymus Bosch, *Cutting the Stone*, before 1521, oil on panel.

spirit. We are reminded of the characters in *The Haywain* when we look at the drunken monk with the wine jug and the nun supporting her head, a mark of the cardinal sin of sloth. Curiously, she is not reading the book but has it perched on her head. They are the embodiment of the corruption of the world, found even among the clergy, summed up by the gallows shown on the left behind the quack. The version of the picture now in the Prado is definitely not an original by Bosch, though comparison of the surviving copies provides proof that this version comes nearest to the works of his own hand.

Bosch's graphic inventions are behind a whole tradition of Dutch representations of fools, a flowering dating back to the sixteenth century. The subject was widely adopted, especially through the medium of illustrated prints, finding its way into burghers' collections. The inscription of the Prado version can be read as an indication that Bosch's graphic inventions were originally aimed at a courtly public. The calligraphic decoration is most closely paralleled by the coats of arms designed in 1481 by Pierre Coustain for the knights of the Order of the Golden Fleece (illus. 56).[3] In the place where the coats of arms of the honourable members of the Order are arranged on the shields, Bosch puts a parable of human gullibility and folly. Philip of Burgundy, who had been accepted into the Order of the Golden Fleece in 1501, would have understood the reference.

Another of Bosch's works that was intended to appeal to the eye of courtiers has survived only as fragments of the two wings of a triptych.[4] Even if some of them have survived only in fragments, most of Bosch's approximately twenty

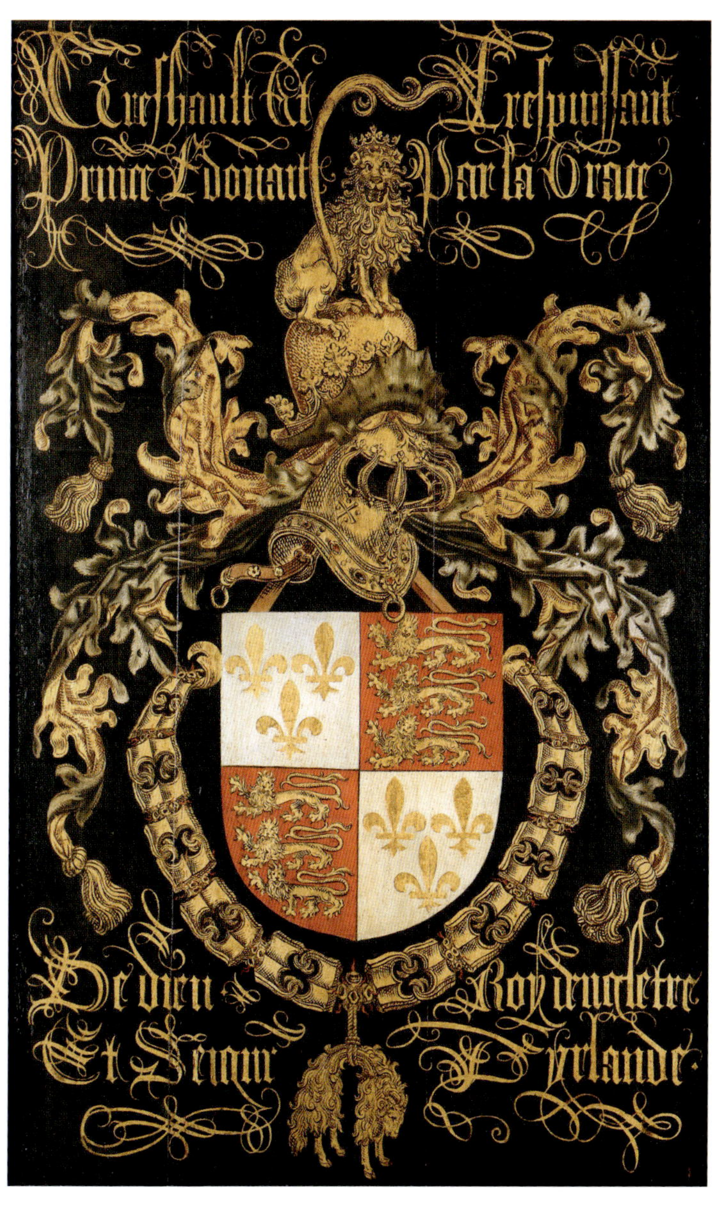

56 Pierre Coustain, shield of Edward IV as a Knight of the Order of the
Golden Fleece, *c.* 1481, oil on panel.

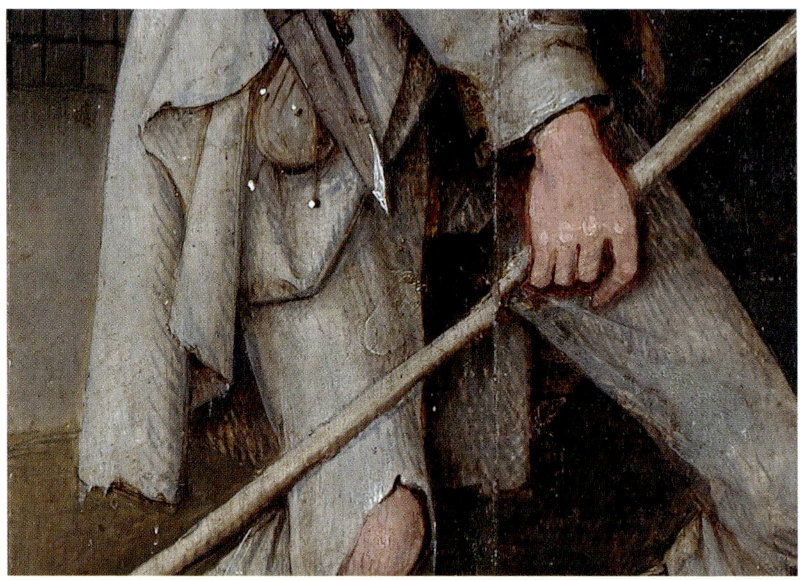

surviving works were, after all, originally conceived as triptychs. Like *The Haywain* (see illus. 49), this work, dating from
the period between 1500 and 1510, also showed a wayfarer on
the outer sides when closed (see illus. 50), again meant to be
read as an allegory of life's journey. This picture, consisting
almost entirely of tonalities of grey and brown, is particularly remarkable for the way it was painted; the paint was
thinly applied as a glaze while still wet. The painting process
was so spontaneous that the painter's thumbprint, carrying
out a correction with his bare fingers, has left its mark in the
damp layer of paint on the figure's upper right leg (illus. 57).
The underdrawing can still be made out, as in the panel with
the *Death and the Miser* (see illus. 39), which once formed the
right-hand inner wing. Death comes to fetch the old man
sitting in bed, while in vain an angel indicates the crucifix

57 Detail from Hieronymus Bosch, *The Wayfarer* (illus. 50).

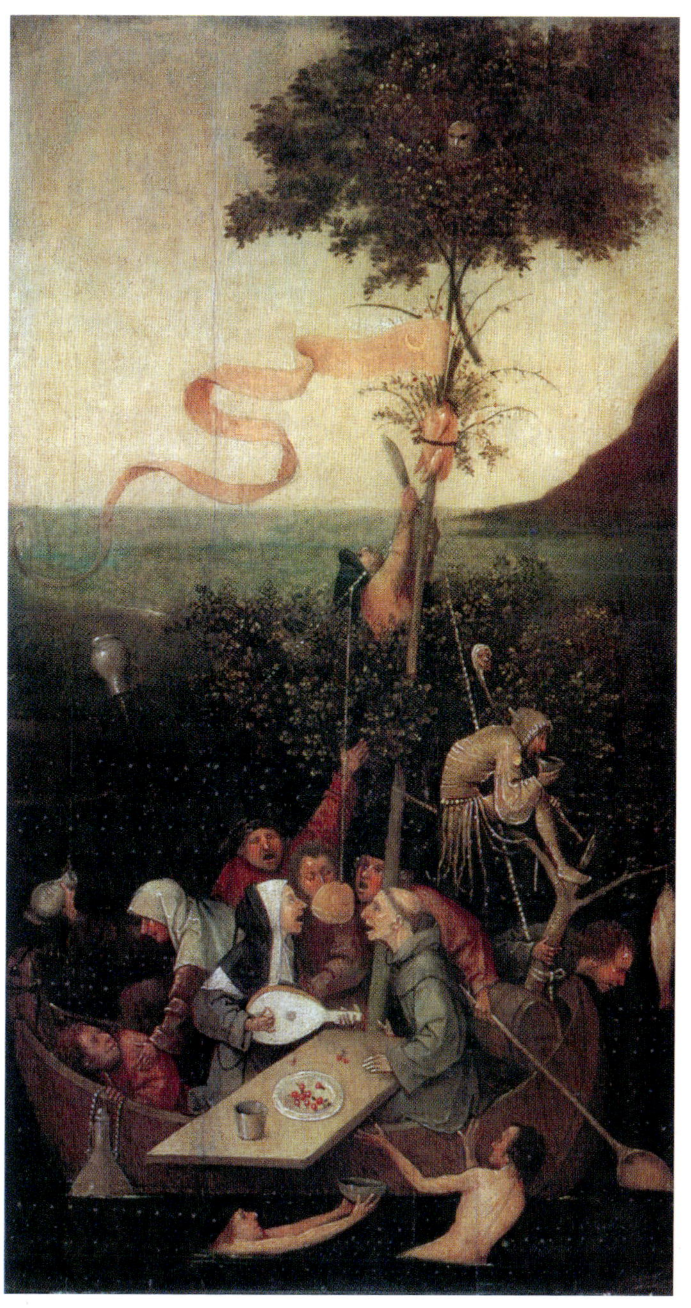

58 Hieronymus Bosch, *Ship of Fools*, c. 1500–1510, oil on panel.

promising salvation. The dying man prefers to bargain with the Devil, selling his soul to him or trying to bribe him. He is no better than the legacy hunter in the foreground who, taking no notice of the dying man, is not concerned with the salvation of his soul, preferring to reach into the chest of money where evil is lurking. Strewn around on the floor in the foreground are the weapons of the Christian soldier, abandoned as if to symbolize the vanity of the ephemeral. The old fool's soul can no more be saved than the crew of the Ship of Fools shown on the other wing, which is now

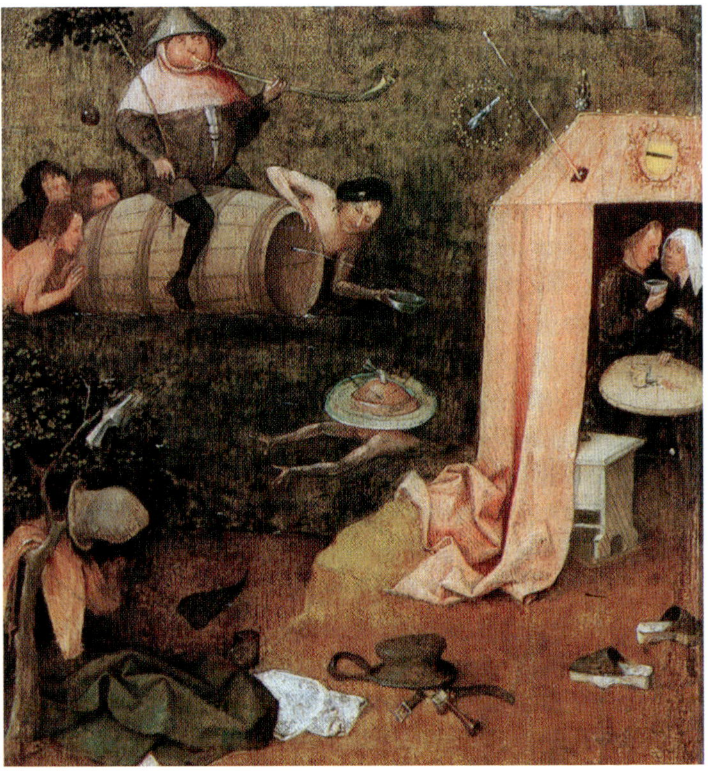

59 Hieronymus Bosch, *Allegory of Gluttony and Lust*, c. 1500–1510, oil on panel.

divided in two (illus. 58). The accompanying lower part of
the panel, now at Yale University, is intended as an allegory
of gluttony and lust (illus. 59). It shows a pot-bellied peasant
straddling a wine barrel, and an amorous couple in a tent.
The unchristian attitude of the company assembled in the
boat is demonstrated by the waving banner bearing a Turkish
crescent instead of the Cross, while a monk and a nun are
among the revellers. The fool sitting in the rigging draws
an inevitable parallel to Sebastian Brant's *Ship of Fools*, first
printed in 1494, which also appeared only a few years later
in Dutch and Latin versions. In its prologue, there is clear
criticism of the godless world of the present, also reflected
in Bosch's pictures:

> Yes, Scripture and Law are scorned,
> The world lives in darkest night
> And blindly persists in sinning.
> All the alleys and streets are full of fools.[5]

The inadequacies of mankind that are unfurled in Brant's
book are depicted by Bosch. And we can take it that, rather
like Brant's description in his prologue, Bosch was not just
aiming at entertaining the public. He too was adding 'whole-
some instruction' to his pictures for an increase in public
awareness and moral improvement.

There has been much speculation about the possible subject of the central panel, a lot of which has seemed perfectly
reasonable. One possibility that has been put forward is that
the depiction of the Marriage Feast at Cana (illus. 60), surviving only in copies, once formed the central panel.[6] Evidence

in favour of this is the format of the surviving copies, which correspond exactly to the central panels of the remaining triptychs by Bosch. However, attempts to identify any direct connection in terms of subject-matter have not proved to be very convincing. It is true that the Marriage Feast at Cana described in St John's Gospel can be associated with the Eucharist and interpreted as a parable on moderation, chastity and loving one's neighbour (John 2:1–11). It would therefore serve as a critical commentary, rich in allusion, on what is represented on the side wings, one of which deals with lack of moderation and lust, the other with egoistical greed only out for selfish gain even in the presence of a dying man. The way the table is laid with the sideboard shown at the back, and the fact that a swan and a pig are on the menu, has caused interpreters to come up with terms like 'richly clustered associations'.[7] The painting, whose subject is actually plain to see, has been read as a 'document of Semitic Gnosis', leading to the suggestion that the events in the picture have some sort of esoteric, occult or heretical significance.[8]

Such claims have been totally disproved by recent research.[9] As in the case of Bosch's *The Conjuror*, the surviving drawings have allowed us to identify all the important details relating to the subject and pinpoint exactly what the painted copies were all about. Analysis of the artistic technology of the painting materials has suggested a date for the picture of some time after 1540, and dating by dendrochronology to some time after 1553.[10] It has never been in doubt that it is a product of Bosch's graphic invention. Based on a critical comparison of the surviving copies, the date of the lost original has been put at around 1510, a period when the painter, who had in the

60 After Hieronymus Bosch, *Marriage Feast at Cana*, after 1553, oil on panel.

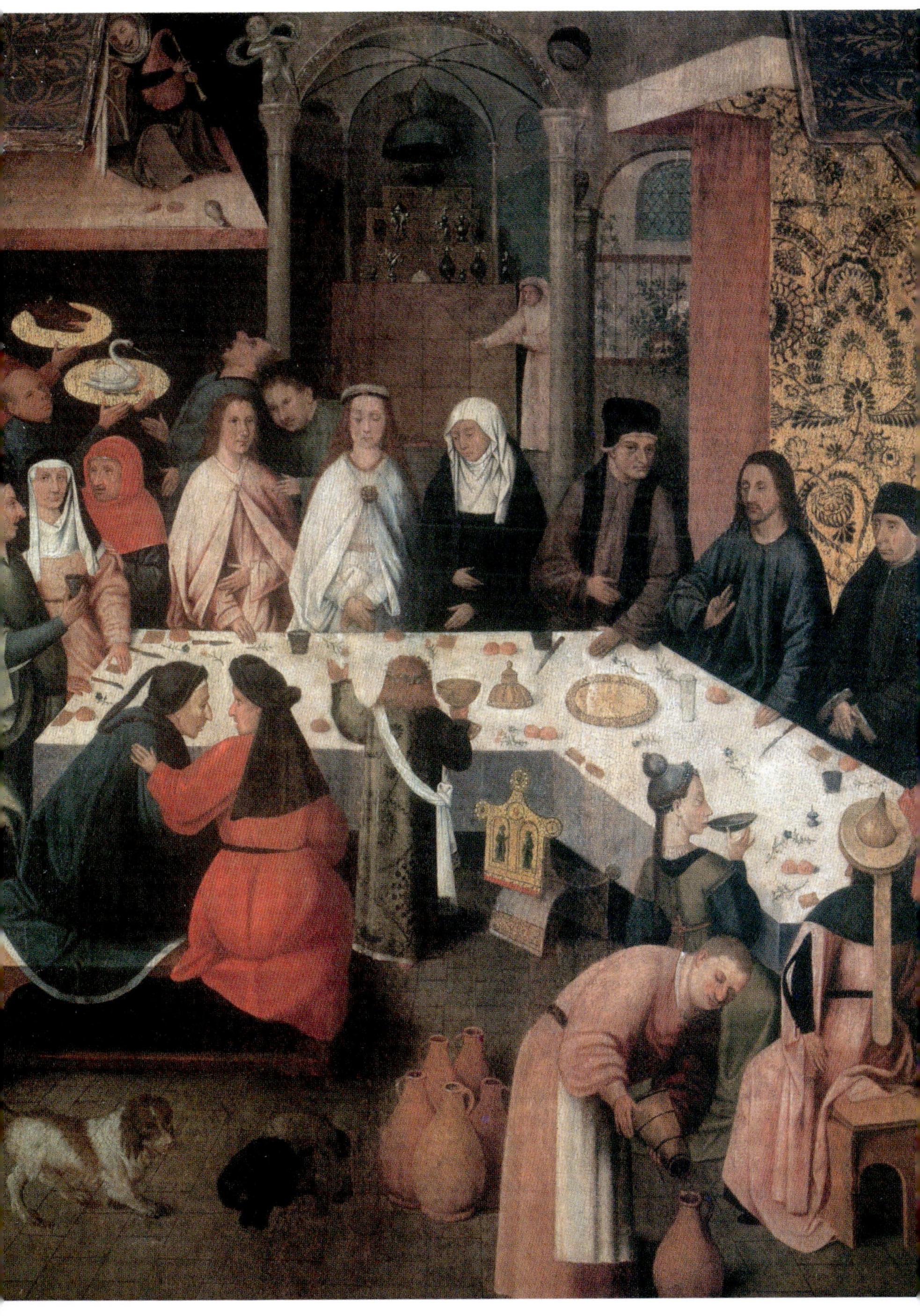

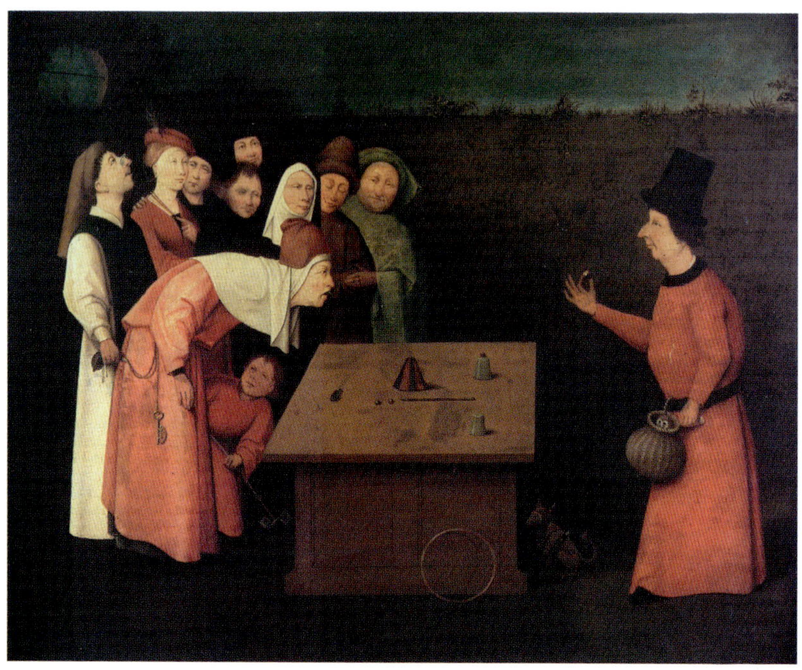

meantime become fairly well known, was producing more and more for a public made up of collectors who clearly appreciated these depictions of worldly subject-matter, as well as his moralizing triptychs. The surviving copies prove the popularity of these pictures and that they were in wide circulation, an example of which is a surviving painting depicting something totally unmysterious. It shows a conjuror captivating his audience with all sorts of mountebankery and magic tricks while his accomplice is among the spellbound onlookers, robbing them (illus. 61).[11] An engraving published around the middle of the sixteenth century, made from one of the surviving versions of the picture, makes plain what is going on as a warning against mountebanks abroad in the world.[12] Just like

61 Hieronymus Bosch, *The Conjurer*, before 1520, oil on panel.

Cutting the Stone, the scene comes over as a painting of a popular farce. The characters in it, however, are the embodiment of faithless humankind, those 'lost and misguided people' whose vices and follies are also on display in the *Seven Deadly Sins* and *The Haywain*.

Just as in a picture from the history of religion, the subjects and motifs of Bosch's worldly paintings can be interpreted allegorically in a range of different ways. Of course, the symbolic interpretation of such a depiction and its motifs is and was dependent on the educational level of each individual viewer. Certainly, a contemporary who had received an academic education or even one who taught as a theologian at a university would no doubt have discovered more symbolic references in a painting by Bosch than a relatively less educated noble or merchant, for example. Nevertheless, one can take it for granted that there was a basic repertoire of shared motifs that was widely understood and accepted as the common currency of pictures. Thus the individual, symbolically charged pictorial signs sufficed to instigate a complex process of imagination and understanding, since the knowledge of the issues behind the formula was common knowledge. In fact a simply incredible wealth of constantly repeated motifs was very much part and parcel of the visual culture of the period, which is now only vaguely accessible to us. It is surely obvious that their message is a moral one given the religious consensus over norms and values. This is another part of the reason why Bosch's pictures cannot be reduced to readily identifiable moral examples.

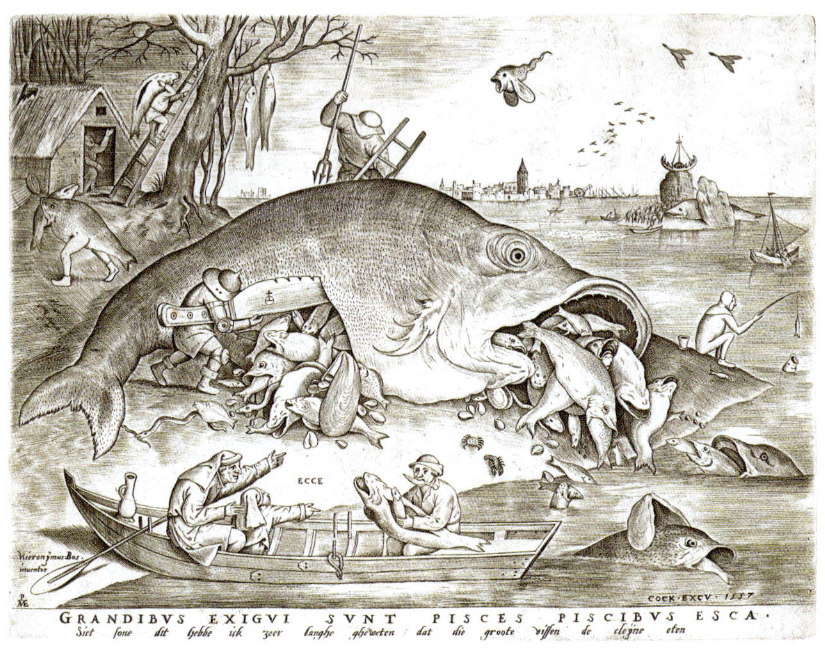

GRANDIBVS EXIGVI SVNT PISCES PISCIBVS ESCA.

Siet sone dit hebbe ick zeer langhe gheweten dat die groote vissen de cleyne eten

TEN

Interpretations

ARTS OF WHAT WAS ONCE a large body of work by Bosch are now known only in copies of variable quality.[1] Many of the products of graphic invention attributed to him in old inventories have completely disappeared, such as the picture mentioned by Marcantonio Michiel in 1521 as the 'picture of the fate of the whale in the process of swallowing Jonah' or the picture of a country festival owned by Guevara along with *The Haywain*.[2] Above all, the pictures on canvas attributed to Bosch are completely lost, a large number of which are known to have been in art collections, especially in Antwerp.[3] Nevertheless the relevant entries in the inventories may be misleading since by no means all of the pictures attributed to Bosch at the time are now thought actually to be by him. Instead it seems as if the name 'Bosch' had come to be identified as more or less interchangeable with the highly popular genre of pictures depicting Hell known as *Helleken*. His *St Anthony* triptych alone gave rise to more than thirty copies in the course of the sixteenth century. Even in his lifetime more scenes of Hell were attributed to him than he could have painted. In other words, Bosch's name therefore often appears in catalogues of paintings for the simple reason

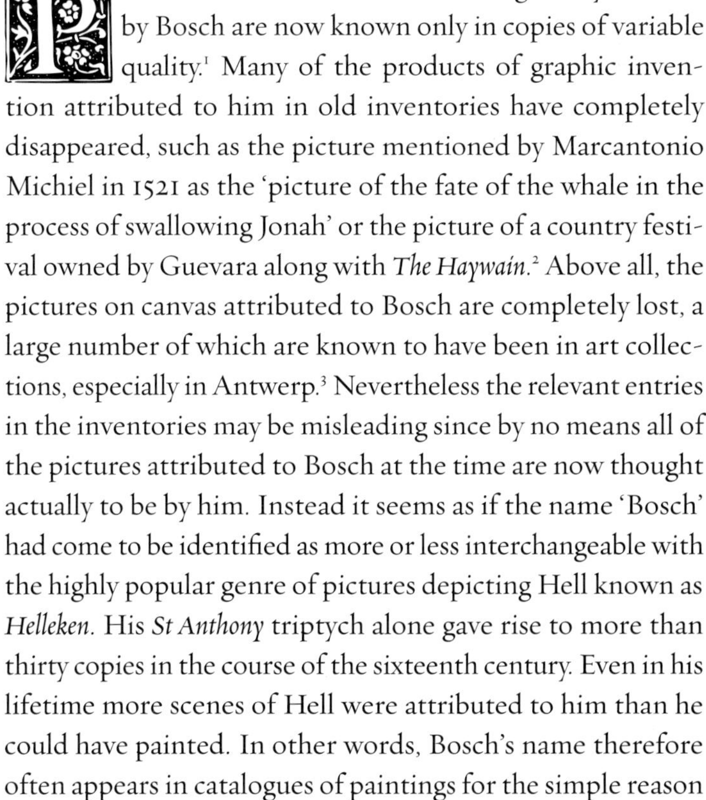

62 Pieter van der Heyden after Pieter Bruegel the Elder, *The Big Fish Eat the Little Fish*, 1557, engraving.

that his imitators did not hesitate to add his signature to their
pictures. Felipe de Guevara was already aware of this around
1560, reporting in his *Comentarios de la pintura* that numerous
pictures were to be found

> which are signed with the name of Hieronymus Bosch
> but are in fact fraudulently inscribed: pictures to which
> he would never have thought of putting his hand but
> which are in reality the work of smoke and of short-
> sighted fools who smoked them in fireplaces in order
> to lend them credibility and an aged look.[4]

This brief mention is evidence, not just of the existence of
such forgeries, but of the fact that they presented a problem for collectors. Bosch lived and worked at a time when
there was a growing interest in the aesthetic dimension of
works of visual art and in their creators. Felipe de Guevara
himself owned six works by Bosch that he had presumably
inherited from his father who died in 1520. In his lifetime
Diego de Guevara had been a confidant of the Spanish kings
at the court of Philip the Handsome and had joined the
Brotherhood of Our Lady in 's-Hertogenbosch in 1498–9.
He would have been in a position to buy the pictures from
Bosch himself. He must also have passed on his knowledge of
Bosch's artistic signature to his son along with the originals
and *The Haywain* painted by his gifted pupil.

Contemporaries of Bosch collecting his pictures and
paying a lot for them wanted to make sure they were get-
ting works by his hand, rather than those by imitators and
copyists. Historical paintings were of increasing interest

for collectors in the sixteenth century. In court collections, inherited Old Masters underlined the noble status of the owners. After all, historical paintings were proof of the fact that even one's ancestors had appreciated and promoted the arts. Copying this habit of the court, the city fathers started to take an interest in old pictures, particularly if they were of local origin, as historical evidence of cultural traditions. At the same time they tried to acquire paintings by those painters whose works also hung in the exemplary collections of the upper nobility. This was how a demand arose that had not previously existed, and which was not satisfied by the extant originals. The consequence of this tendency can be seen in a decree by Antwerp City Council of 3 October 1575 which, along with the other privileges of the Guild of St Luke, authorized the copying of known pictures.[5] It should never be the case, it stated, that 'honourable gentlemen and citizens would be defrauded as a result of suchlike purchases in buying the works of known and famous masters, they being only authentic copies of the same'.[6] The copies and imitations of Bosch's pictures, often originating in Antwerp, were done almost entirely by painters whose names are for very good reasons no longer known.[7] Nevertheless, the personalities of some of the artists stand out from the mass of nameless imitators, showing evidence of a remarkable oeuvre in their own right. The most prominent of these is surely Pieter Breughel the Elder (illus. 62). Just over halfway through the sixteenth century, still at the start of his career, his drawings, which displayed an inventiveness that was entirely his own, were circulated by the publisher Hieronymus Cock as products of Bosch's invention. Karel van Mander wrote in 1604 that Pieter Breughel painted very much in the style of Hieronymus Bosch, with ghostly images and comic scenes, which is why they called him 'Pier den Drol' – 'Pieter the joker': 'This is why one sees few pictures by him which a spectator can contemplate seriously and without laughing.'[8] It is significant that van Mander said that Bosch's paintings were 'usually not so much kindly as ghastly to look upon'.[9] Where Bosch depicted a gloomy vision of the future as a result of the abominable acts of a godless mankind, his followers were happy to portray the horrors of Hell as picturesque and in as many different ways as possible. Moral instruction was replaced by entertainment, focusing more on the comic than was the case in Bosch's art and the way his contemporaries saw it. Particularly towards the end of the sixteenth century, when a real 'Bosch Renaissance' took off, many imitators were keen to highlight what was to a great extent already there in the way of comic elements in Bosch's art.

Other imitators made ornamental arrangements out of Bosch's ghastly visions of Hell. This can be seen from the many drawings done by Bosch's followers, and in a fragment of a *Last Judgment* probably dating from the time he was still alive (illus. 63).[10] To judge by analysis of the age of the wooden panel, this picture could date from as early as the middle of the fifteenth century. Bosch's motifs are clearly at work here, like calligraphy spread all over the dark background of the picture. The individual monsters, totally unlike Bosch's, have a functional appearance. Arranged like a grotesque butterfly collection, they have been turned into brightly coloured arabesques.

The many imitations of Bosch and the pictures done by his followers are worthy of further study in their own right. It is therefore easier to list the enormous number of imitations than to explain them. One thing for sure is that Alart du Hameel's engravings contributed to the spread of Bosch's vocabulary of imagery (see illus. 40).[11] They were both of a similar age and must have known one another, because du Hameel was a member of the Brotherhood of Our Lady. From 1478 to 1494 he was the chief mason of the cathedral of 's-Hertogenbosch. He signed his fantastical inventions using the name and inscription 'Bosche', also found on a dozen engravings.[12] Some of these drawings are closely related to Bosch's world of imagery, without exactly reproducing it. In his engravings, du Hameel works with Bosch's motifs, but with other models as well. With unbridled enjoyment he depicts the foolish goings-on of small, mainly humanoid demons that are only distantly related to Bosch's hybrid creatures. Misunderstandings over how to classify their origin have also led to the false assumption, until recently, that the engravings were reproductions of lost paintings by Bosch.[13] After all, it was precisely fantastical inventions like these that made his reputation in the first place.

Around the middle of the sixteenth century Marcus van Vaernewijck, Lodovico Guicciardini and Giorgio Vasari were already praising Bosch's 'fantastical and odd' inventions. At the end of the century, by which time his reputation as a 'devil maker' was firmly established, he came in for similar praise from Giovanni Paolo Lomazzo, Ambrosio de Morales and Gonzalo Argote de Molina, the last of whom called the pictures that Bosch was particularly famous for 'farces'.[14] Up

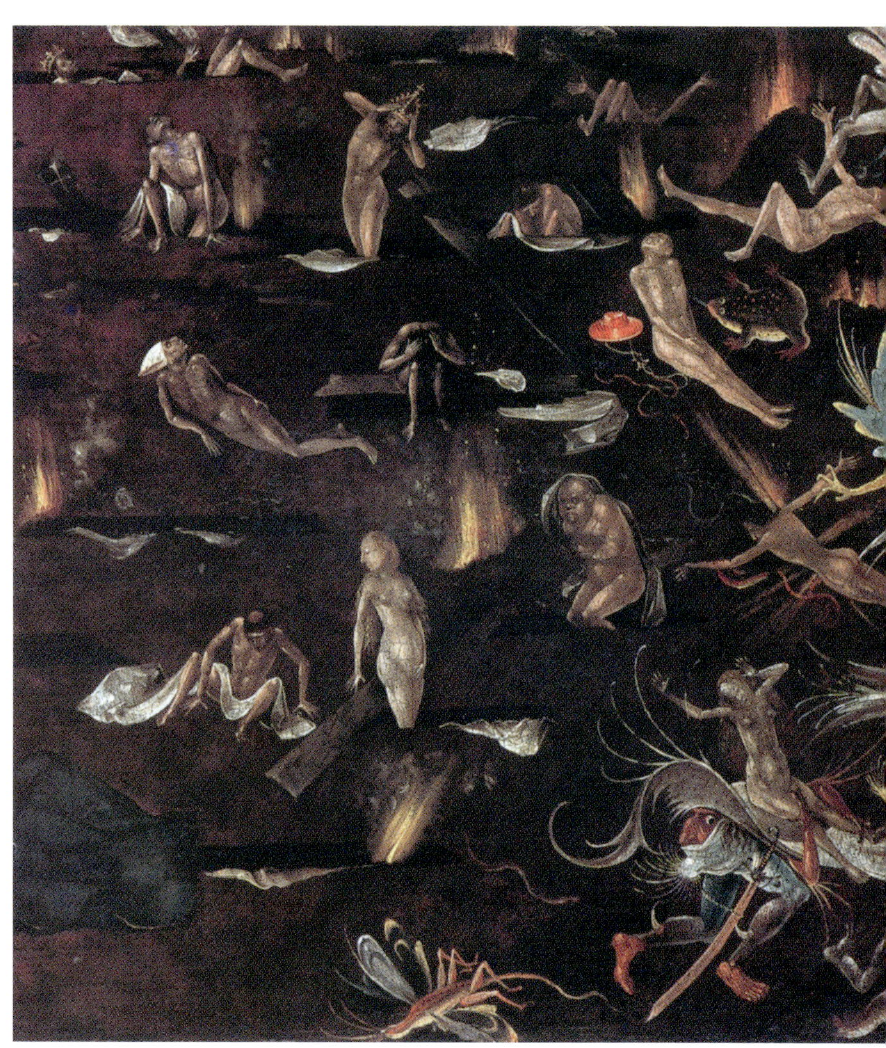

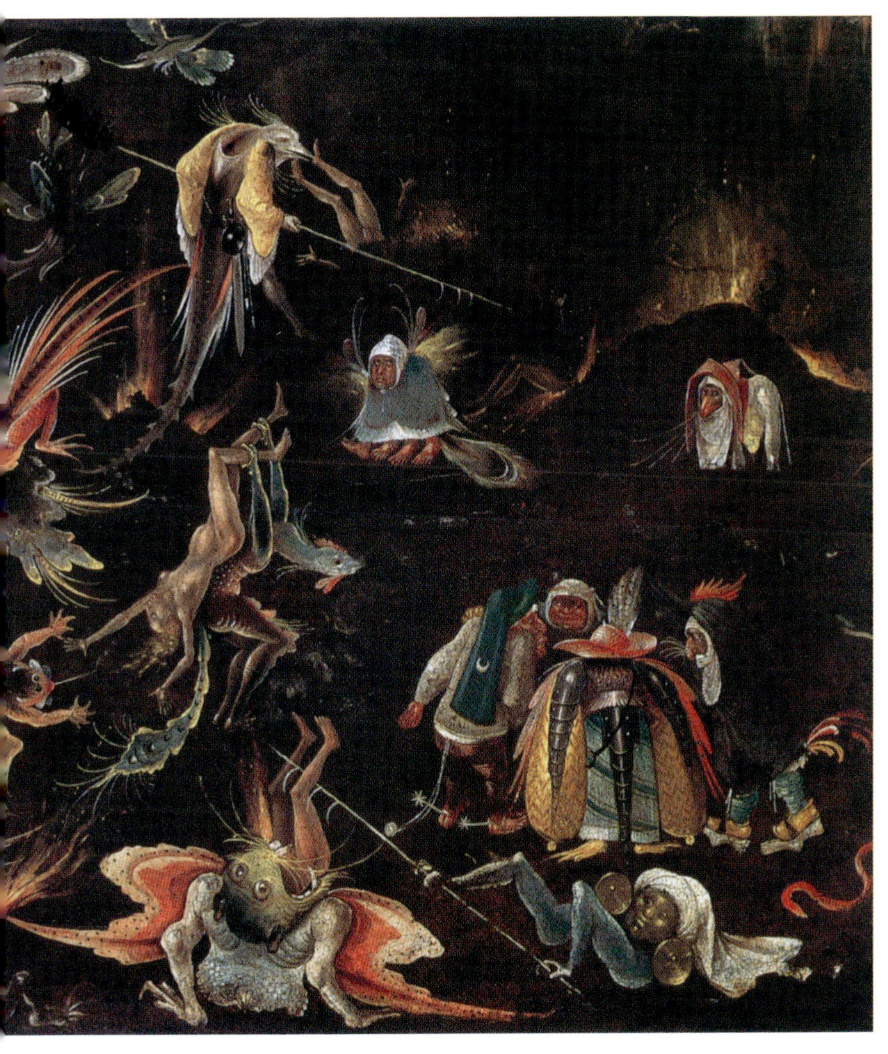

63 Imitator of Hieronymus Bosch, fragment of a *Last Judgment*, c. 1510–20, oil on panel.

until today, Bosch's oeuvre has been obscured by the many farces and imitations of varying quality. Guevara was the first to recommend distinguishing them from the original pictures by focusing on the motifs, Bosch having worked hard on these:

> Granted, he endeavoured to find for his fantastic pictures the rarest objects, but they were always true to nature; thus one can consider it a safe rule that any painting (even though provided with his signature) which contains a monstrosity or something else that goes beyond the confines of naturalness is a forgery or imitation, unless as I said before the picture represents Hell or a part of it.[15]

These graphic inventions would live on in the highly valued works of his faithful pupil who,

> either out of reverence for his master or in order to increase the value of his own works, signed them with the name of Bosch rather than with his own . . . In their execution he was even more meticulous and patient than Bosch and did not deviate from the lively and fresh qualities and colouring of his teacher.[16]

This statement is illustrated by the way the background in Guevara's copy of *The Haywain* (see illus. 48) was carefully done, the figures meticulously added to the spaces previously left blank. As the works that are unquestionably by his hand show, this painstaking process would have been alien to

Bosch. In 1604 van Mander pinpointed a certain painterly efficiency as a characteristic of Bosch's pictures. He was also less occupied with reproducing complicated folds in clothing than were his contemporaries: 'He had a steady hand and a very adroit and subtle working manner, usually finishing his works in one layer which nevertheless remains bright without discolouration.'[17] Unfortunately, in what follows, van Mander does not mention a single picture that is now recognized as an original.[18] Hence his comments, along with Guevara's statements, are now mainly interesting as evidence that in Bosch's day people were already interested in the questions of attribution that are current today.

Because it has not become any easier to distinguish between works by the artist's own hand and works that are copies or imitations, many recent commentators on art history have favoured the suggestion of a family workshop in which the father, the brothers and the sister produced the works regularly signed 'Jheronimus Bosch' as a joint venture.[19] What is the point, however, of making an unprovable suggestion that Bosch was related to his assistants? There is no doubt that Bosch ran a workshop and had pupils and assistants. He was also no doubt involved at every stage in the production of a great altarpiece, supervising his assistants, as was normal for medieval workshop practice. In addition, however, his signature – for example on the *Adoration of the Magi* (see illus. 13) – is like a modern trademark, a guarantee of quality based on the method of production. It is what links the works that are now accepted to be by Bosch's hand, the number of which has grown smaller and smaller over the years.[20] Those who try to prove that Bosch, as a member of a clandestine sect, produced picture puzzles and riddles tend to be no more interested in questions pertaining to the attributions of paintings than those who study aspects of cultural and religious history. But how can such questions be resolved, if the dates of the works and the specific context of their reception are unknown?

Bosch's work has in the end proved puzzling because of the fact that it has mystified modern interpreters trying to place his work as part of a process of development. In descriptions of the historical development of art, they like to see Bosch as belonging to a third generation, one of the last representatives of Early Netherlandish painting founded by Jan van Eyck.[21] Such authors never tire of placing Bosch's puzzling distinctiveness in the context of those painters who are also called 'Flemish Primitives'. This clear development, however, does not exist; it is constructed by art historians. Rather than Bosch's pictures, it is this type of historical projection that is problematic. It has also made sure that speculative explanations were constructed for those pictures that seemed not to fit into the art-historical development. Whether these pictures were seen to comprise astrological or alchemical messages, heretical content or that relating to secret societies, they also had to yield to a preconceived interpretation. These often highly speculative theories are not based on any documentary evidence, and the lack of focus on the historical perspective has resulted in the existing sources being ignored. Only by taking these into account is there a way into the wealth of possible contexts and interpretations that are so important for understanding Bosch. Above all, along with the fact that the pictorial expression is so wide open to interpretation, the ambiguous nature of the documentary evidence leaves room for more and more new interpretations of Bosch's works. Susan Sontag complains that he has become an artist 'around whom thick encrustations of interpretation have taken hold'.[22] The conception of art current in Bosch's day was based on an ambiguity that confounds all attempts to reduce the works of art to a single meaning. Therefore there is surely no *right* interpretation of his pictures, but by the same token there are a host of wrong ones. The general reading public must in the end gain the impression, from the steadily growing number of interpretations, that Bosch's pictures are essentially not capable of being understood, and that what they are is, in the end, the story of their interpretations. The different interpretations and ways of reading the pictures have piled up over time and have merged with Bosch's fantastical inventions, living on in the popular culture of our time. His hybrid creatures come alive again in comics and three-dimensional versions offered on sale at fashionable 'medieval markets'; on the Internet his works are everywhere and permanently available for all to think about. There is no doubt that over the last five hundred years Hieronymus Bosch's pictures have lost none of their fascination.

REFERENCES

Titles and dates of publications refer to the editions given in the
Bibliography. References to classical works as regards edition and
type of reference (paragraph, book, page number and so on) are
given according to the *Thesaurus linguae latinae*.

1 Visions and Nightmares

1 Vasari/Milanesi 1878–85, V, 439.
2 Vaernewijck/Vanderhaeghen 1872–6, i, 156.
3 Guicciardini 1567, 98.
4 Büttner 2015, 171–84.
5 Van Mander/Miedema 1994–8, I, 124–5.
6 Ilsink 2013, 272–3; Meiers 2006, 1–16.
7 MS 266, Bibliotheque Médiathèque d'Arras, fol. 275; see Châtelet
2007; Dijck 2001, 75.
8 Vrij 2013, 73–4.
9 Büttner 2014 (b), 27–40; Unverfehrt 1980.
10 Iffland 1978–82, II, 43–4.
11 Snyder 1973, 34; Siguença 1605, 837.
12 Van Mander/Miedema 1994–8, I, 125.
13 Büttner 2015, 171–84.
14 Gossart 1907.
15 Fraenger 1947.
16 Tolnay 1937, 87–106; Tolnay 1965, 335–77.
17 Unverfehrt 1980, 26–7; Marijnissen 1987, 9, counts 24 paintings;
Fischer 2013, 240–60, counts 20.
18 Klein 2001, 121–31
19 Koselleck 1995, 206.

2 A Painter in Den Bosch

1 Smulders 1957, 70; Gorissen 1973, 1134; Dijck 2001, 166.

2 Dijck 2001, 44; Fischer 2009, 17, note 22.

3 Marijnissen 1987, 13–14; Gerlach 1988, 48; Dijck 2001, 182; Fischer 2013, 289.

4 Gorissen 1973, 113; Dijck 2001, 160.

5 Cuperinus/Hermans 1846, 12; Mosmans 1947, 20.

6 Dijck 2001, 15, 78–9.

7 Gorissen 1973, 1134–8.

8 Dijck 2001, 27; Unverfehrt 2003, 89.

9 J. Koldewij, in Koldeweij 2001, 54; Unverfehrt 2003, 89.

10 Unverfehrt 2003, 89.

11 Marijnissen 1987, 11; Gerlach 1988, 44; Dijck 2001, 167; Fischer 2013, 288.

12 Mosmans 1947, 207, note 8; Marijnissen 1987, 11; Gerlach 1988, 44; Dijck 2001, 170; Fischer 2013, 288.

13 Gorissen 1973, 1134.

14 Mosmans 1947, 26f.

15 Dijck 2001, 44, 72–4.

16 Gorissen 1973, 1134–8.

17 Dijck 2001, 46, 168.

18 Dijck 2001, 47.

19 Smulders 1957, 71.

20 Vink 2001, 28–9; Unverfehrt 2003, 89.

21 Unverfehrt 2003, 89.

22 Unverfehrt 2003, 88; Koldeweij 1990, 100.

23 Vink/Vos 2001, 81; Unverfehrt 2003, 90.

24 Unverfehrt 2003, 89; Unverfehrt 1980, 233–4; Vandenbroeck 1987, 181; Fischer 2009, 118.

25 Dijck 2001, 175; Unverfehrt 2003, 89.

26 Blondé/Vlieghe 1989, 699–700.

27 Dijck 2001, 50.

28 Cf. Kuijer 2000, 229; ibid., P. Th. J. Kuijer in Koldeweij 1990, 395–6; Gerlach 1988, 19; Blondé/Vlieghe 1989, 699–700.

29 Marijnissen 1987, 13.

30 Fischer 2009, 20.

31 Fischer 2009, 20.

32 Büttner 2003, 67, 76, note 74.

33 Friedländer 1927, 81.

34 Fischer 2009, 95–102.

35 Marijnissen 1987, 12; Gerlach 1988, 44; Dijck 2001, 173;
    Unverfehrt 2003, 56; Fischer 2009, 23f.; Fischer 2013, 288.

36 Fischer 2009, 23.

37 Dijck 1973, 72.

38 Dijck 1973, 70f., 107–12; Unverfehrt 2003, 83.

39 Koldeweij 1990, 119.

40 Unverfehrt 1980, 61; Delevoy 1960, 13.

41 Unverfehrt 2003, 56.

42 Unverfehrt 2003, 58.

43 Gerlach 1988, 53; Unverfehrt 1980, 62f.; Unverfehrt 2003, 56.

44 Dijck 2010, 115.

45 Marijnissen 1987, 18; Dijck 2001, 174; Vink 2001, 93; Unverfehrt
    2003, 56.

46 Fischer 2009, 27.

47 Marijnissen 1987, 13; Gerlach 1988, 47; Dijck 2001, 178; Fischer
    2013, 288.

48 Dijck 2001, 77–8.

49 Mosmans 1947, 78; Goertz 1977, 16; Harris 1996, 78; Unverfehrt
    2003, 83.

50 Dijck 1973, 69–70; Unverfehrt 2003, 84.

51 Unverfehrt 2003, 84.

52 Fischer 2009, 48–62.

53 Dijck 1973, 85–96; Unverfehrt 2003, 87.

54 Dijck 1973, 70, 79–81, 81–5, 444–6; Unverfehrt 2003, 86.

55 Dijck 1973, 70, 79–81; Unverfehrt 2003, 86.

56 Belting 2002, 71–84.

57 Marijnissen 1987, 13–14; Gerlach 1988, 48; Dijck 2001, 182;
    Fischer 2013, 289.

58 Unverfehrt 2003.

59 Dijck 1973, 70f., 178; Unverfehrt 2003, 86.

60 Unverfehrt 2003, 84.

61 Cuperinus/Hermans 1846, 79; Dijck 2001, 186; Unverfehrt
    2003, 60.

62 Marijnissen 1987, 14; Gerlach 1988, 48; Dijck 2001, 182; Fischer 2013, 289.

63 Marijnissen 1987, 14; Gerlach 1988, 48; Dijck 2001, 182; Fischer 2013, 289.

3 Pious Donations

1 Dijck 2001, 174; Fischer 2013, 288; for the 'Geefhuis' see Kappelhof 1981, 1–54.

2 Vink 2001, 102f.

3 Vink 2001, 103f.

4 Marijnissen 1987, 12; Gerlach 1988, 45; Dijck 2001, 175; Fischer 2013, 288.

5 Marijnissen 1987, 12; Gerlach 1988, 45; Dijck 2001, 176–7; Fischer 2013, 288.

6 Marijnissen 1987, 13; Gerlach 1988, 48; Dijck 2001, 182; Fischer 2013, 289.

7 Marijnissen 1987, 14; Gerlach 1988, 49; Dijck 2001, 183; Fischer 2013, 289.

8 Marijnissen 1987, 14; Gerlach 1988, 49; Dijck 2001, 183; Fischer 2013, 289.

9 Gramaye 1610, 13 (recte 21).

10 Gerlach 1988, 59–60; Vink 2001, 102.

11 Gerlach 1988, 60.

12 Vandenbroeck 2002, 326–7, 399, note 1411.

13 J. Koldewij, in Koldeweij 2001; Vink 2001, 101; Wattel 2001, 13; Fischer 2009, 90.

14 Fischer 2013, 242.

15 Physiologus VI.

16 Marijnissen 1987, 287; Silver 2006, 206.

17 Silver 2006, 206.

18 Silver 2006, 206.

19 R. Van Schoute, H. Verougstraete and C. Garrido, in Koldeweij/Vermet/van Kooij 2001, 108–10; Koldeweij 2001, 72–8, 88, 94–5, 97.

20 Klein 2001, 123–30.

21 Jezler 1994, 13–26.

22 Oexle 1995.
23 Fischer 2013, 240.
24 Fischer 2009, 82.
25 Friedländer 1927, 95; Friedländer 1969, 52.
26 Dijck 2001, 25–6; 149–56; Fischer 2009, 82–3.
27 Fischer 2013, 242.
28 Sander 1993, 34–5.
29 Wattel 2001, 10–17; R. Trnek, in Timmermans 2014, 264–83.

4 From Christmas to Easter

1 Rupprich 1956–69, II, 113 ('Dan dy kunst des molens würt geprawcht jm dinst der kirchen vnd dordurch angetzeigt daz leiden Christi, behelt awch die gestalt der menschen noch jrem absterben').
2 Fischer 2013, 243–4.
3 Hymans 1893, 234; Huys Janssen 2005.
4 Marijnissen 1987, 234.
5 Dijck 2001, 104–6.
6 Gramaye 1610, 13 (recte 21).
7 Panofsky 1953; Eclercy 2008, 133–47.
8 Peukert 1948, 152–3.
9 Schlie 2002, 157.
10 Graus 1987, 530–31.
11 Revelation 20:8; Peukert 1948, 121–2, 164–5.
12 Meier 2006, 141.
13 Stock 1993.
14 Fischer 2013, 245.
15 Boon 1967, no. 28.
16 Bax 1949, 127.
17 Fischer 2013, 244–5.
18 Fischer 2013, 242–3.
19 Elsig 2004, 88–91; Spronk 2011, esp. 26–7; Fischer 2013, 266.
20 Tolnay 1965, Kat. 36; Unverfehrt 1980, 26f., no. 25.
21 Spronk 2011, esp. 26–7; Fischer 2013, 266.
22 Elsig 2004.

23 Fischer 2009, 204.
24 Koreny 2002–3, 49.
25 Friedländer 1927, 110.

5 Devout Examples

1 Dijck 2001, 59, 91–2; Fischer 2009, 98.
2 Eichberger 2002, 269–70.
3 'Superstitiosus imaginum cultus', Erasmus 1515, fol. 29, recto [cv]; Hofmann 1983–4, 130–31; Fuhrmann 2002, 218–19.
4 Nicholas of Lyra, Gal. com. 4, 3: 'Littera gesta docet, quid credas allegoria, moralis quid agas, quo tendas anagogia.'
5 Luther WA, I, vol. 63, III.
6 Hecht 2012, 160.
7 Melanchthon/Wels 2011, 214–16.
8 Henkelum 1865, 27.
9 Fischer 2013, 240–41.
10 *Letters of St Jerome*, 22.
11 Marijnissen 1987, 390.
12 Fischer 2013, 251–2.
13 Fischer 2013, 257–8.
14 Fischer 2013, 249–50.
15 E. Pokorny, in Schröder 2013, 90; Koreny 2012, 230–35.
16 Bambeck 1987, 43–8; Fischer 2009, 167.
17 Fischer 2013, 246–7.
18 Fischer 2009, 100.
19 Unverfehrt 1980, 146f.
20 Koreny 2002–3, 48.
21 Unverfehrt 1980, 12.

6 The Art of Invention and the Invention of Art

1 Hor. ars., 361.
2 Registrum XI, 10, ed. Norberg II, 874; Hecht 2012, 63–4.
3 Koreny 2012, 170–75.
4 Buck 2001, 197–206; Koreny 2012, 170–75.
5 Stadlober 2006, 335.

6 'Docet fabula, loquacitatem semper esse detrimentosam'.
   Camerarius 1538, fol. 102.
7 Bebel/Suringar 1879, 34, 247, no. 102: 'Campus habet oculos; silua
   aures dicitur quod nihil faciamus in siluis & campo (vbi homines
   esse possunt) quod occultum esse volumus'.
8 Bambeck 1987; Buck 2001, 197–206, nr. 1.31; Ilsink 2009, 34–89;
   Koreny 2012, 170–75.
9 'Miserrimi quippe est ingenii semper uti inventis et nunquam
   inveniendis'.
10 Vandenbroeck 2002, 186.
11 Gasser 2007, 106.
12 Hor. ars., 128f.
13 Buck 2001, 207–15; Koreny 2012, 178–83.
14 Koreny 2012, 184–9.
15 Unverfehrt 1980, 43.
16 Unverfehrt 1980, 44, 48, 78–9, 89; Koreny 2012, 242–4.
17 Unverfehrt 1980, 78.
18 Vaernewijck/Vanderhaeghen 1872–76, I, 156.
19 Rupprich 1956–69, I, 209: 'im sein hand zw weisen'.
20 Belting 2002, 8.
21 Friedländer 1927, 109.
22 Unverfehrt 1980, 241–2; Rijen 1993, 427–39.
23 Friedländer 1927, 110.
24 Friedländer 1927, 123.

7 The *Seven Deadly Sins* and the *Last Judgment*

1 Snyder 1973, 28; Guevara/Ponz 1788, 41.
2 Pliny, *Natural History* xxxv, 114.
3 Snyder 1973, 28–9; Guevara/Ponz 1788, 41–2.
4 Snyder 1973, 29; Guevara/Ponz 1788, 41–2.
5 Snyder 1973, 29; Guevara/Ponz 1788, 41–2; Fischer 2013, 252–3.
6 Belting/Kruse 1994, 270.
7 Gibson 1974, 35.
8 Fischer 2009, 156, note 846.
9 Marijnissen 1987, 97–9.
10 Snyder 1973, 37; Siguença 1605, 838–9.

11 Snyder 1973, 37, 35; Siguença 1605, 838–9.

12 Snyder 1973, 39; Guevara/Ponz 1788, 43.

13 Snyder 1973, 39; Guevara/Ponz 1788, 43–4.

14 Pliny, *Natural History* xxxv, 98–100.

15 Dijck 2001, 99.

16 Dijck 2001, 106.

17 Vandenbroeck 2009, 212–69.

18 Gossart 1907, 59.

19 Belting 2002, 74; Dijck 2001, 91.

20 Fischer 2013, 250–51.

21 R. Trnek, in Timmermans 2014, 266.

22 Fischer 2013, 250; Fischer 2009, 96; Bax 1983, 319.

23 J. Koldeweij, in Timmermans 2014, 400–433.

24 Klein 2001, 124.

25 Bax 1983, 319f.

26 Marijniissen 1987, 493–4; Palmer 1982.

27 Palmer 1982, 210.

28 Marijnissen 1987, 217.

29 Hecht 2012, 250.

30 Durand, Rationale Divinorum Officiorum, Lib. i, cap. iii, sect. 4:
    'Pictura namque plus vedetur movere animum, quam scriptura'.

31 Büttner 2005, 37–56.

32 Fischer 2013, 253–4.

33 Song of Songs 4:12/15.

34 Dijck 2001, 93.

8 *The Haywain* and *The Garden of Earthly Delights*

1 Unverfehrt 1980, 18f., 85f.; De Bruyn 2001, 34f.; Dijck 2001, 94f.;
   Fischer 2009, 101.

2 Dijck 2001, 102.

3 Koldeweij 2001, 23f., 71, 74, 77–80, 97f., 153, 159; Koreny 2012,
   69, 89.

4 Koreny 2004, 58; Koreny 2012, 69, 89.

5 Fischer 2013, 254–5.

6 Bax 1956, 129–31.

7 Traeger 1970, 298–331.

8 Belting/Kruse 1994, 268–83; Salazar 1955, 117–38.
9 De Bruyn 2001, 36.
10 Snyder 1973, 31–3; Morales 1586, 316–20.
11 Snyder 1973, 31; Morales 1586, 316.
12 Snyder 1973, 31; Morales 1586, 316.
13 Büttner 2014 (b), 274–5, note 3.
14 Koreny 2004, 51.
15 Unverfehrt 2003, 25.
16 Beatis/Hale 1979, 94f.
17 Rupprich 1956–69, I, 155; Unverfehrt 2007, 70.
18 Rupprich 1956–69, I, 155: 'das groß beth do 50 Menschen mügen innen liegen'.
19 Beatis/Hale 1979, 94f.
20 Marijnissen 1987, 98; Fischer 2013, 248.
21 Marijnissen 1987, 23: 'Una pintura de la variedad del mundo'.
22 Snyder 1973, 38; Siguença 1605, 838.
23 Wirth 2000; Belting 2002.
24 Büttner 2014 (b), 291, note 39: 'Nec est turpior in mundo cloaca, quam peccator impoenitens, vitiosusque homo: qui tamen in sua natura et specie multum naturalis pulchritudinis habet'.
25 Snyder 1973, 28–9; Guevara/Ponz 1788, 41.
26 Freud 1955, 241.
27 Augustine of Hippo, conf. XIII, lib. X, 35, 55, pl 32, 802.

9 The Folly of the World

1 Unverfehrt 1980, 111.
2 Koldeweij 1991, 7: 'Een taeffereel van Lubbertas, die men de keye snyt'.
3 Koldeweij 1990, 106–7.
4 Fischer 2013, 255–6.
5 Brant 1494, fol. 3: 'Die gantz welt lebt in vinstrer nacht Und důt in sünden blint verharren All strassen / gassen / sindt voll narren Die nüt dañ mit dorheit vmbgan.'
6 Fischer 2009, 243–5.
7 Holländer 1988, 8.
8 Fraenger 1950.

9 Unverfehrt 2003, 27–36; Silver 2006, 150.
10 Klein 2001, 129; Spronk 2011, 10.
11 Fischer 2013, 265–6.
12 Koldeweij 1990, 252, no. 153.

10 Interpretations

1 Unverfehrt 1980.
2 Dijck 2001, 93: 'La tela della fortuna con el ceto che ingiotte Giona fu de man de l'istesso'.
3 Maroto 2001, 41–8.
4 Snyder 1973, 29; Guevara/Ponz 1788, 42.
5 Vermeylen 2003, Appendix 5, 199; Van der Straelen 1855, 63–5.
6 Van der Straelen 1855, 64; Vermeylen 2003, Appendix 5, 132, 199.
7 Büttner 2014 (a), 27–40.
8 Van Mander 1604, fol. 233r; Van Mander/Miedema 1994–8, 1, 190.
9 Van Mander/Miedema 1994–8, 1, 125.
10 Unverfehrt 1980, 46–7; Koreny 2013, 296–303, 312–18.
11 Unverfehrt 1980, 241–2; Rijen 1993, 427–39.
12 Kuijer 2000, 213.
13 Unverfehrt 1980, 210–14.
14 Molina 1582, fol. 20r–v.
15 Snyder 1973, 29; Guevara/Ponz 1788, 42–3.
16 Snyder 1973, 29; Guevara/Ponz 1788, 43.
17 Van Mander/Miedema 1994–8, 1, 125.
18 Büttner 2014 (a), 31–2.
19 Koldeweij 2001, 16, 21, 54, 70, 83, 85, 93; Belting 2002, 59.
20 Tolnay 1937, 87–106; Tolnay 1965, 335–77; Unverfehrt 1980, 26–7; Marijnissen 1987, 9, counts 24 paintings; Fischer 2013, 240–60, counts 20.
21 Panofsky 1953.
22 Sontag 1961, 14.

BIBLIOGRAPHY

A Note on the Literature

Since the end of the nineteenth century, when research began into Hieronymus Bosch, more than a thousand publications have appeared about his life and work. An almost complete bibliography of works published up until 2000 can be found in van Dijck 2001. An indispensable source is still the bibliography in Gibson 1983. Further sources include Vandenbroeck 1987; Mund/Stroo 1998, 29–46; Pokorny 2007, 129–33. Further sources are available in the bibliographies to Fischer 2009 and Fischer 2013. In addition to this rich volume of illustrations, mention should be made of two informative studies in which Bosch's works are presented in their historical and iconographic context: Marijnissen 1987 and Silver 2006. On so-called Early Netherlandish painting in general and on Bosch in relation to this context, see Belting/Kruse 1994; Van Schoute/De Patoul 1994. On the history of 's-Hertogenbosch, see Kuijer 2000.

A summary of documents relating to Bosch is available in Huys Janssen 2007. See also van Dijck 1973; Gorissen 1973, 1134–8; Gerlach 1988; Vink 2001; van Dijck 2001 (translated into Dutch), also giving early literary references. For these, see also Beatis/Hale 1979; Snyder 1973; Guevara/Ponz 1788, 41–4; Salazar 1955, 117–38; Van Mander 1604, fol. 216v; Siguença 1605, 837–41; Gramaye 1610, 21.

On Bosch's works and influence, catalogues still in use are those by Friedländer [1927] 1969; Tolnay 1965. For the ensuing debate around the oeuvre, see the summary in Fischer 2013; cat. Rotterdam 2001, as well as the supplementary volume to Koldeweij/Vermet/van Kooij 2001, particularly the contribution by Peter Klein: 'Dendrochronological Analysis of Works by Hieronymus Bosch and his Followers' (121–32).

On the drawings, see Koreny 2012. On the underdrawings of the paintings, see Filedt Kok 1972/73; Verougstraete/Van Schoute 2003. On Bosch's followers and reception, Unverfehrt 1980 is an indispensable standard work.

There has emerged a consensus in academic studies that Bosch was not an isolated figure in the art and society of his time. On such interpretations, based on historical research into the sources and everyday reality, in addition to those mentioned above (Marijnissen, Silver, Fischer) are: Bax 1949; Gibson 1974; Bruyn 2001; Unverfehrt 2003. The studies by Vandenbroeck 1987 and 2002 are particularly rewarding as regards material.

Sources

Bambeck, Manfred, *Das Sprichwort im Bild: 'Der Wald hat Ohren, das Feld hat Augen': zu einer Zeichnung von Hieronymus Bosch* (Stuttgart, 1987)

Bax, Dirk, *Beschrijving en poging tot verklaring van het tuin der onkuisheiddrieluik van Jeroen Bosch: Gefolgd door kritiek op Fraenger* (Amsterdam, 1956)

—, *Hieronymus Bosch and Lucas Cranach: Two Last Judgement Triptychs: Description and Exposition* (Amsterdam, 1983)

—, *Ontcijfering van Jeroen Bosch* (The Hague, 1949)

Beatis, Antonio de, *The Travel Journal of Antonio de Beatis: Germany, Switzerland, the Low Countries, France and Italy, 1517–1518*, ed. John R. Hale (London, 1979)

Bebel, Heinrich, *Proverbia germanica* [1508], ed. Willem H. D. Suringar (Leiden, 1879)

Belting, Hans, *Hieronymus Bosch: Garten der Lüste* (Munich, 2002)

—, and Christiane Kruse, *Die Erfindung des Gemäldes: das erste Jahrhundert der niederländischen Malerei* (Munich, 1994)

Blondé, Bruno, and Hans Vlieghe, 'The Social Status of Hieronymus Bosch', *Burlington Magazine*, 131 (1989), 699–700

Brant, Sebastian, *Das Narrenschiff* (Basel, 1494)

Bruyn, Eric de, *De vergeten beeldentaal van Jheronimus Bosch* ('s-Hertogenbosch, 2001)

Buck, Stephanie, *Die niederländischen Zeichnungen des 15. Jahrhunderts im Berliner Kupferstichkabinett: kritischer Katalog* (Turnhout, 2001)

Büttner, Nils, '"Where is Paradise?": Imagining Heaven and Hell in Early Modern Times', in *Imagined Worlds: Willful Invention and the Printed Image, 1470–2005*, ed. Amy Baker Sandback (New York, 2005), 37–56

—, 'Fälschung, Plagiat und Kopie nach – Hieronymus Bosch?', in *Fälschung – Plagiat – Kopie: Künstlerische Praktiken in der Vormoderne*, ed. Birgit Ulrike Münch et al. (St Petersberg, 2014) (a), 27–40

—, 'No Flesh in the "Garden of Earthly Delights": On the Paintings of Hieronymus Bosch', in *Aesthetics of the Flesh*, ed. Felix Ensslin and Charlotte Klink (Berlin, 2014) (b), 273–99

—, 'Paintings as Historical Evidence of Artistic Emotions: The Art of Hieronymus Bosch and the Soul of the Artist in Critical Discourse in the Seventeenth Century', in *Facts and Feelings: Retracing Emotions of Artists, 1600–1800*, ed. Hannelore Magnus and Katlijne Van der Stighelen (Turnhout, 2015), 171–84

—, 'Wer war "Meister Gielesz"? Der Vertrag über das Dortmunder Retabel und die Werkstattpraxis in Antwerpen', in *Das 'Goldene Wunder' in der Dortmunder Petrikirche*, ed. Barbara Welzel (Bielefeld, 2003), 57–76

Camerarius, Joachim, *Aesopi Phrygis Fabularum Celeberrimi Autoris Vita, Fabellae Aesopicae Plures Quadringentis: quaedam prius etiam, multae nunc primum editae* (Tübingen, 1538)

Châtelet, Albert, ed., *Visages d'antan: Le Recueil d'Arras* (Lathuile, 2007)

Cuperinus, Albertus, *Die Chronicke vander vermaerder ender vromer Stadt van Tsertogenbosch, in Verzameling Van Kronyken: Charters En Oorkonden Betrekkelijk de Stad en Meijerij van 's-Hertogenbosch*, ed. Cornelis Rudolphus Hermans, vol. I ('s-Hertogensbosch, 1846)

Delevoy, Robert L., *Bosch: Biographical and Critical Study* (Geneva, 1960)

Dijck, Godfried C. van, *De Bossche Optimaten: geschiedenis van de Illustere Lieve Vrouwebroederschap te 's-Hertogenbosch, 1318–1973* (Tilburg, 1973)

—, *Op zoek naar Jheronimus van Aken alias Bosch* (Zaltbommel, 2001)

Dijck, Lucas van, 'Jheronimus Bosch Inspired by People in his Environment: Research from the Archival Sources', in *Jheronimus Bosch: His Sources: 2nd International Jheronimus Bosch Conference, May 22–5, 2007*, ed. Jill Bradley et al. ('s-Hertogenbosch, 2010), 112–27

Eclercy, Bastian, 'Von Mausefallen und Ofenschirmen: zum Problem des "disguised symbolism" bei den frühen Niederländern', in *Der Meister von Flémalle und Rogier van der Weyden*, exh. cat.,

Städel-Museum, Frankfurt am Main; Gemäldegalerie, Staatliche
    Museen, Berlin (2008), 133–47
Eichberger, Dagmar, *Leben mit Kunst, Wirken durch Kunst: Sammelwesen und
    Hofkunst unter Margarete von Österreich* (Turnhout, 2002)
Elsig, Frédéric, *Jheronimus Bosch: la question de la chronologie* (Geneva, 2004)
Erasmus, Desiderius, *Morias enkomion, id est stultitiae laus* (Basel, 1515)
Filedt Kok, Jan Piet, 'Underdrawing and Drawing in the Work of
    Hieronymus Bosch: A Provisional Survey in Connection with the
    Painting by Him in Rotterdam', *Similous*, 6 (1972–3), 133–62
Fischer, Stefan, *Hieronymus Bosch: Malerei als Vision, Lehrbild und Kunstwerk*
    (Cologne, 2009)
—, *Hieronymus Bosch: The Complete Works* (Cologne, 2013)
Fraenger, Wilhelm, *Die Hochzeit zu Kana: ein Dokument semitischer Gnosis bei
    Hieronymus Bosch* (Berlin, 1950)
—, *Hieronymus Bosch: das Tausendjährige Reich. Grundzüge einer Auslegung*
    (Coburg, 1947)
Freud, Sigmund, 'The Uncanny' [1919], in *The Standard Edition of the
    Complete Psychological Works of Sigmund Freud*, vol. XVII, trans. James
    Strachey (London, 1955), 219–50
Friedländer, Max J., *Early Netherlandish Painting*, vol. V: *Geertgen tot Sint Jans
    and Jerome Bosch* (Leiden, 1969)
—, *Die altniederländische Malerei*, vol. V: *Geertgen van Haarlem und Hieronymus
    Bosch* (Berlin, 1927)
Fuhrmann, Horst, *Überall ist Mittelalter: Von der Gegenwart einer vergangenen
    Zeit* (Munich, 2002)
Gasser, Markus, *Die Sprengung der platonischen Höhle: Roman und Philosophie
    im Widerstreit* (Göttingen, 2007)
Gerlach, Pater O.F.M., *Jheronimus Bosch: Opstellen over leven en werk*
    ('s-Hertogensbosch, 1988)
Gibson, Walter S., *Hieronymus Bosch* (Frankfurt am Main, 1974)
Goertz, Heinrich, *Hieronymus Bosch* (Reinbek, 1977)
Gorissen, Friedrich, *Das Stundenbuch der Katharina von Kleve: Analyse und
    Kommentar* (Berlin, 1973)
Gossart, Maurice, *Jérôme Bosch: Le 'faizeur de Dyables' de Bois-le-Duc* (Lille,
    1907)
Gramaye, Jean-Baptiste, *Taxandria* (Brussels, 1610)
Graus, František, and Geissler Pest, *Judenmorde* (Göttingen, 1987)

Guevara, Felipe de, *Comentarios de la pintura* [1560], ed. Antonio Ponz
    (Madrid, 1788)
Guicciardini, Lodovico, *Descrittione . . . di tutti i Paesi Bassi* (Antwerp, 1567)
Harris, Lynda, *Hieronymus Bosch und die geheime Bildwelt der Katharer*
    (Stuttgart, 1996)
Hecht, Christian, *Katholische Bildertheologie der frühen Neuzeit* (Berlin,
    2012)
Henkelum, G. W. van, *Van sunte Cristoffels heelden* (Utrecht, 1865)
Hofmann, Werner, ed., *Luther und die Folgen für die Kunst*, exh. cat.,
    Kunsthalle, Hamburg (Munich, 1983)
Holländer, Hans, *Hieronymus Bosch: Weltbilder und Traumwerk* (Cologne,
    1988)
Hymans, Henri, 'Les Musées de Madrid: Le Musée du Prado', *Gazette
    des Beaux-Arts*, XXXV/3 (1893), 223–36
Iffland, James, *Quevedo and the Grotesque*, 2 vols (London, 1978–82)
Ilsink, Matthijs, 'Bosch, Bruegel and the Netherlandish Tradition', in
    Hieronymus Cock: The Renaissance in Print, ed. Joris Van Grieken, Ger
    Luijten and Jan van der Stock (Brussels, 2013), 243–77
——, *Bosch en Bruegel als Bosch: Kunst over kunst bij Pieter Bruegel (c. 1528–1569)
    en Jheronimus Bosch (c. 1450–1516)* (Edam, 2009)
Janssen, Paul Huys, 'Hieronymus Bosch: Facts and Records
    Concerning his Life and Work', *Wallraf-Richartz-Jahrbuch*, 68
    (2007), 239–54
Jezler, Peter, 'Jenseitsmodelle und Jenseitsvorsorge: eine Einführung',
    in *Himmel, Hölle, Fegefeuer: das Jenseits im Mittelalter* (Zurich, 1994),
    13–26
Jheronimus Bosch, exh. cat., Het Noordbrabants Museum,
    's-Hertogenbosch ('s-Hertogenbosch, 1967)
Kappelhof, A.C.M., 'Het Bossche geefhuis, het inkomen uit het
    vermogen van de Tafel van de Heilige Geest van Den Bosch,
    1450–1810', *Varia Historica Brabantica*, 10 (1981), 1–54
Klein, Peter, 'Dendrochronological Analysis of Works by Hieronymus
    Bosch and his Followers', in *Hieronymus Bosch: New Insights into his
    Life and Work*, ed. Jos Koldeweij, Bernard Vermet and Barbera van
    Kooij (Ghent, 2001), 121–31
Koldeweij, Adrianus M., ed., *In Buscoducis: Kunst uit de Bourgondische
    tijd te 's-Hertogenbosch, de cultuur van late middeleeuwen en renaissance,*

exh. cat., Het Noordbrabants Museum, 's-Hertogenbosch
('s-Hertogenbosch, 1990)

—, *De 'Keisnijding' van Hieronymus Bosch* (Zutphen, 1991)

Koldeweij, Jos, Bernard Vermet and Barbera van Kooij, eds, *Hieronymus Bosch: New Insights into his Life and Work* (Ghent, 2001)

Koldeweij, Jos, Paul Vandenbroeck and Bernard Vermet, eds, *Hieronymus Bosch: The Complete Paintings and Drawings*, exh. cat. (Rotterdam, 2001)

Koreny, Fritz, 'Hieronymus Bosch: Überlegungen zu Stil und Chronologie: Prolegomena zu einer Sichtung des Œuvres', *Jahrbuch des Kunsthistorischen Museums Wien*, IV/5 (2002–3), 46–75

—, *Hieronymus Bosch: die Zeichnungen. Werkstatt und Nachfolge bis zum Ende des 16. Jahrhunderts* (Turnhout, 2012)

Koselleck, Reinhart, *Vergangene Zukunft* (Frankfurt am Main, 1995)

Kuijer, P. Th. J., *'s-Hertogensbosch: Stad in het hertogdom Brabant ca. 1185–1629* (Zwolle, 2000)

Luther, D., *Martin Luthers Werke: Kritische Gesamtausgabe (Weimarer Ausgabe)*, 120 vols (Weimar, 1883–2009)

Marijnissen, Roger H., and Peter Ruyffelaere, *Hieronymus Bosch*, trans. Ted Alkins et al. (Antwerp, 1987)

Maroto, Pilar Silva, 'Bosch in Spain: On the Works Recorded in the Royal Inventories', in *Hieronymus Bosch: New Insights into his Life and Work*, ed. Jos Koldeweij, Bernard Vermet and Barbera van Kooij (Ghent, 2001), 41–8

Meier, Esther, *Die Gregorsmesse: Funktionen eines spätmittelalterlichen Bildtypus* (Cologne, 2006)

Meiers, Sarah, 'Portraits in Print: Hieronymus Cock, Dominicus Lampsonius, and "Pictorum aliquot Germaniae Inferioris Effigies"', *Zeitschrift für Kunstgeschichte*, LXIX/1 (2006), 1–16

Melanchthon, Philipp, *Elementa rhetorices* [1531], ed. Volkhard Wels (Potsdam, 2011)

Molina, Gonzalo Argote de, *Libro dela Monteria* (Seville, 1582)

Morales, Ambrosio de, *Las obras del maestro Fernán Pérez de Oliva, con otras cosas que van añadidas* (Cordoba, 1586)

Mosmans, Jan, *Jheronimus Anthonis-zoon van Aken alias Hieronymus Bosch* ('s-Hertogensbosch, 1947)

Mund, Hélène, and Cyriel Stroo, *Early Netherlandish Painting (1400–1500): A Bibliography (1984–1998)* (Brussels, 1998)

Oexle, Otto Gerhard, ed., *Memoria als Kultur* (Göttingen, 1995)

Palmer, Nigel F., *'Visio Tnugdali': The German and Dutch Translations and their Circulation in the Later Middle Ages* (Munich, 1982)

Peuckert, Will-Erich, *Die grosse Wende* (Hamburg, 1948)

Pokorny, Erwin, 'Hieronymus Bosch hält sich bedeckt: zu Forschungsstand und rezenter Literatur', *Kunstchronik*, 60 (2007), 129–33

Rijen, Jean-Pierre van, 'De kunstreis van het Bernulphusgilde naar de Sint-Jan: Alart du Hamel en Lambert Hezenmans', in *Bouwkunst: Studies in vriendschap voor Kees Peeters*, ed. Willem F. Denslagen (Amsterdam, 1993), 427–39

Rupprich, Hans, *Dürer Schriftlicher Nachlass*, 3 vols (Berlin, 1956–69)

Salazar, Abdon M., 'El Bosco y Ambrosio de Morales', *Archivo Espanol de Arte*, 28 (1955), 117–38

Sander, Jochen, *Niederländische Gemälde im Städel, 1400–1550. Kataloge der Gemälde im Städelschen Kunstinstitut Frankfurt am Main*, II (Mainz, 1993)

Schlie, Heike, *Bilder des Corpus Christi: Sakramentaler Realismus von Jan van Eyck bis Hieronymus Bosch* (Berlin, 2002)

Schröder, Klaus Albrecht, ed., *Bosch, Bruegel, Rubens, Rembrandt: Meister-werke aus der Albertina*, exh. cat., Albertina, Vienna (Vienna, 2013)

Siguença, Fray Joseph de, *Tercera parte de la Historia de la Orden de S. Geronimo* (Madrid, 1605)

Silver, Larry, *Hieronymus Bosch* (New York, 2006)

Smulders, F. W., 'De ooms van Jeroen Bosch', *De Brabantse Leeuw*, 6 (1957), 55–6

Snyder, James, ed., *Bosch in Perspective* (Englewood Cliffs, NY, 1973)

Sontag, Susan, *Against Interpretation and Other Essays* (New York, 1961)

Spronk, Ron, *Eigenhandig? Opmerkingen bij de schildertechniek en toeschrijvingsproblematiek bij Jheronimus Bosch* (Nijmegen, 2011)

Stadlober, Margit, *Der Wald in der Malerei und der Graphik des Donaustils* (Vienna, 2006)

Stock, Jan van der, ed., *Antwerp, Story of a Metropolis: 16th–17th century*, exh. cat., Hessenhuis, Antwerp (Antwerp, 1993)

Timmermans, Jo, ed., *Jheronimus Bosch: His Patrons and his Public: 3rd International Jheronimus Bosch Conference, September 16–18, 2012* ('s-Hertogensbosch, 2014)

Tolnay, Charles de, *Hieronymus Bosch* (Baden Baden, 1965)

—, *Hieronymus Bosch* (Basel, 1937)

Traeger, Jörg, 'Der "Heuwagen" des Hieronymus Bosch und der eschatologische Adventus des Papstes', *Zeitschrift für Kunstgeschichte*, 33 (1970), 298–331

Unverfehrt, Gerd, *Da sah ich viel köstliche Dinge: Albrecht Dürers Reise in die Niederlande* (Göttingen, 2007)

—, *Hieronymus Bosch: die Rezeption seiner Kunst im frühen 16. Jahrhundert* (Berlin, 1980)

—, *Wein statt Wasser: Essen und Trinken bei Jheronimus Bosch* (Göttingen, 2003)

Van der Straelen, Jan Baptist, *Jaerboek der vermaerde en kunstrijke gulde van Sint Lucas binnen der stad Antwerpen*, ed. Philippe Theodoor Moons-Van der Straelen (Antwerp, 1855)

Van Mander, Karel, *Het Schilder-boeck* (Haarlem, 1604)

—, *The Lives of the Illustrious Netherlandish and German Painters, from the First Edition of the Schilder-boeck (1603–1604)*, ed. Hessel Miedema, 6 vols (Doornspijk, 1994–8)

Van Schoute, Roger, and Brigitte De Patoul, *Les primitifs flamands et leur temps* (Louvain-la-Neuve, 1994)

Vandenbroeck, Paul, 'Meaningful Caprices: Folk Culture, Middle Class Ideology (ca 1480–1510) and Aristocratic Recuperation (ca 1530–1570): A Series of Brussels Tapestries after Hieronymus Bosch', in *Antwerp Royal Museum Annual* (2009), 212–69

—, *Jheronimus Bosch: De verlossing van de wereld* (Ghent and Amsterdam, 2002)

—, *Jheronimus Bosch: Tussen volksleven en stadscultuur* (Berchem, 1987)

Vaernewijck, Marcus van, *Van die beroerlicke tijden in die Nederlanden en voornamelijk in Ghendt, 1566–1568*, ed. Ferdinand Vanderhaeghen, 4 vols (Ghent, 1872–6)

Vasari, Giorgio, *Le vite de' più eccellenti pittori, scultori ed architettori*, ed. Gaetano Milanesi, 9 vols (Florence, 1878–85)

Vermeylen, Filip, *Painting for the Market: Commercialization of Art in Antwerp's Golden Age* (Turnhout, 2003)

Verougstraete-Marcq, Hélène, and Roger Van Schoute, *Jérôme Bosch et son entourage et autres études: le dessin sous-jacent et la technologie dans la peinture* (Louvain, 2003)

Vink, Ester, *Jeroen Bosch in Den Bosch: De schilder tegen de achtergrond van zijn stad* (Nijmegen, 2001)

Vrij, Marc Rudolf de, *Jheronimus Bosch: An Exercise in Common Sense* (Hilversum, 2012)

Wattel, Arvi, 'Stichterportretten bij Jheronimus Bosch', *Desipientia: Jheronimus Bosch, kunsthistorisch tijdschrift*, VIII/2 (September 2001), 10–17

Wirth, Jean, *Hieronymus Bosch: Der Garten der Lüste: Das Paradies als Utopie* (Frankfurt am Main, 2000)

PHOTO ACKNOWLEDGEMENTS

The author and publishers wish to express their thanks to the below sources of illustrative material and / or permission to reproduce it.

Akademie für Bildende Künste, Vienna: 21, 42, 43; Albertina, Vienna: 30; Art Institute of Chicago: 40; Gemäldegalerie, Berlin: 6, 7, 8; Graphische Sammlung Albertina, Vienna: 37; Kunsthistorisches Museum, Vienna: 16, 17; The Metropolitan Museum of Art, New York: 62; Museum Boijmans Van Beuningen, Rotterdam: 22, 24, 26, 26, 27, 49, 50, 56, 60; Musée du Louvre, Paris: 38, 58; Musée Municipal, Saint-Germain-en-Laye: 61; Museu Nacional de Arte Antiga, Lisbon: 31, 32, 33; Museo del Prado, Madrid: 2, 4, 10, 13, 14, 15, 36, 48, 51, 52, 53, 55; Museum voor Schone Kunsten, Ghent: 20, 23; National Gallery, London: 19; National Gallery of Art, Washington, DC: 39; Noordbrabants Museum, 's-Hertogenbosch: 3; Palacio Real, Madrid: 18, 42, 54; Palazzo Ducale, Venice: 12, 26, 27, 44, 45, 46, 47; Rijksmuseum, Amsterdam: 56; Royal Museums of Fine Arts of Belgium, Brussels: 11; Staatliche Museen, Berlin: 34, 35; Städel Museum, Frankfurt: 9; Yale University Art Gallery, New Haven: 59.

INDEX

Illustration numbers are indicated by *italics*.